CAMBRIDGE LIBRARY COLLECTION

Books of enduring scholarly value

History

The books reissued in this series include accounts of historical events and movements by eye-witnesses and contemporaries, as well as landmark studies that assembled significant source materials or developed new historiographical methods. The series includes work in social, political and military history on a wide range of periods and regions, giving modern scholars ready access to influential publications of the past.

The Case of Labourers in Husbandry Stated and Considered

David Davies (1742–1819) was an English clergyman and social commentator, best remembered for this survey of the lives of rural agricultural labourers. Raised and educated in the West Indies, Davies acted as a schoolmaster, plantation manager (which confirmed his abolitionist views) and private tutor until he was ordained in 1782 and became the rector of Barkham, Berkshire, where he remained incumbent until his death. This volume, first published in 1795, contains Davies' discussion of the living conditions of agricultural labourers in England. Davies discusses in detail the causes of the poverty of labourers, linking the high prices of goods with poverty, and proposes measures to relieve the labourers, including linking their daily wage to the price of bread. Davies' observations also demonstrate the failings of the contemporary Poor Laws. Originally focusing on the annual expenditure of labourers in Davies' own parish, this volume was expanded to include accounts of expenditure from elsewhere in Britain. This meticulously researched volume provides valuable evidence for the increase in rural poverty in the late eighteenth century.

T0382487

Cambridge University Press has long been a pioneer in the reissuing of out-of-print titles from its own backlist, producing digital reprints of books that are still sought after by scholars and students but could not be reprinted economically using traditional technology. The Cambridge Library Collection extends this activity to a wider range of books which are still of importance to researchers and professionals, either for the source material they contain, or as landmarks in the history of their academic discipline.

Drawing from the world-renowned collections in the Cambridge University Library, and guided by the advice of experts in each subject area, Cambridge University Press is using state-of-the-art scanning machines in its own Printing House to capture the content of each book selected for inclusion. The files are processed to give a consistently clear, crisp image, and the books finished to the high quality standard for which the Press is recognised around the world. The latest print-on-demand technology ensures that the books will remain available indefinitely, and that orders for single or multiple copies can quickly be supplied.

The Cambridge Library Collection will bring back to life books of enduring scholarly value (including out-of-copyright works originally issued by other publishers) across a wide range of disciplines in the humanities and social sciences and in science and technology.

The Case of Labourers in Husbandry Stated and Considered

David Davies

CAMBRIDGE UNIVERSITY PRESS

Cambridge, New York, Melbourne, Madrid, Cape Town, Singapore,
São Paolo, Delhi, Dubai, Tokyo, Mexico City

Published in the United States of America by Cambridge University Press, New York

www.cambridge.org
Information on this title: www.cambridge.org/9781108024747

© in this compilation Cambridge University Press 2010

This edition first published 1795
This digitally printed version 2010

ISBN 978-1-108-02474-7 Paperback

This book reproduces the text of the original edition. The content and language reflect the beliefs, practices and terminology of their time, and have not been updated.

Cambridge University Press wishes to make clear that the book, unless originally published by Cambridge, is not being republished by, in association or collaboration with, or with the endorsement or approval of, the original publisher or its successors in title.

THE CASE

OF

LABOURERS IN HUSBANDRY

STATED AND CONSIDERED,

IN THREE PARTS.

PART I.

A VIEW OF THEIR DISTRESSED CONDITION.

PART II.

THE PRINCIPAL CAUSES OF THEIR GROWING DISTRESS AND NUMBER, AND OF THE CONSEQUENT INCREASE OF THE POOR-RATE.

PART III.

MEANS OF RELIEF PROPOSED.

WITH

AN APPENDIX;

CONTAINING

A COLLECTION of ACCOUNTS,

SHEWING

THE EARNINGS AND EXPENCES OF LABOURING FAMILIES, IN DIFFERENT PARTS OF THE KINGDOM.

BY

DAVID DAVIES,

RECTOR OF BARKHAM, BERKS.

THE LABOURER IS WORTHY OF HIS HIRE. *LUKE* x. 7.

BATH, PRINTED BY R. CRUTTWELL,

FOR

G. G. AND J. ROBINSON, PATER-NOSTER-ROW, LONDON.

1795.

TO

THE HONOURABLE

THE BOARD OF AGRICULTURE.

AFTER ſpending a great deal of time in examining the circumſtances of *Labourers in Huſbandry*, I have thought it my duty to lay the following facts and obſervations before the publick. I hope they will be uſeful in drawing once more the attention of conſiderate perſons to what appears to be a caſe of real, wide-ſpread, and increaſing diſtreſs; and be inſtrumental in procuring for the numerous claſs of people in queſtion that redreſs, to which they ſeem to have the juſteſt claim. At all events the motive will excuſe me with the candid and humane for committing this work to the preſs.

It ſeems to lie peculiarly within the province of a Board inſtituted for the improvement of Agriculture, to enquire into the ſtate and condition of that denomination of people, by whom the buſineſs of agriculture is carried on. That Board have it more in their power than any private individual, to obtain the moſt authentick information with reſpect to labouring families; and I underſtand that they have notified their intention of making this one object of their

their particular enquiry. If the refult fhould be, *that the pay of the day-labourer is not adequate to his neceffities;* then, on their reprefentation of the matter, a rational plan may eafily be devifed for his fpeedy relief. For thefe reafons I have thought that the prefent publication might with propriety be addreffed to that Board.

To that Board, therefore, I take the liberty to infcribe it; earneftly hoping that, fuch as it is, it may prove of fome fervice in the farther profecution of thefe ufeful enquiries. Heartily wifhing them fuccefs in all their views for the publick good,

I remain,

with the greateft refpect,

their moft obedient

and moft humble fervant,

BARKHAM, BERKSHIRE,
MARCH 26TH, 1795.

DAVID DAVIES.

CONTENTS.

PART I.

PART II.

SECTION

PART III.

APPENDIX.

A VIEW OF THE

DISTRESSED CONDITION

OF

LABOURING FAMILIES.

SECTION I.

INTRODUCTORY OBSERVATIONS CONCERNING THE POOR AND THE POOR LAWS.

IN every nation the welfare and contentment of the lower denominations of people are objects of great importance, and deserving continual attention. For the bulk of every nation consists of such as must earn their daily bread by daily labour. It is to the patient industry of these that the higher ranks are every where indebted for most of their enjoyments. It is chiefly on these that every nation depends for its population, strength, and security. All reasonable persons will therefore acknowledge the equity of ensuring to them at least the necessary means of subsistence.

But of all the denominations of people in a state, *the labourers in husbandry* are by far the most valuable. For these are the men, who, being constantly employed in the cultivation of the earth, provide the staff of life for the whole nation. And it is the wives of these men, who rear thofe hardy broods of children, which, befides fupplying the country with the hands it wants, fill up the voids which death is continually making in camps and cities. And fince they have thus a peculiar title to public regard, one might expect to fee them every where comfortably accommodated. Yet even in this kingdom, diftinguifhed as it is for humanity and political wifdom, they have been for fome time paft fuffering peculiar hardfhips. To make their cafe known, and to claim for them the juft recompence of their labour, is the chief purpofe of this publication.

It has however, indirectly, a refpect to the cafe of the poor in general. For, in tracing the unufual diftrefs of day-labourers to the feveral caufes in which it has originated, I could not but obferve that the fame caufes would alfo account for that general diftrefs which is fo heavily felt, and fo much complained of, by all the lower ranks of people. And this led me to conclude, that if means could be devifed for removing or leffening the exifting evils in the former cafe, the fame would probably be found efficacious for the fame purpofe univerfally.

The defign of our poor laws is to provide for the employment of the able and induftrious, for the correction of the idle and vicious, and for the maintenance of the aged and impotent. They appear in theory admirably calculated to anfwer thefe ends. Yet men of learning and judgment have entertained very different opinions concerning them: fome regarding them as ufeful regulations for the government of the poor, though ftill imperfect and requiring amendment; fome, as forming a complete fyftem incapable of further improvement, and only wanting a better execution; and others, as a pernicious code, encouraging idlenefs and profligacy, and which ought therefore to be abolifhed.

It may be admitted that these laws are imperfect, and that they have been but imperfectly executed; yet I think it undeniable that they have on the whole produced a great deal of good. They have undoubtedly saved thousands of families from perishing by hunger and nakedness. The poor themselves are sensible of their excellent tendency; and when their wrongs go unredressed, they do not blame the laws. It seems therefore probable that the repealing them now, or even greatly altering them, would be attended with the most serious consequences. Either of these measures might drive the people to despair, to insurrection, to every evil work.

It has been, however, the general opinion for some time past, that some kind of reform is become necessary. For the *rich* have complained loudly of the great and rapid increase of the poor-rate: and the late returns made to Parliament by the overseers of the poor are full evidence of the fact. In the mean while the *poor* have been more than ever dissatisfied with the relief afforded them by means of this tax; and every body sees that their numbers and distresses have increased amazingly. In consequence of this discontent on both sides, several plans have been offered to the public with the twofold design of providing more effectually for the poor, and of gradually reducing the rate. But either because they appeared impracticable in themselves, or because they innovated too much on our established system of poor laws, none of them has hitherto received the public approbation. Further light seems to be required, before any plan of this kind can be properly adjusted to the present circumstances of the nation.

I dare not flatter myself that I am able to furnish all the light that is wanted, well knowing that many wise and benevolent men have employed their talents upon this difficult subject without much success.

If

If I ſhould only have the good fortune to point out the right way of proceeding in our enquiries reſpecting the poor, this will be one material point gained. Hereafter ſome perſon of a more ſagacious mind may ſee more clearly how to introduce ſuch improvements of our poor laws, as may give them the greateſt efficacy for the valuable purpoſes they aim at.

Of this, however, I am confident. When the caſe of labouring families comes to be fully known and conſidered, it cannot fail to awaken the general compaſſion in their favour; to ſilence the abſurd complaints ſo frequently made on account of the great progreſſive increaſe of the rate; and to procure for this deſerving claſs of people able and zealous advocates, who will plead their cauſe with effect, and reſcue them from that abject ſtate into which they are ſunk.

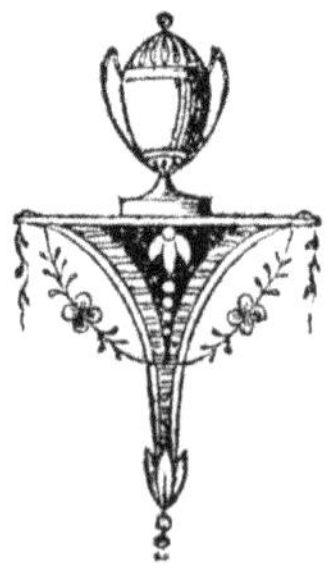

SECTION

SECTION II.

AN ENQUIRY INTO THE STATE OF THE POOR, NECESSARY, PREVIOUS TO A REFORM OF THE POOR LAWS—THE MANNER IN WHICH THE FOLLOWING ACCOUNTS OF THE EARNINGS AND EXPENCES OF LABOURING FAMILIES WERE OBTAINED—THE ACCOUNTS THEMSELVES, WITH AN ABSTRACT OF THE SAME.

WHEN the Parliament in the years 1775 and 1785 ordered returns to be made of the poor-rates throughout the kingdom, another matter, at leaft equally neceffary as a ground of reform, feems not to have been thought of. To render the information complete, an enquiry fhould at the fame time have been directed to be made into the actual circumftances of poor families. For certainly a perfect knowledge of the ftate of the poor, is the only bafis upon which any new regulations refpecting them can be fafely raifed. And as labourers in hufbandry form the moft numerous, as well as the moft ufeful clafs of the community, a careful enquiry into *their* circumftances was efpecially neceffary, previous to the framing of fuch regulations.

I hope that omiffion will be fupplied in fome meafure, though doubtlefs very imperfectly, by the *accounts* I am about to produce of the earnings and expences of labouring families in different parts of the kingdom. But as thefe accounts form the groundwork of what I have

I have to advance on the behalf of the poor, it is proper that I ſhould here deſcribe the manner in which they were obtained.

In viſiting the labouring families of my pariſh, as my duty led me, I could not but obſerve with concern their mean and diſtreſſed condition. I found them in general but indifferently fed; badly clothed; ſome children without ſhoes and ſtockings; very few put to ſchool; and moſt families in debt to little ſhopkeepers. In ſhort, there was ſcarcely any appearance of comfort about their dwellings, except that the children looked tolerably healthy. Yet I could not impute the wretchedneſs I ſaw either to ſloth or waſtefulneſs. For I knew that the farmers were careful that the men ſhould not want employment; and had they been given to drinking, I am ſure I ſhould have heard enough of it. And I commonly found the women, when not working in the fields, well occupied at home; ſeldom indeed earning money; but baking their bread, waſhing and mending their garments, and rocking the cradle.

Theſe poor people, in aſſigning the cauſe of their miſery, agreed in aſcribing it to the high prices of the neceſſaries of life. "Every thing (ſaid they) is ſo dear, that we can hardly live." In order to aſſure myſelf, whether this was really the caſe, I enquired into the particulars of their earnings and expences; and wrote the ſame down at the time, juſt as I received them from each family reſpectively, guarding as well as I could againſt error and deception. The following accounts are the reſult of that enquiry, and they ſhew that the cauſe aſſigned is founded in fact.

Theſe accounts of the earnings and expences of labouring families, in my own pariſh, were collected about *Eaſter* 1787, when affairs relating to the poor were under the conſideration of the Parliament and

and the public. From what loose information I could then gather near home, I saw sufficient reason to believe, that they presented but too faithful a view of the general distress of such families throughout this and the neighbouring counties. And the vast increase of the poor-rate, at that time every where a subject of complaint, rendered it very probable that the same misery had overspread the kingdom.

On my suggesting this to some friends who interest themselves in the welfare of the poor, we thought this matter deserving of a fuller scrutiny. And in order to collect information, an abstract of these accounts was printed, and many copies were distributed. We supposed that two or three papers returned from every county, carefully filled up, would furnish us amply with the information we desired. I have to regret that a greater number of those distributed papers has not been returned. The few I have received confirm the opinion previously entertained of the general distress of labouring people, and of the insufficiency of their wages for the supply of their wants. But the accounts themselves will evince this much better than many words.

Accounts of the Expences and Earnings of Six Labouring Families in the Pariſh of Barkham in the County of Berks, taken at Eaſter 1787.

No. I.

Weekly Expences of a Family, conſiſting of a Man and his Wife, and five Children, the eldeſt eight years of age, the youngeſt an Infant.

	s.	*d.*
FLOUR: 7 $\frac{1}{2}$ gallons, at 10d. *per* gallon - - - - - - -	6	3
Yeaſt, to make it into bread, 2$\frac{1}{2}$d; and ſalt 1$\frac{1}{2}$d. - - - - - -	0	4
Bacon, 1lb. boiled at two or three times with greens: the pot-liquor, with bread and potatoes, makes a *meſs* for the children - -	0	8
Tea, 1 ounce, 2d.;—$\frac{3}{4}$ lb. ſugar, 6d.;—$\frac{1}{2}$ lb. butter or lard 4d. -	1	0
Soap, $\frac{1}{4}$ lb. at 9d. *per* lb. - - - - - - - - - - -	0	2$\frac{1}{4}$
Candles, $\frac{1}{3}$ lb. one week with another at a medium, at 9d. - -	0	3
Thread, thrum, and worſted, for mending apparel, &c. - - -	0	3
Total	8	11$\frac{1}{4}$

Weekly Earnings of the Man and his Wife, viz.

The man receives the common weekly wages 8 months in the year	7	0
By taſk-work the remaining 4 months he earns ſomething more: his *extra* earnings, if equally divided among the 52 weeks in the year, would increaſe the weekly wages about - - - - -	1	0
The wife's common work is to bake bread for the family, to waſh and mend ragged clothes, and to look after the children; but at bean-ſetting, haymaking, and harveſt, ſhe earns as much as comes one week with another to about - - - - - - - -	0	6
Total	8	6

Weekly expences of this family - - - - -	8	11$\frac{1}{4}$
Weekly earnings - - - - - - - -	8	6
Deficiency of earnings - - - - - -	0	5$\frac{1}{4}$

No. 2.

No. 2.

Weekly Expences of a Family, confifting of a Woman, whofe Hufband is run away, and fix Children, the eldeft 16 years of age, the youngeft 5: four of the Children too young to earn any thing.

	s.	*d.*
Flour for bread, 6 gallons, at 10d. *per* gallon - - - - -	5	0
Ditto $\frac{1}{2}$ gallon for puddings, and thickening the children's meffes -	0	5
Yeaft for the bread, 2d.;—falt $1\frac{1}{2}$d. - - - - - - - -	0	$3\frac{1}{2}$
Bacon, 2lbs. at 8d. (with fometimes a fheep's head) - - -	1	4
Tea, $1\frac{1}{2}$ ounce, 4d.;—fugar, $\frac{1}{2}$lb. 4d.;—butter, $\frac{1}{4}$lb. 4d. - -	1	0
Soap, fomething more than $\frac{1}{4}$lb. at 9d. *per* lb. - - - -	0	$2\frac{1}{2}$
Candles, $\frac{1}{3}$lb. one week with another, at 9d. *per* lb. - - -	0	3
Thread, worfted, &c. - - - - - - - - - -	0	3
Total	8	9

Weekly Earnings of this Family, with the Parifh Allowance.

This family receives from the parifh weekly - - - -	5	0
The eldeft boy earns *per* week - - - - - - - - -	2	6
The next, aged 13 years, earns, but not conftantly - - -	1	6
The mother, whilft an old woman looks after the younger children, earns, one week with another, about - - - - - -	1	6
The amount, fuppofing none of them to lofe any time, is - -	10	6
But fome deduction muft be made from this fum, becaufe they are an unhealthy family, one or other of them being often laid up with the ague or rheumatifm; diforders to which poor people, from low living and working in the wet, are very fubject. The woman affures me that their earnings with the parifh allowance do not exceed 9s. *per* week on an average; therefore deduct - - - - -	1	6
Total of earnings, with the parifh allowance	9	0
Surplus of earnings - - - - -	0	3

No. 3.

No. 3.

Weekly Expences of a Family, confifting of a Man and his Wife, with four fmall Children, the eldeft under 6 years of age, the youngeft an Infant.

	s.	d.
Flour, 6 gallons, at 10d. per gallon - - - - - - - -	5	0
Yeaft, 2d.—falt 1½d. - - - - - - - - - -	0	3½
Bacon, 1 lb. - - - - - - - - - - - - -	0	8
Tea, 1 ounce, 2d.—fugar, ¾ lb. 6d.—butter, ½ lb. 4d. - - -	1	0
Soap, ¼ lb. 2¼d.—candles, ⅓ lb. 3d.—thread, &c. 3d. - - -	0	8¼
Total	7	7¾

Weekly Earnings of the Man and his Wife, viz.

The hufband, if he has conftant health and conftant employment, earns on an average - - - - - - - - - - -	8	0
The wife, like No. 1, does not earn above - - - - - -	0	6
Total	8	6

Weekly earnings of this family - - - - -	8	6
Weekly expences - - - - - -	7	7¾
Surplus of earnings	0	10¼

No. 4.

No. 4.

Weekly Expences of a Man and his Wife, with three Children, the eldeft under 5 years of age, the youngeft an Infant.

	s.	d.
Flour, 3 gallons *per* week, at 10d. - - - - - - - -	2	6
Yeaft, 1d.—falt 1½d. - - - - - - - - - - - -	0	2½
Bacon: the farmer, of whom they rent their dwelling, lets them have a fatted hog, weight about 14 fcore, (on condition of their not keeping any pigs or poultry) at 1s. *per* fcore under the market price: this at 6s. 6d. *per* fcore (1787) comes to 4l. 11s. and as it lafts the family the whole year, it is *per* week exactly - - - - - -	1	9
Cheefe, about 28lb. at 4½d. *per* lb.; 10s. 6d. *per ann.*—*per* week - -	0	2½
Tea, ¼lb. *per* month, at 3s. *per* lb. *per* week 2¼d.; fugar 8d.; butter 4d.	1	2¼
The wife having an infant at the breaft, and fancying *very* fmall beer better than mere water, brews a peck of malt once a month, which cofts 1s. 4d.—hops ¼ lb. 4d.—this is *per* week - - - -	0	5
Soap, 3 lbs. at 9d. *per* lb. lafts 2 months, this is *per* week 3d. -	0	3
Candles, ⅓ lb. at a medium, 3d.—thread and worfted 2d. - -	0	5
Total	6	11¼

Weekly Earnings of this Family, viz.

	s.	d.
The man's bufinefs is to follow a farmer's team, for which he has 8s. a week throughout the year - - - - - - - -	8	0
He has, befides, either his diet in his employer's houfe 6 weeks in harveft, or inftead of it 18s.; which divided into 52 parts, is *per* week	0	4
The wife earns at a medium about 8d. *per* week - - - -	0	8
Total	9	0

	s.	d.
Weekly earnings of this family - - -	9	0
Weekly expences - - - - - -	6	11¼
Surplus of earnings	2	0¾

No. 5.

No. 5.

Weekly Expences of another Family, confifting of a Man and his Wife, with three Children, the eldeft 6 years of age, the youngeft an Infant.

	s.	d.
Flour, ½ a fack *per* month, or nearly 5 gallons per week, fay 4½, at 10d.	3	9
Yeaft and falt - - - - - - - - - - - - -	0	3
Meat:—bought a pig and fatted it: price of the pig 10s. 6d.; coft 6d. a week for 42 weeks before fatting, 1l. 1s.; was fatted with one fack of beans 15s. one fack of peafe 16s. and 5 bufhels of ground barley 25s.; total 4l. 7s. 6d.—when killed it was eftimated to weigh about 14 fcore pounds; it coft therefore 6s. 4d. *per* fcore; this, with a few fheep's heads and fhins of beef, will laft all the year, and is *per* week	1	8
Beer; they feldom brew but againft a chriftening - - - -	0	0
Tea, fugar, and butter - - - - - - - - - -	1	0
Soap, ftarch, candles, worfted, on an average - - - - -	1	0
Total	7	8

Weekly Earnings of this Family, viz.

	s.	d.
The man has, fummer and winter, the common pay, 7s.; and he has alfo a mefs of milk for breakfaft, and fmall beer, worth at leaft 1s. more - - - - - - - - - - - - -	8	0
The woman earns, as fhe believes, by wafhing and needle-work, by breeding poultry, and at harveft work when fhe has no child to nurfe, about 1s. *per* week - - - - - - -	1	0
	9	0

	s.	d.
Weekly earnings of this family - - - -	9	0
Weekly expences - - - - - - - -	7	8
Surplus of earnings	1	4

No. 6.

Weekly Expences of a Family, confifting of a Man and his Wife, with two young Children, the eldeft 7 years of age, the youngeft 4.

	s.	d.
Flour, 5 gallons, at 10d. - - - - - - - -	4	2
Yeaft and falt - - - - - - - - - - -	0	3
Bacon, $1\frac{1}{2}$ lb. at 8d. - - - - - - - - - -	1	0
Tea, 1 ounce, 2d.;—fugar, $\frac{1}{2}$ lb. 4d.;—butter, $\frac{1}{4}$ lb. 4d. - -	0	10
Soap, $\frac{1}{4}$ lb. $2\frac{1}{4}$d.;—candles, 3d.;—worfted, 3d. - - - - -	0	$8\frac{1}{4}$
Total	6	$11\frac{1}{4}$

Weekly Earnings of this Family, viz.

The man earns, one week with another, if conftantly employed	8	0
The woman, on an average, not more than - - -	0	6
Total	8	6

Weekly earnings of this family - - - - -	8	6
Weekly expences - - - - - - -	6	$11\frac{1}{4}$
Surplus of earnings	1	$6\frac{3}{4}$

N. B. The weekly expences and earnings of another family, confifting of the fame number of perfons, are fo nearly the fame with the above, that it is not worth while to fet them down feparately.

Note 1.

Note 1. It is not eaſy to come at the exact earnings of a day-labourer, as the farmers keep no regular account of the diſtinct payments made to each labourer. A great deal of huſbandry work is done by the *piece*, or by *taſk*; ſuch as hoeing turnips, beans, and peaſe; mowing graſs and ſpring corn; reaping, threſhing, hedging and ditching, draining, coppice work, &c. Intelligent farmers ſay, that the men are thus employed about four months in the year, and that they then earn from eight to twelve ſhillings a week, according to circumſtances. Suppoſe them to earn at a medium 10s.

	£.	s.	d.
Then a man's work 35 weeks, at 7s. comes to	12	5	0
And ——— 17 weeks, at 10s. - -	8	10	0
Amount *per annum* - -	20	15	0
Add the wife's earnings, at 6d. *per* week -	1	6	0
Total of earnings *per annum*	22	1	0

This is at the rate of 8s. 6d. a week nearly: and Nos. 4 and 5 of the foregoing accounts *prove*, that the *men*'s earnings on an average do not much, if at all, exceed 8s. a week.

Note 2. If any one ſhould think that the *women*'s earnings are ſtated too low in theſe accounts, he will be convinced they are not, on conſidering that theſe women commonly begin the world with an infant, and are mere nurſes for ten or twelve years after marriage, being always either with child, or having a child at the breaſt; conſequently incapable of doing much other work beſides the neceſſary buſineſs of their families, ſuch as baking, waſhing, and the like. In winter they earn next to nothing, few of them having in their youth learnt to knit and ſpin: and if in ſummer they are able to go to harveſt work, they muſt pay ſome perſon a ſhilling a week out of their earnings for looking after

after their children. It is probable therefore that from 6d. to 9d. a week is as much as labourers' wives in general, hereabout, earn on an average the year through.

THE expences already ſet down are only the *weekly outgoings*, excluſive of houſe-rent, fuel, clothing, lying-in, ſickneſs, and burials: theſe being beſt allowed for by the year, may be called *annual outgoings*, and are as under:

	£.	s.	d.
Rent of a cottage, or part of an old farm-houſe, with a ſmall piece of garden ground, for a family, is from two pounds to two guineas: ſay - - - - - - - - - - -	2	0	0
Fuel: this is turf from the Common, and when bought coſts 12s. *per* family; but as a man can cut in a week nearly enough to ſerve his family all the year, and the farmers (if the diſtance be not great) will give the carriage for the aſhes, let this be charged at a little more than one week's wages - - - -	0	10	0
Clothing: 1. The man's: wear of a ſuit *per annum* 5s.; wear of a working jacket and breeches 4s.; two ſhirts 8s.; one pair of ſtout ſhoes nailed 7s.; two pair of ſtockings 4s.; hat, handkerchief, &c. 2s. Sum 1l. 10s.——2. The *wife*'s: wear of gown and petticoats 4s.; one ſhift 3s. 6d.; one pair of ſtrong ſhoes 4s.; one pair of ſtockings 1s. 6d.; two aprons 3s.; handkerchiefs, caps, &c. 4s. Sum 1l.——3. The *children*'s: their clothing is (uſually) partly made up of the parents' old clothes, partly bought at ſecond-hand: what is bought (ſuppoſing *three* children to a family) cannot well be reckoned at leſs than 1l.: where there are more than three children, 7s. may be added; and where there are fewer, 7s. may be deducted, for each.—Let the whole be eſtimated at	3	10	0
Carried over	6	0	0

[*Note.*

	£.	s.	d.
Brought over	6	0	0
[*Note.* Very few poor people can afford to lay out this ſum in clothes; but they ſhould be enabled to do it: ſome cottagers breed a few fowls, with which they buy what ſheets and blankets they want: but thoſe who live in old farmhouſes are ſeldom allowed (to uſe their own words) *to keep a pig or a chick.*]			
Lying-in: the child's linen 3 or 4s.; the midwife's fee 5s.; a bottle of gin or brandy always had upon this occaſion, 2s.; attendance of a nurſe for a few days, and her diet, at leaſt 5s.; half a buſhel of malt brewed, and hops, 3s.; to the miniſter for churching 1s.;— call the ſum 1l. and ſuppoſe this to happen but once in two years; this is *per annum* - - - - - - - - - -	0	10	0
Caſualties: 1. In *ſickneſs* there is the phyſick to be paid for, and the loſs of time to be allowed for:—2. *Burials*; poor people having many children, ſometimes loſe one:—for both theſe together it ſeems moderate to allow *per annum* - - - - - -	0	10	0
Sum of theſe annual outgoings	£.7	0	0

This ſum (7l.) being divided by 52, the number of weeks in a year, gives 2s. 8¼d. *per* week. If therefore any one deſires to know the *whole* weekly expence of a family, (conſiſting of a man and his wife with three children) in order to compare it with the *whole* of their weekly earnings, he muſt add 2s. 8¼d. to the *current* weekly expence of the family, as before ſet down at the foot of its account.

Suppoſe, for inſtance, it were required to find the whole weekly expence of No. 5, in order to compare the ſame with the whole of the weekly earnings of that family:

	s.	d.
To the current weekly expence, p. 12, - - - -	7	8
Add one 52d part of the *annual outgoings*, or - -	2	8¼
The whole weekly expence -	10	4¼
The whole weekly earnings, p. 12	9	0
Weekly deficiency	1	4¼

In other cafes: where there are *more* than three children, two-pence more muft be added for each; and where there are *fewer*, two-pence muft be deducted; the reafon of which may be feen under the article *Clothing*, in p. 15. Thus,

To the current weekly expence of No. 3, p. 10 -	7	$7\frac{3}{4}$
Add, as in the former inftance - - - - - -	2	$8\frac{1}{4}$
Add alfo, towards clothing the *fourth* child - -	0	2
The whole weekly expence -	10	6
The whole weekly earnings, p. 10	8	6
Weekly deficiency	2	0

PARISH OF BARKHAM, BERKS.

EASTER, 1787.

An Abſtract of the Expences and Earnings of the foregoing ſix Families of Labourers, by the Week, and by the Year.

	No. 1. 7 Persons.			No. 2. 7 Persons.			No. 3. 6 Persons.			No. 4. 5 Persons.			No. 5. 5 Persons.			No. 6. 4 Persons.		
Expences per Week.	£.	s.	d.	£.	s.	d.	£.	s.	d.	£.	s.	d.	£.	s.	d.	£.	s.	d.
Bread or Flour - - - -	0	6	3	0	5	5	0	5	0	0	2	6	0	3	9	0	4	2
Yeast and Salt - - - -	0	0	4	0	0	3½	0	0	3½	0	0	2½	0	0	3	0	0	3
Bacon or other Meat -	0	0	8	0	1	4	0	0	8	0	1	9	0	1	8	0	1	0
Tea, Sugar, Butter - - -	0	1	0	0	1	0	0	1	0	0	1	2¼	0	1	0	0	0	10
Cheese (seldom any) - -	0	0	0	0	0	0	0	0	0	0	0	2½	0	0	0	0	0	0
Beer (seldom any) - - -	0	0	0	0	0	0	0	0	0	0	0	5	0	0	0	0	0	0
Soap, Starch, Blue, - - -	0	0	2¼	0	0	2½	0	0	2¼	0	0	3	0	0	6	0	0	2¼
Candles - - - - - - -	0	0	3	0	0	3	0	0	3	0	0	3	0	0	3	0	0	3
Thread, Thrum, Worsted -	0	0	3	0	0	3	0	0	3	0	0	2	0	0	3	0	0	3
Total	0	8	11¼	0	8	9	0	7	7¾	0	6	11¼	0	7	8	0	6	11¼
Amount *per annum*	23	4	9	22	15	0	19	17	7	18	0	9	19	18	8	18	0	9
Earnings per Week.	£.	s.	d.	£.	s.	d.	£.	s.	d.	£.	s.	d.	£.	s.	d.	£.	s.	d.
The Man earns at a medium	0	8	0	Pariſh pay	5	0	0	8	0	0	8	4	0	8	0	0	8	0
The Woman - - - - -	0	0	6	0	1	0	0	0	6	0	0	8	0	1	0	0	0	6
The Children - - - -	0	0	0	0	3	0	0	0	0	0	0	0	0	0	0	0	0	0
Total	0	8	6	0	9	0	0	8	6	0	9	0	0	9	0	0	8	6
Amount *per annum*	22	2	0	23	8	0	22	2	0	23	8	0	23	8	0	22	2	0
	£.	s.	d.	£.	s.	d.	£.	s.	d.	£.	s.	d.	£.	s.	d.	£.	s.	d.
To the above Amount of Expences *per annum* -	23	4	9	22	15	0	19	17	7	18	0	9	19	18	8	18	0	9
Add Rent, Fuel, Clothes, Lying-in, &c. - -	7	14	0	7	14	0	7	7	0	7	0	0	7	0	0	6	14	0
Total of Expences *per annum*	30	18	9	30	9	0	27	4	7	25	0	9	26	18	8	24	14	9
Total of Earnings *per annum*	22	2	0	23	8	0	22	2	0	23	8	0	23	8	0	22	2	0
Deficiency of Earnings - -	8	16	9	7	1	0	5	2	7	1	12	9	3	10	8	2	12	9

PARISH OF BARKHAM.

Account of the Families.

No. 1. A man and his wife, with five children, the eldest eight years of age, the youngest an infant.

No. 2. A woman whose husband is run away, and six children; the eldest a boy of sixteen years of age, the next a boy of thirteen, the youngest five: four of the children too young to earn any thing.

No. 3. A man and his wife, with four small children, the eldest six years of age, the youngest an infant.

No. 4. A man and his wife, with three small children, the eldest under five years of age, the youngest an infant.

No. 5. A man and his wife, with three young children, the eldest six years of age, the youngest an infant.

No. 6. A man and his wife, with two young children, the eldest seven years of age, the youngest four.

Note. Such families as these are numerous in country parishes: in this parish they make above two-fifths of the inhabitants.

Annual Outgoings.

	£.	s.	d.
1. *Rent* of a cottage and garden, or of a part of an old farm-house and garden, for a family	2	0	0
2. *Fuel*, being turf cut on the common, from 8 to 12s.—say	0	10	0
3. *Clothing*:— The man's £.1 10 0; The wife's 1 0 0; Allow for three children - - 1 0 0	3	10	0
4. *Lying-in*, one year with another	0	10	0
5. *Casualties*, including sickness, loss of time thereby, and burials; estimated at - - -	0	10	0
Sum of these outgoings	7	0	0
Price of the half-peck loaf of houshold wheaten bread -	0	0	11½
Price of the gallon of flour -	0	0	10
—— of a week's labour in winter	0	7	0
—— of a week's labour, where the labourer is employed constantly all weather the year through - - - - - - -	0	8	0

NOTES.

Few poor families can afford themselves more than 1lb. of meat weekly.

The tea used per family is from 1 to 1½ oz. per week, at 2d. per oz.

Soft sugar, ½lb. at 7d. to 8d. per lb.

Salt butter, or lard, ½lb. at 7½lb. to 8d. per lb.

Suckling is here so profitable (to furnish veal for London) that the poor can seldom either buy or beg milk.

Poor people reckon cheese the dearest article they can use.

Malt is so dear, that they seldom brew any small beer, except against a lying-in or a christening.

To eke out soap, they burn *green* Fern, and knead the ashes into balls, with which they make a lye for washing.

In No. 4, the charge for bread is considerably less than in the others, because that family is favoured by its employer in the article of meat: *See the Account.*

In No. 5, the woman washes for one or two single labourers, for which reason 6d. is charged for soap.

SECTION III.

OBSERVATIONS SUGGESTED BY THE FOREGOING ACCOUNTS, AND CONFIRMED BY OTHERS RECEIVED FROM DIFFERENT PARTS OF THE KINGDOM.

1. THESE accounts fuppofe that a labouring man may always have work, when he is well and willing to work, without regard to any other lofs of time than what may be occafioned by ficknefs alone: but as this is in reality the cafe of very few labourers comparatively, moft of them lofing fome time from other accidents, it is certain that in general they muft feel additional diftrefs from this circumftance.

2. It deferves to be remarked, that the outgoings called *annual* in thefe accounts, to diftinguifh them from thofe that recur weekly, amount to a *third part* nearly of the whole annual earnings of a labouring family. And they would exceed this proportion, were not the charge for *fuel* here much below what that article cofts in many places; for in a great part of the kingdom *thirty fhillings* will fcarcely purchafe fuch a quantity, as is abfolutely neceffary for a family.

3. Every body muft have obferved, that families with four or five young children are common in country parifhes. As *bread* makes the principal part of the food of all poor families, and almoft the whole of the food of all fuch large families, it is manifeft that whatever caufes operate in raifing at any time the price of corn, the fame muft neceffarily bring heavy diftrefs upon families of this defcription.

4. It

4. It appears that in fuch families as No. 1, in which there are five children, all unable to work, the whole of their earnings nearly goes for *food* alone, even when the price of bread (as here reckoned) is rather low than moderate. Alfo, that the weekly earnings of fuch families are not fufficient for fupplying them in the fcantieft proportion with the common weekly neceffaries, exclufive of the annual outgoings.

5. But in moft country parifhes there are *fome* families with even fix children, all incapable of earning a maintenance. Confequently the weekly earnings of fuch as thefe muft fall fhort in a ftill greater degree than in the preceding inftance, of what is abfolutely neceffary for fupplying their common weekly neceffities.

6. No. 2 is a family deferted by the father, and thereby thrown on the parifh; which fometimes happens from the fault of overfeers in refufing timely relief. This family has received from the parifh, during fome years, a weekly penfion of 5s.; lives in the parifh-houfe rent free; and is fupplied with fuel, and fome clothing, at the parifh expence. And though the mother is a hard-working woman, the expence of this family to the parifh, fince the man went away, has been about 15l. a year. Such is the *folly* of bearing hard upon the poor!

7. The weekly furpluffes, which appear in Nos. 2 and 3, are fo trifling, that if they were expended on the weekly fubfiftence of thofe families refpectively, no reafonable perfon could think that they fared too well. It is probable that in moft inftances thofe apparent furpluffes are fo expended by fuch families. And then the whole amount of the annual outgoings of thefe (as well as of No. 1) for rent, fuel, clothing, lying-in, and cafualties, muft either come out of the poor-rate, or thefe families muft neceffarily run in debt, fteal, or ftarve.

8. Nos.

8. Nos. 4, 5, 6, have, each, a weekly furplus confiderable enough to be applied to fome ufe: but it is obfervable that the furplus in No. 4 exceeds that of all the reft. This happens, *1ft*, becaufe that family is favoured in the article of meat;—*2dly*, becaufe it has at prefent credit enough to buy a fack of flour at a time, by which fomething is gained in bread;—and *3dly*, becaufe it has fufficient garden-ground for planting a good patch of potatoes, which alfo fave bread.

9. Let us now fuppofe all the *weekly furpluffes*, which appear in thefe accounts, really to exift and to be faved. Then, on comparing the *yearly* amount of the earnings with the *yearly* amount of the expences, we fhall fee in every inftance a confiderable deficiency: which deficiency, unlefs it be made up by poaching, ftealing, and other bad practices, or be fupplied by the charity of individuals, muft neceffarily come out of the poor-rate.

10. If, omitting Nos. 1 and 2, whofe earnings are fo inadequate to the fupply of their wants, we add together *all* the expences of the remaining *four* families, confifting of twenty perfons, the fum 103l. 18s. 9d. divided by 4, the number of families, gives 26l. very nearly for the whole yearly expence of a family of five perfons. And if we confider that *three* of thefe four families have, each, a fucking child who eats but little bread, and that none of them can afford to drink fmall beer in common, we fhall be fatisfied that 26l. is the leaft fum that will fuffice for the annual maintenance of fuch a family, wherever bread made of wheat is commonly eaten. But the fum of the earnings of the fame four families, fuppofing them conftantly employed, is only 91l. which, divided by 4, gives 22l. 15s. for the mean amount

amount of the earnings of a family of five perſons. Therefore the mean deficiency of the earnings of ſuch a family is at the leaſt 3l. 5s.

11. But if it be thought reaſonable (and ſurely it *is* reaſonable) that labouring people ſhould have the ability to brew ſmall beer for themſelves; then, ſuppoſing each family to uſe only *one* buſhel of malt *per* month of four weeks, which will make about 28 gallons of very ſmall drink; this, reckoning the malt at 5s. 6d. *per* buſhel, with three or four ſhillings worth of hops, will add about 3l. 15s. to the above expences. And if it be alſo thought right that they ſhould be enabled to give a child or two a little ſchooling, 10s. more muſt be added on *this* account. Both theſe articles together make 4l. 5s. which, added to the 26l. above, makes the total of the expences 30l. 5s. And this ſum, I think, labouring families ſhould earn yearly, to enable them to provide for themſelves all neceſſaries, and to live in tolerable comfort, independent of parochial aſſiſtance. But it appears that in fact they do not earn above 23l. *per annum.* Therefore the mean deficiency of their earnings is, on this ſuppoſition, at leaſt 7l.

12. However, taking the matter as it is ſtated in Obſervation 10, the deficiency of 3l. 5s. there ſhewn, would well maintain one young child. Whence we may infer, that the preſent wages of a labouring man conſtantly employed, together with the uſual earnings of his wife, are barely ſufficient to maintain in all neceſſaries, independent of pariſh relief, the man and his wife with two children: And that the ſum of their earnings would be inſufficient for this, if poor people were to allow themſelves *ſmall beer* in common. But it is a fact, in which old people uniformly agree, that the joint earnings of a labouring man and his wife were ſufficient to maintain themſelves and three children, and

in

in a better manner too, about the middle of this century. Therefore the price of day-labour has not, in this interval, kept pace with the prices of the neceſſaries of life; and the condition of a labouring family is now become, from this circumſtance alone, worſe than it was then, by ſo much as would ſuffice for the maintenance of one child.

13. In truth, various cauſes, as I ſhall ſhew preſently, have concurred to raiſe the nominal prices of the neceſſaries of life a great deal higher than they were forty or fifty years ago. And various cauſes have likewiſe concurred, as I ſhall alſo ſhew, to keep down the nominal price of labour nearly as low as it was at that time. Add to this, that the labouring poor have been gradually deprived of ſome advantages which they formerly enjoyed, and ſubjected to ſome hardſhips from which they were formerly exempt. Thus the *ſubſiſtence* of poor families in general is become far more expenſive and difficult than it was in the former part of this century: in conſequence of which the *number* of the poor depending on pariſh relief is greatly increaſed. And this obſervation (when theſe facts are proved) will ſerve to explain that augmentation of the general amount of the poor-rates, which has been continually going on from about the year 1750 to the preſent day.

14. It is manifeſt from *Obſ.* 10, that the poor-rate is now in part a *ſubſtitute for wages*. And a miſerable ſubſtitute it is, for the following reaſons:—1ſt. Becauſe the diſtribution of it being left very much in the diſcretion of the overſeers of the poor, who in ſaving the pariſh money ſave their own, and who in diſtributing it do not always regard ſtrict juſtice, many modeſt and deſerving families, that cannot live entirely without relief, receive not ſufficient relief from it, chuſing rather to ſuffer oppreſſion than to incur the ill-will of their ſuperiors

 by

by applying to a magiſtrate for redreſs. 2dly. Becauſe the receiving that from the pariſh in the precarious way of alms, which they ought to receive in wages as the reaſonable recompence of labour, is a great diſcouragement to the induſtrious poor, tends to ſink their minds in deſpondency, and to drive them into deſperate courſes. 3dly. Becauſe ſometimes the men, either from reſentment at the hard uſage they have met with, are provoked to deſert their families; or elſe too often, from mere deſpair of being able to maintain them honeſtly, they and their wives betake themſelves to wicked courſes: the example corrupts their children, whoſe minds being thus tainted remain ever after dead to all virtuous impreſſions. 4thly. Becauſe, wherever large ſums of money are raiſed for the uſe of the poor, a great temptation is laid in the way of unprincipled overſeers, who, by embezzling a part of what comes into their hands, rob the poor in the firſt inſtance; and afterwards, to cover the villainy, perjure themſelves in ſwearing to their accounts.

15. I have read ſomewhere, that about the beginning of this century, the poor of this country receiving relief were computed to be about 600,000. I think it probable that their number is now (1787) almoſt tripled. In this pariſh the poor-rate is ſomewhat lower than in any of the contiguous pariſhes.* Here is no work-houſe, nor any manufacture carried on. Tilling the ground is the only occupation. The number of the inhabitants being only 200, every one is known, and no one can well be idle. The overſeers, being frugal farmers, keep down the rate as low as they can. No expence for law or entertainments has of late been incurred. The rental of the pariſh is about 750l.; the poor-

* It has riſen faſt ſince.

rate

rate 2s. in the pound, or 75l. *per annum:* befides which, the parifh-houfe, confifting of four tenements, faves houfe-rent to four poor families. The number of poor receiving relief, either individually or by families, (including thofe in the poor-houfe) is about forty, befides others affifted occafionally in ficknefs: that is, the number of individuals affifted by the rate is about *one fifth* of the whole. Suppofing this proportion to hold throughout the kingdom, and our population to be 8,000,000, the number of paupers comes out 1,600,000. I give this merely as a *rude guefs* at the number of our poor: but on comparing the above-recited circumftances of *this* parifh with thofe of fome neighbouring parifhes, I am induced to believe that this calculation is not very far from the truth.

16. Two millions of pounds *fterling*, and upwards, raifed for the poor (befides *charitable donations*, amounting to a quarter of a million more) founds largely. And indeed the *net* revenue of the kingdom a little more than a *hundred years* ago did not amount to fo much. But, if we confider how fmall a proportion *this* fum bears to the whole collective income of the nation at prefent, which probably exceeds 120 millions; this tax muft then appear to every humane perfon to be by no means immoderate. And if we confider further, how wretchedly the poor actually live *with* this aid; far from entertaining the vain hope of the *extinction* of the rate by any plan whatever, we fhall fee little room even to expect any material *reduction* of it, whilft the price of day-labour remains fo low as it now is, and whilft the churchwardens and overfeers are permitted, as they have long been, to neglect their duty in fetting the poor to work. Under thefe circumftances it is manifeftly impoffible to diminifh the rate in any great degree, without greatly increafing the miferies of the poor.

17. Since

17. Since labouring families are generally in real diſtreſs, (*per* Obſ. 12) when they come to have more than *two* children unable to earn their living; it ſeems indiſputable, that ſuch families have then an equitable claim upon their pariſh, by the very *principle* which forms the baſis of our poor laws, for the ſupport of all above two, whilſt things continue on the preſent foot. For it is manifeſt that our laws conſider all the inhabitants of a pariſh as forming one large family, the higher and richer part of which is bound to provide employment and ſubſiſtence for the lower and labouring part.

18. I have ſaid that I found our poor families very meanly clothed. In this reſpect No. 4 was no exception. And this is viſibly the caſe of the poor in general. In fact it is but little that in the preſent ſtate of things the belly can ſpare for the back. Even ſuch perſons as may have been provident enough, when ſingle, to ſupply themſelves with a ſmall ſtock of clothes, are, after marriage, from inability to buy more, ſoon reduced to ragged garments. And then the women ſpend as much time in tacking their tatters together, as would ſerve for manufacturing new clothing, had they the ſkill to do it, and materials to do it with. One bad conſequence of this meanneſs of dreſs is, that many of the poor are aſhamed to appear among decent people at our churches; they either neglect the duty of public worſhip altogether, or they aſſemble at places where they are ſure of meeting with people as ill-clothed as themſelves.

19. Since the day-labourer can ſcarcely with his utmoſt exertions ſupply his family with the daily bread which is to ſuſtain their bodies, no wonder that he ſhould ſo ſeldom ſtrive to procure for them that other bread, which is to nouriſh their ſouls, and prepare them for a future ſtate of being. For though the ſchooling of a child coſts but two-pence

two-pence or three-pence a week, yet this pittance is wanted for fo many other purpofes, that it would be miffed in the family. And thus the children of the poor are too commonly left to wafte thofe early years in idlenefs and vice, which they fhould be made to employ in learning their duties to God and man, and in laying the foundations of a religious and virtuous life.

20. Such being the unhappy condition of poor people, particularly of day-labourers: left, for the moft part, deftitute of inftruction in their early years, and copying as they grow up the example of vicious parents; being, in confequence of this, thoughtlefs, improvident, and irreligious in youth; unable, when married, by inceffant labour, to provide for the neceffities of even a moderate family; their fpirits finking, as children come on, under a growing weight of wretchednefs and woe; their applications for affiftance often treated with contempt by the perfons appointed to relieve them; can we wonder, if, thus circumftanced, they receive occafional favours without gratitude, and brood over their miferies in fulky filence? Can we wonder at that wide-fpread difhonefty, and profligacy of manners, the fatal effects of which we are daily lamenting? Our aftonifhment will affuredly ceafe, if we do but reflect that the very beft education will fcarcely keep a man honeft and virtuous, whofe family is perifhing for want of neceffaries.

21. The preceding obfervations may fuggeft one valuable precaution to *Juftices of the Peace*, who are the legal guardians and protectors of the poor. When a family, having been denied relief by the overfeers of their parifh, comes to the magiftrate for redrefs, the magiftrate would do well to inform himfelf minutely, not only of the *weekly* earnings and expences, but alfo of the *annual* earnings and outgoings of fuch

ſuch family; becauſe it is from a compariſon of the *whole* of the one with the *whole* of the other, that he can alone form a right judgment what relief he ſhould order to be given to the party ſo applying to him.

SECTION IV.

AN APOLOGY FOR THE POOR—EATING WHEATEN BREAD—NEGLECTING POTATOES—DRINKING TEA.

POOR people are often cenfured for want of frugality and œconomy in the management of their earnings. In particular, they are accufed of extravagance in eating wheaten bread; of being over-nice in neglecting as they do the ufe of potatoes; and of a luxurious excefs in drinking tea. It may be proper to fee what force there is in thefe charges.

Firft; It is afked, Why fhould our labouring people eat wheaten bread? Were they content, as the poor of this country were formerly, and as the poor of other countries are ftill, with bread of an inferior quality, they might then fpare money for other purpofes, and live with more comfort than they ufually do. It is wonderful how readily even men of fenfe give into this cenfure, neither confidering the different circumftances of different countries at the fame time, nor the different circumftances of the fame country at different times. They affume that the condition of the working people of this kingdom is the fame now, in all *other* refpects, as it was formerly; which is by no means the cafe. If the working people of other countries are content with bread made of rye, barley, or oats, have they not milk, cheefe, butter, fruits, or fifh, to eat with that coarfer bread? And was not this the cafe of our own people formerly, when thefe grains were the common productions

ductions of our land, and when ſcarcely wheat enough was grown for the uſe of the nobility and principal gentry? Fleſh-meat, butter, and cheeſe, were then at ſuch moderate prices, compared with the preſent prices, that poor people could afford to uſe them in common. And with a competent quantity of theſe articles, a coarſer kind of bread might very well ſatisfy the common people of any country.

Time, which changes all things, has gradually changed the circumſtances of this kingdom. Our lands have been ſo much improved, that wheat is as common now as rye and barley were formerly. A ſufficient quantity of wheat is now annually produced for the conſumption of, probably, three-fourths of our people. In the corn counties it is chiefly on the crop of wheat that the farmer relies for the ability to pay his rent; which cauſes ſuch care to be taken in preparing the land for this grain, as almoſt to enſure a plentiful crop. And if the labouring people, of whom the maſs of every nation conſiſts, were to ceaſe to eat it when produced, how, let me aſk, would the farmer then diſpoſe of his corn? And how could he pay his landlord the high rent now demanded of him? But this is not all. The prices of meat, butter, and cheeſe, are ſo much increaſed, in conſequence of the increaſe of riches, luxury, and taxes, that working people can now ſcarcely afford to uſe them in the ſmalleſt quantities. So that they depend almoſt entirely upon the bread they eat for ſtrength to perform their daily labour. That bread ſhould therefore be of a good kind. But it is certain that wheaten bread contains much more nouriſhment than barley bread*; and it is probable that the difference in this reſpect is

* It is ſaid, however, that the people of *Cornwall*, who eat barley bread, prefer it, ſaying, that it has more *heart* in it than wheaten bread.

ſuch

ſuch as to compenſate for the difference of price. (See *Tracts on the Corn Trade*, p. 199.) The old man there mentioned, who fed his family with barley bread in *dear* times, found it as cheap to feed them with wheaten bread, unleſs he could buy barley at two-thirds of the price of wheat. I believe the price of barley for ſome years paſt has been but little, if any thing, ſhort of this proportion : and it is manifeſt that if this grain were commonly uſed for bread, as well as for drink, the price of it muſt ſtill advance conſiderably. Working people ſeem therefore to judge rightly in giving wheaten bread the preference, ſince it is the only good thing of which they can have a ſufficiency. And it is obviouſly not leſs for the *intereſt* of the rich, than it is for the *comfort* of the poor, that the latter ſhould eat wheaten bread, wherever wheat is the common produce of the land. In ſuch parts of the kingdom, where the lands have not been ſo highly improved as to produce plenty of wheat, barley, oatmeal, or maſlin bread is ſtill in common uſe.

It appears then that the œconomy of eating inferior bread is, in the preſent ſtate of things, at leaſt very queſtionable. But, were it otherwiſe, a change in this reſpect is ſcarcely practicable. The corn buſineſs is now carried on in a ſyſtematical way, from which the dealers will not depart. Formerly the labourer could have corn of different kinds mixed in any proportion, in exchange for his labour, even more readily than he could get money. His wife carried it to the mill, had it ground and dreſſed, and then brought it home, and baked it for the family. There was no intermediate perſon except the miller, between the farmer and the conſumer, to receive a profit. But now it is out of the courſe of buſineſs for the farmer to retail corn by the buſhel to this or that poor man; except in ſome particular places, as a matter of

 favour,

favour, to his own labourers. The great farmer deals in a wholefale way with the miller; the miller with the mealman; and the mealman with the fhopkeeper; of which laft the poor man buys his flour by the bufhel. For neither the miller, nor the mealman, will fell the labourer a lefs quantity than a *fack* of flour *under* the retail price at fhops: and the poor man's pocket will feldom allow of his buying a whole fack at once. Formerly then the wife faved the profits of the mealman and fhopkeeper, who now, without adding to the value of the manufacture, do each receive a profit out of the poor man's earnings. It has been afferted by a good judge of thefe matters, that this is a difadvantage to the poor of at leaft *ten per cent.* upon this prime neceffary of life. (See Mr. Kent's *Hints to Gentlemen of Landed Property*, p. 277.) In fhort, the poor man buys *every thing* at the higheft price; at a higher price than the rich do. He cannot help this; but muft fubmit to the eftablifhed order. It is not poffible for him, nor is it eafy for his fuperiors, to effect a change, where things have gone on for a long time in a certain train.

Upon the whole, labouring people, having neither meat, nor cheefe, nor milk, nor beer, in fufficient quantities, eat good bread where every body elfe eats it. You fay, they cannot afford to do this; and you blame their extravagance. But can you, who blame them, give a reafon, why they, whofe hands have tilled the ground, and fown and reaped the grain, are not as well entitled to eat good bread, as manufacturers? or, as the fervants in gentlemen's families? or, as the paupers in houfes of induftry and parochial work-houfes? or, as the felons in your gaols?

2dly. It

2dly. It is ſometimes ſaid that poor people neglect too much the uſe of potatoes; as potatoes would not only ſave bread, but, by helping to keep a pig, give them more meat than they can now afford themſelves. Though the potatoe is an excellent root, deſerving to be brought into general uſe, yet it ſeems not likely that the uſe of it ſhould ever be general in this country. The uſe of wheat, ſpreading with improvements in huſbandry, will probably ſuperſede it in many places where it is now in requeſt. The potatoe has the advantage in cheapneſs only: wheat is ſuperior in all other reſpects. Beſides, there are two circumſtances which forbid the common people in the richer counties from cultivating potatoes ſo much as they might otherwiſe be inclined to do; namely, the want of ſufficient garden ground, and the difficulty of procuring milk.

1ſt. The want of ſufficient garden ground. This appears truly ſtrange in a country, where a third part of the land at leaſt lies waſte; and where, if every poor family were allowed as much of this waſte land as they could, when not otherwiſe employed, cultivate with the ſpade and the pick-axe, it would be undoubtedly a great public benefit. Yet ſuch is the fact. In conſequence of the law of ſettlements, it has been, and is, the policy of pariſhes (in order to eaſe the rates and check their increaſe, and alſo to render labourers entirely dependent on their employers) to deſtroy cottages, ſome of which had ground about them. And this deſtruction has been greatly promoted by the ſyſtem of engroſſing farms. For the engroſſing farmer, occupying ſometimes half a dozen farms, converts all the farm-houſes, except that in which his own family reſides, into dwellings for the poor. After taking ſuch part of the garden belonging to each houſe as he chooſes, for his own uſe, he he divides the reſt, as he had before divided the houſe, into ſeveral portions, allotting to each of his under-tenants about a quarter of a rood of ground, with perhaps an apple-tree or two. The occupier of this ſcanty bit of ground, deſiring ſome variety in his food, (and variety is known to be wholeſome) inſtead of planting the whole in potatoes, produces from it a little of many things; beans, peaſe, cabbages, onions, and ſome potatoes too. He works at it early and late to make it yield him ſomething conſtantly. And it is hard to ſay what better uſe he can poſſibly put it to.

But, 2dly, If the labouring man has ground enough, as is here and there the caſe, the want of milk is another impediment to the uſe of potatoes. Wheaten bread may be eaten alone with pleaſure; but potatoes require either meat or milk to make them go down: you cannot make many hearty meals of them with ſalt and water only. Poor people indeed give them to their children in the greaſy water, in which they have boiled their greens and their morſel of bacon: and, bleſſed be God! children will thrive, if they have but enough of any thing. As to meat, we know very well how little of that they are obliged to content themſelves with. Butter-milk is the thing, if they could get it. In Wales and Ireland, (and in ſome parts of England too) potatoes and butter-milk make one meal a day in moſt families almoſt all the year. But taking England in general, butter-milk is too little regarded as an article of diet. The method of churning in the ſouthern counties makes it only fit for ſwine. Where the method of churning is ſuch as to produce it ſweet and good, there a poor family may always either beg or buy a jug of butter-milk; and there too we find potatoes in uſe. But the uſe of potatoes muſt be very limited, where

milk

milk cannot be cheaply procured. And, if they were brought into general uſe, would not this materially affect the intereſt of the land-holder, by leſſening the conſumption of wheat and other grain? But,

3dly. The topic on which the declaimers againſt the extravagance of the poor diſplay their eloquence with moſt ſucceſs, is *tea-drinking*. Why ſhould ſuch people, it is aſked, indulge in a luxury which is only proper for their betters; and not rather content themſelves with milk, which is in every form wholeſome and nouriſhing? Were it true that poor people could every where procure ſo excellent an article as milk, there would be then juſt reaſon to reproach them for giving the preference to the miſerable infuſion of which they are ſo fond. But it is not ſo. Wherever the poor can get milk, do they not gladly uſe it? And where they cannot get it, would they not gladly exchange their tea for it? The truth is, that very few labouring people can afford to purchaſe a cow; for a cow would coſt the earnings of almoſt half a year. But, were they able to purchaſe one, where could they find paſture for her? The commons are ſo covered with the rich farmer's herds and flocks, that the poor man's cow would ſoon be ſtarved there. And the little ground about their cottages is barely ſufficient for garden ſtuff. They cannot therefore produce milk for themſelves. And as to buying milk, it is not to be had in many places for love or money. In ſuch places as are within reach of the capital and other great towns, (and the influence of theſe now extends a vaſt way) the farmers find the moſt profitable uſe of a cow to be *ſuckling*, in order to ſupply the markets with veal. Beſides, it is an obſervation of Mr. Kent, (ſee *Hints to Gentlemen*, &c.) that there are thouſands of pariſhes, which, ſince little farms have been ſwallowed up in greater, do not ſupport ſo many cows as they

they did by fifty or ſixty in a pariſh. And thus the poor are very much at a loſs for due ſupplies of milk.

Is there any thing elſe that they can ſubſtitute for milk? Time was when *ſmall beer* was reckoned one of the neceſſaries of life, even in poor families: and it ſeems to have been deſigned by Providence for the common drink of the people of this country, being deemed a preſervative againſt ſome of its worſt diſeaſes. Were the poor able to afford themſelves this wholeſome beverage, it would well enough compenſate for the ſcarcity of milk. But, on account of the dearneſs of *malt*, which is, moſt unfortunately for them, a principal ſubject of taxation, ſmall beer has been theſe many years far beyond their ability to uſe in common.

Under theſe hard circumſtances, the dearneſs of malt, and the difficulty of procuring milk; the only thing remaining for them to moiſten their bread with, was *tea*. This was their laſt reſource. Tea (with bread) furniſhes one meal for a whole family every day, at no greater expence than about one ſhilling a week at an average. If any body will point out an article that is cheaper and better, I will venture to anſwer for the poor in general, that they will be thankful for the diſcovery.

It was aſſerted in a work of reputation, many years ago, that as much ſuperfluous money was then expended upon tea, ſugar, &c. as would, upon a moderate calculation, maintain four millions more of ſubjects in bread. (Harte's *Eſſays*, p. 166.) It is not ſufficiently clear upon what grounds this calculation was made; but it ſeems to have been made upon pretty good grounds. Certain it is that the conſumption of theſe articles has increaſed prodigiouſly ſince that time. In the

higher

higher and middling ranks it is very great; and in manufacturing families, living in towns, it is confiderable. But, though the ufe of tea is more common than could be wifhed, it is not yet general among the labouring poor: and if we have regard to numbers, *their* fhare of the confumption is comparatively fmall; efpecially if we reckon the *value* in money.

Still you exclaim, *Tea is a luxury*. If you mean fine hyfon tea, fweetened with refined fugar, and foftened with cream, I readily admit it to be fo. But *this* is not the tea of the poor. Spring water, juft coloured with a few leaves of the loweft-priced tea, and fweetened with the browneft fugar, is the luxury for which you reproach them. To this they have recourfe from mere neceffity: and were they now to be deprived of this, they would immediately be reduced to bread and water. Tea-drinking is not the caufe, but the confequence, of the diftreffes of the poor.

After all, it appears a very ftrange thing, that the common people of any European nation fhould be obliged to ufe, as a part of their daily diet, two articles imported from oppofite fides of the earth. But if high taxes, in confequence of expenfive wars, and the changes which time infenfibly makes in the circumftances of countries, have debarred the poorer inhabitants of this kingdom the ufe of fuch things as are the natural products of the foil, and forced them to recur to thofe of foreign growth; furely this is not *their* fault. I have no pleafure, however, in defending this practice of tea-drinking among the lower people; becaufe I know it is made the occafion of much idle goffiping among the women; and alfo becaufe the money thus expended, though far from fufficient to fupply a family with beer, would yet go fome way towards it.

In

In fine; this charge of miſmanagement made againſt labouring people, ſeems to reſt upon no ſolid ground. For a long time paſt their condition has been going from bad to worſe continually. Small indeed is the portion of worldly comforts now left them. Inſtead therefore of grudging them ſo ſmall an enjoyment as a morſel of good bread with their miſerable tea; inſtead of attempting to ſhew how it may yet be poſſible for them to live *worſe* than they do; it well becomes the wiſdom and humanity of the preſent age to deviſe means how they may be better accommodated. Give to ſome the ability to keep a cow; and then all will have milk. Give to all the ability to drink ſmall beer at home; and then few will frequent alehouſes. He that can procure for them theſe two benefits, nay, he that can procure for them *one* of theſe two, will receive the bleſſing of the grateful poor, and deſerve the applauſe of all good men.

PART THE SECOND.

THE

PRINCIPAL CAUSES

OF THE

Growing Diftrefs and Number of the Poor,

AND OF THE

CONSEQUENT INCREASE

OF

THE POOR-RATE.

PART II.

SECTION I.

A VIEW OF THE PROGRESSIVE ADVANCE OF THE POOR-RATE.

IT appears from the foregoing accounts and obſervations, that both the diſtreſſes and the numbers of the dependent poor have been increaſing rapidly together in the latter half of the preſent century. And this fact will explain, generally, that vaſt augmentation of the poor-rate which has taken place within the ſame ſpace of time. But it is proper, now, to note more particularly the ſeveral circumſtances which have conſpired to bring things into this ſituation. In doing this, we may perhaps diſcover what meaſures ought to be adopted, on the return of peace, for remedying the evils complained of. But as few perſons ſeem to have a diſtinct notion of the celerity with which the poor-rate has of late advanced, the following view of its progreſs, though not accurate, may be acceptable to many.

The firſt general aſſeſſment made for the poor was in the 14th of *Q. Elizabeth*, anno 1572: ſee *Burn's Hiſt. of P. Laws*, p. 74. It does not appear what the amount was at that time: but from the complaints then made of the burdenſomeneſs of the poor, and the endeavours uſed in preceding reigns to check their growing number, I *gueſs*

it

it might be about 200,000l. I have accordingly begun the following table with *this* ſum.

A Table, ſhewing the Amount of the Poor-Rate in different years, its Increaſe in the Intervals, and its progreſſive Annual Increaſe.

Year.		Amount of the Poor-Rate.	Inter-val.	Increaſe in the Interval.	Annual Increaſe.
		£.		£.	£.
1572	Suppoſed amount - - - - -	200,000			
1685	At the cloſe of the reign of Charles II. the amount, according to *Davenant*, was - - - - - - - -	665,362	113	465,362	4,118
1753	*H. Fielding*, in his Propoſal for making an effectual Proviſion for the Poor, &c. printed this year, (ſee *Burn*'s H. P. L. p. 196) reckons it at - - - - - - - - - - -	1,000,000	68	334,638	4,921
1776	According to the returns made to Parliament by the Overſeers of the Poor, the medium annual expence of 3 years, ended at Eaſter 1776, was net money paid to poor - -	1,529,780	23	529,780	23,034
1785	According to the like returns, the medium expence of 3 years, ended at Eaſter 1785, was* - - -	2,004,238	9	474,458	52,719

This table exhibits an amazing acceleration of the rate between the years 1753 and 1785, and thereby ſuggeſts what was undoubtedly the

* This was excluſive of the charitable donations, the annual amount of which appears, by the returns then made by the clergy, to be 258,711l.

chief

chief though not the ſole cauſe of that acceleration. For it muſt be aſcribed to the quick and powerful operation of events which happened in that interval. And what could thoſe events be, but the two expenſive wars in which this nation was involved; and which occaſioned ſuch a number of new taxes to be impoſed on neceſſaries as well as luxuries? Notwithſtanding this, the progreſs of luxury in the ſame period was extremely rapid, and muſt have contributed greatly to the advancement of the prices of all things. With theſe two grand cauſes, many inferior circumſtances have co-operated in producing the effect in queſtion.

In the three following ſections I ſhall conſider, 1ſt, Thoſe circumſtances which have enhanced directly the *prices* of neceſſaries, and by conſequence increaſed the *number* of dependent poor, thereby *doubly* augmenting the rate. 2dly, I ſhall mention ſuch as have augmented the rate by *only* increaſing the number of the poor. And, *laſtly*, I ſhall note briefly ſuch prevailing neglects and abuſes on the part of overſeers of the poor, as have cauſed a conſiderable direct augmentation of the rate itſelf.

SECTION

SECTION II.

THE PRINCIPAL CAUSES WHICH HAVE ENHANCED THE NECESSARIES OF LIFE, AND BY CONSEQUENCE INCREASED THE NUMBER OF THE POOR, THEREBY DOUBLY AUGMENTING THE RATE.

1. THAT the NEW TAXES have had a great influence in raiſing prices, may be fairly inferred from the following ſketch, ſhewing the progreſs of the Public Revenue, of the National Debt and its Intereſt, and of the Poor-Rate.

Year.	Revenue.	National Debt.	Inter. of N. Debt.	Poor-Rate.
1685	2,061,856			665,362
1703	5,561,944	16,394,702	1,310,942	700,000
1753	6,690,000	74,571,840	2,396,717	1,000,000
1775	10,000,000	135,943,051	4,440,821	1,529,780
1786	14,405,702	239,154,880	9,275,769	2,004,238

Thus has this nation, in the ſpace of a century, augmented its net revenue from about two millions to near fourteen millions and a half *ſterling*. Of this ſum near eight millions have been added between the years 1750 and 1786, on account of the debts contracted for carrying on the two laſt wars. And now (May 1794) the *groſs* revenue, or the total of money drawn from the people in taxes, is probably eighteen millions. If therefore we conſider the unavoidable effect of taxes in raiſing prices, we cannot doubt but that the rapid progreſs of the Poor-Rate from one million to two, in the ſame ſpace of time, muſt have been very much owing to *their* accumulation. For it is an unqueſtionable truth, that

that a tax impofed on any *one* article of general confumption, raifes the price not only of the article taxed, but of *all* other articles alfo. We may be fure, therefore, that the numerous taxes, which have been laid on the nation fince the year 1750, have caufed a prodigious advance in the prices of all the neceffaries of life. And the *experience* of every perfon, who was a houfekeeper then, and is a houfekeeper ftill, will furnifh abundant evidence of this fact.

2. LUXURY *attends wealth.* The influx of wealth into this kingdom has for many years been prodigious. And the diffufion of this wealth through the higher and middling ranks has tempted them all into very expenfive habits of living. *Luxury* raifes the prices of the moft neceffary articles, by *wafting* on a few what would fuffice for the maintenance of many.

It is pretended that moderate luxury is falutary, becaufe it promotes induftry and population, by creating employment. But how is luxury to be confined within moderate limits? Is not its progrefs ufually rapid; and does it not foon become exceffive? And what is the effect produced by it then? By rendering fubfiftence dear, it firft produces diftrefs, and afterwards depopulation. Many, dreading the expence of a family, avoid marriage; and many emigrate to cheaper countries.

But it is needlefs to dwell on the bad effects of luxury in general. The following particulars deferve notice, as having contributed materially to raife the price of provifions.

1ft. *The greater and more general confumption of Butcher's Meat among us.* Queen Elizabeth, to keep the price low for the poor, iffued proclamations againft eating flefh in Lent and on fifh-days; but every body now eats meat at all times without fcruple. In great families the luxury

of

of the table waſtes vaſt quantities of fleſh-meat in ſoups and ſauces. "And many ranks of people, whoſe ordinary diet was in the laſt century prepared almoſt entirely from milk, roots, and vegetables, now "require every day a conſiderable portion of the fleſh of animals. "Hence a great part of the richeſt lands of the country are converted "to paſturage. Much alſo of the bread-corn, which went directly to "the nouriſhment of human bodies, now only contribute to it by fattening the fleſh of ſheep and oxen. The maſs and volume of proviſions are hereby diminiſhed." (*See Mr. Dean Paley's M. Phil.* vol. ii. p. 360, 8vo. ed.) It is manifeſt that this continually-growing demand for animal food muſt continually have enhanced the price, not only of butcher's meat, but alſo of corn and all other neceſſaries.

2dly. *The great increaſe in the number of Horſes throughout the kingdom.* It was ſuppoſed many years ago, by competent judges, that more of our land was then appropriated to the maintenance of horſes than of men. It is certain that a vaſt addition has been made to the number ſince. Suppoſe an addition of 200,000 to have taken place in the laſt forty or fifty years. Many thouſand acres of our beſt land muſt now be employed in producing food for theſe additional horſes, which would otherwiſe be employed in producing food for man. And ſince the maintenance of a horſe coſts as much as the maintenance of a labouring family does, theſe additional horſes may be ſaid to devour the ſubſiſtence of 200,000 families.

3dly. The following circumſtances have alſo operated conſiderably to the diminution of the quantity of land in tillage. 1ſt. *The increaſed number of gentlemen-farmers*; who are in general fond of graſs-farms, as requiring the leaſt trouble; and the produce of theſe is frequently con-

ſumed

ſumed by the cattle kept on them. 2dly. Huſbandry has ſuſtained a loſs by the converſion of many thouſand acres of good land, arable and paſture, into *roads*, *canals*, *parks*, and *pleaſure-grounds.*

4thly *The Diſtillation of Wheat*:—a wicked abuſe of the greateſt bleſſing that Providence has beſtowed on our country. For this proceſs converts a conſiderable quantity of that moſt valuable article of human ſubſiſtence into a ſuperfluous and pernicious liquor. If only 100,000 quarters of wheat are thus wantonly deſtroyed in a year, this is the ſame thing as deſtroying the bread of the ſame number of individuals; that is, of 20,000 families. I know no reaſon why this abuſe ſhould be tolerated, except that it contributes ſomething to the exciſe. It ought ſurely to be prohibited.

5thly. *Wheaten Bread has been conſtantly growing more and more into general uſe among the lower claſſes of people.* This is their luxury. The increaſed demand for it has undoubtedly been owing, in a great meaſure to their inability to buy meat; the want of which they ſupply with bread of a better quality. For the ſame money, that will only purchaſe one pound of raw meat with its proportion of bone, will purchaſe about three pounds of wheaten bread. But this quantity of bread will go at leaſt twice as far as one pound of meat. It is obvious, that this increaſed demand for wheaten bread muſt have raiſed the price of bread-corn, unleſs the quantity annually produced has increaſed proportionably along with it; which there is good reaſon to believe has not been the caſe.*

* In the Repreſentation of the Lords of the Committee of Council on Corn, (printed for *Stockdale*, 1790) it is ſtated, that on an average of 19 years, ending in 1765, the corn exported from this country produced a clear profit of not leſs than 651,000l. but that on an average of 18 years, ending in 1788, we have paid to foreigners for a ſupply of corn no leſs than 291,000l. which makes an annual difference to this country of 942,000l.

Thus

Thus wherever *taxes* and *luxury* go on continually increaſing together, for a ſeries of years, their combined effect in raiſing prices (unaſſiſted by other cauſes) muſt ſoon come to be ſeverely felt by the inferior claſſes of people.

III. Depreciation of Money. By this term I mean ſimply that decreaſe in the value of money, which has gradually taken place throughout Europe, in conſequence of the greater plenty of it now than formerly. For ſince the diſcovery of *America*, many thouſand tons of the precious metals have been imported from thence into Europe; and the greater abundance of them has cauſed their value to ſink gradually in this quarter of the world. The effects of this depreciation appear, 1ſt. in the higher prices of all things; and 2dly, in the lower intereſt of money. In this kingdom in particular the change in theſe reſpects has been conſiderable, as is well known to thoſe who have attended to theſe matters. And without doubt this depreciation has been going on during the preſent century, as well as before.

It is probable, too, that the emiſſion of ſo much *paper* by banking companies, in almoſt every great town, has, beſides promoting luxury, contributed to *overload* the circulation, and to lower the value of money. Theſe banking companies, coining their credit into this ſort of caſh, have *forced* a great deal of it upon the publick, thereby baniſhing not only *ſpecie*, but even the notes of the Bank of England, from their reſpective neighbourhoods. While this paper paſſes as money, it is in effect the ſame thing as ſo much coin iſſued out of the mint, only that *it has no intrinſic value*. The uſe of it may be convenient; but it is evidently attended with much danger.

IV. The

IV. The price of *wheat* (and indeed of every ſpecies of grain) has been of late years uniformly higher than it was about the middle of the preſent century. Whatever circumſtances have had a ſhare in producing this effect, the ſame have an eſpecial claim to our notice. For of nothing are the lower people ſo apt to complain, as of the dearneſs of bread. And not without reaſon. For ſince, from the exceſſive dearneſs of proviſions in general, they are reduced to ſubſiſt almoſt entirely on bread; when bread is dear too, their caſe becomes truly deplorable. They know that the crops have for many years paſt been apparently plentiful, and yet they experience no *permanent* fall of price. They conclude that large quantities of corn are carried out of the kingdom; and, attributing the dearneſs of bread to this circumſtance, they ſometimes proceed to vent their indignation in a riotous manner.

But, as violence commonly increaſes the evils which it wiſhes to remedy; ſo is it obviouſly miſchievous in this particular caſe. It is therefore of conſequence that all people ſhould think rightly on this ſubject. The obſervations already made will abundantly account for the advanced price of this chief neceſſary of life. To which may perhaps be added the *bounties allowed on the exportation of grain*. But, with reſpect to the influence which *taxes* and *bounties* have on the price of grain, I am deſirous of citing here the opinions of two eſteemed writers.

Mr. Soame Jenyns obſerves, "No tax is immediately laid upon corn, but the price of it muſt neceſſarily be advanced; becauſe, out of that all the innumerable taxes paid by the farmer on windows, ſoap, candles, malt, hops, leather, ſalt, and a thouſand others, muſt be repaid; ſo that corn is as effectually taxed, as if a duty by the buſhel had been primarily laid upon it." And *Dr. Smith*, in his celebrated work *On the Wealth*

H 2 *of*

of Nations, has ſhewn that a bounty granted on exported grain (beſides being itſelf a direct tax on the publick) muſt neceſſarily operate *as a tax* on all remaining within the kingdom, and of courſe enhance the price of this and of all other articles to the conſumer.

If theſe authors argue juſtly, as they appear to do, we are not to expect, under the exiſting circumſtances of the nation, any *permanent fall* in the price of grain. The preſent war will unavoidably increaſe the taxes. And a late Act of Parliament has continued the bounties with ſome little variations. It is therefore more likely that the price of corn will ſtill go on advancing, unleſs effectual meaſures are ſpeedily taken for promoting tillage, and perhaps checking paſturage, ſo as to render the annual produce of grain at leaſt adequate to the annual conſumption.

Without doubt *a high price* is the greateſt encouragement to the farmer to raiſe plenty of corn; and therefore no undue means ſhould be taken to keep the price of it from advancing with that of other things. But, on the other hand, it ſeems abſurd to grant bounties for encouraging the exportation of what we cannot ſpare. [*See the laſt note.*] And let it never be forgotten that the labourer ought to be enabled to ſubſiſt his family; and conſequently that *his pay* ſhould be made to keep pace with the general advance in the prices of neceſſaries, of which wheat is now the principal article.

SECTION

SECTION III.

CIRCUMSTANCES WHICH HAVE DIRECTLY INCREASED THE NUMBER OF THE DEPENDENT POOR, AND BY CONSEQUENCE THE AMOUNT OF THE RATE.

I. OUR *progressive population must have added to the Number of dependent poor*:—1st. *Directly*, the history of the poor laws shewing that an increase of population has been always accompanied in this country by an increased number of poor:—And, 2dly, It has perhaps added to it *indirectly* also, by increasing the demand for necessaries, and thereby causing an advance in their price; which of course has forced more and more persons to come for aid to their parishes.

But it has been a matter of controversy between very able and learned men, whether an increase or a decrease of people has been going on in this country during the present century? And the advocates for each side of the question have supported their respective opinions by plausible arguments. The publick, however, seem to have decided in favour of an increased population: and that apparently on reasonable grounds.

For, 1st, though we should admit, what the late *Dr. Price* contended for, that a decrease has actually taken place of the total number of *houses* in the kingdom; yet it is an undoubted fact, that a great many *farm-houses* in the hands of engrossing farmers, each of which was formerly occupied by *one* farming family only, are now divided into *two*, *three*, and even *four* separate dwellings for labouring families. The like happens where cottages are suffered to fall into decay, and no new ones

ones are built: ſeveral families are forced to lodge together in one poor cottage. And therefore a *ſmall* decreaſe in the number of houſes does not neceſſarily imply *any* decreaſe in the number of families. 2dly. That the decreaſe in the number of houſes (if any) is *but* ſmall, appears probable from a compariſon of the number of chargeable houſes, given in by the ſurveyors of the houſe and window duties, for certain pariſhes and diſtricts, with the total of houſes found by enumeration in the ſame places. [*See the publications of Mr. Wales and Mr. Howlett on this head.*] 3dly. The evidence produced from pariſh regiſters by the two gentlemen juſt mentioned, ſeems, notwithſtanding the objections made againſt it, to afford a *preſumptive* proof that our population has advanced in the courſe of the preſent century. And, 4thly, Whoſoever conſiders the progreſſive improvement of our agriculture, manufactures, commerce, and ſhipping, during this period (as exhibited by *Mr. Chalmers* in his *Comparative Eſtimate*) can ſcarcely forbear concluding, that it has been *really* accompanied by a like improvement of our population alſo.

II. *Increaſed number of Manufacturers.* Whatever opinion we may adopt as to the general population of the kingdom, all will acknowledge that *this* claſs of people is multiplied exceedingly. And depending upon their employers for their daily ſubſiſtence, they are in much the ſame ſituation with reduced farmers and impoveriſhed labourers; that is, they are very liable to come to want. The caprice of faſhion cauſes by fits and ſtarts a great demand for one ſpecies of goods, and a ceſſation of demand for another: and thus workmen, who to-day are fully employed, may be to-morrow in the ſtreets begging their bread. By living in towns, and aſſociating at publick-houſes, they are habitually improvident,

improvident, and mind nothing but prefent enjoyment; and when flung out of work, they are immediately in want. They are alfo, from their fedentary occupations and habitual intemperance, more fhort-lived than day-labourers; and leaving families behind them unable wholly to maintain themfelves, thefe, as the men die off, fall on their parifhes. All this will account for the mifery vifible in manufacturing towns, in moft of which the poor are numerous, and the rates higher than in other places. Manufacturers enjoy, however, one advantage over day-labourers, though they feldom make a right ufe of it. Several manufactories employ women and children, as well as men: and wherever this is the cafe, thefe families might earn a great deal more money, and live better, than labouring families do; but by contracting early the vices of towns, they commonly mis-fpend thofe earnings, which, if ufed with frugality, would render their condition comfortable and themfelves happy.

III. *The practice of enlarging and engroffing of farms, and efpecially that of depriving the peafantry of all landed property, have contributed greatly to increafe the number of dependent poor.*

1ft. The *land-owner*, to render his income adequate to the increafed expence of living, unites feveral fmall farms into one, raifes the rent to the utmoft, and avoids the expence of repairs. The rich farmer alfo engroffes as many farms as he is able to ftock; lives in more credit and comfort than he could otherwife do; and out of the profits of *feveral farms*, makes an ample provifion for *one family*. Thus thoufands of families, which formerly gained an independent livelihood on thofe feparate farms, have been gradually reduced to the clafs of day-labourers. But day-labourers are fometimes in want of work, and are fometimes

times unable to work; and in either cafe their fole refource is the parifh. It is a fact, that thoufands of parifhes have not now half the number of farmers which they had formerly. And in proportion as the number of farming families has decreafed, the number of poor families has increafed.

2dly. The depriving the peafantry of all landed property has beggared multitudes. It is plainly agreeable to found policy, that as many individuals as poffible in a ftate fhould poffefs an intereft in the foil; becaufe this attaches them ftrongly to the country and its conftitution, and makes them zealous and refolute in defending them. But the gentry of this kingdom feem to have loft fight of this wife and falutary policy. Inftead of giving to labouring people a valuable ftake in the foil, the oppofite meafure has fo long prevailed, that but few cottages, comparatively, have now *any* land about them. Formerly many of the lower fort of people occupied tenements of their own, with parcels of land about them, or they rented fuch of others. On thefe they raifed for themfelves a confiderable part of their fubfiftence, without being obliged, as now, to buy all they want at fhops. And this kept numbers from coming to the parifh. But fince thofe fmall parcels of ground have been fwallowed up in the contiguous farms and inclofures, and the cottages themfelves have been pulled down; the families which ufed to occupy them are crouded together in decayed farm-houfes, with hardly ground enough about them for a cabbage garden: and being thus reduced to be *mere* hirelings, they are of courfe very liable to come to want. And not only the *men* occupying thofe tenements, but *their wives and children* too, could formerly, when they wanted work abroad, employ themfelves profitably at home; whereas now, few of *thefe* are conftantly employed,

employed, except in harveſt; ſo that almoſt the whole burden of providing for their families reſts upon the *men*. Add to this, that the former occupiers of ſmall farms and tenements, though poor themſelves, gave away ſomething in alms to their poorer neighbours; a reſource which is now much diminiſhed.

Thus an amazing number of people have been reduced from a comfortable ſtate of partial independence to the precarious condition of hirelings, who, when out of work, muſt immediately come to their pariſh. And the great plenty of working hands always to be had when wanted, having kept down the price of labour below its proper level, the conſequence is univerſally felt in the increaſed number of dependent poor.

IV. *The Deſertion of the Country by the rich Families during the greater Part of the Year has increaſed the Number of the Poor.*—Formerly, when the gentry reſided conſtantly on their eſtates, the crumbs from their tables fed many families; their humanity comforted and relieved the poor under ſickneſs and misfortune; and their influence and authority ſecured them from oppreſſion and injuſtice. But of late, by the nonreſidence of the rich, the poor have loſt that valuable ſupport which they uſed to receive. When (as is too commonly the caſe) families of moderate fortunes have expended two-thirds of their income, in winter, upon the amuſements and accompliſhments in vogue in the capital; and have alſo diſſipated a conſiderable part of the remainder at bathing and water-drinking places during ſome of the ſummer months; they have afterwards but little power to exerciſe hoſpitality, employ the induſtrious, and relieve the ſick and needy, on their return to their manſions. And thus numbers of poor families are come to want parochial aſſiſtance, which, but for this change in the manners of the rich, might have made ſhift without it. This new mode of life has been the fruitful ſource of numerous evils: the worſt of which perhaps is, that it has ſpread the vices of the capital over the whole kingdom, and infected even farm-houſes and cottages.

V. *The Improvidence of the Lower Sort of People brings multitudes of them very early to Poverty and Want.*—This careleſſneſs about the future ſeems to have increaſed in proportion as the ſhame of applying for pariſh-relief has worn off. Few of them, ſtrictly ſpeaking, take any thought for the morrow. Seldom do we ſee any of them making proviſion for marriage, ſickneſs, or old age; much leſs for the relief of infirm parents, or poor relations. Formerly it was not uncommon for young men and women to ſave in ſervice twenty or thirty pounds in money, beſides furniſhing themſelves with a decent ſtock of clothes, &c. But now young people are ſo unfrugal, that few of them have a decent ſuit to appear in even when they come to be married. And as for money, what in time paſt was wont to be laid by againſt a wet day, is all now thoughtleſsly ſpent by the men in drink, and by the women in frippery. "What ſignifies ſaving?" ſay they; "is not the pariſh obliged to maintain us, when we come to want?" Though they ſee continually ſad inſtances of coming to the pariſh, yet have they not the ſenſe to aſk themſelves this ſhort queſtion, How ſhall *I* like to be reduced to this abject condition? The conſequence of this inconſiderateneſs is, that, when married, they come ſoon to feel very ſeverely the effects of that poverty, which, when ſingle, they took no care to prevent. It is indeed ſome excuſe for them, that the number of farmers being ſo much decreaſed, there are not now ſo many

many opportunities, as formerly, for putting out young perſons ſervants in thoſe families where theſe ſavings were chiefly made. Add to this, that theſe people having contracted the ruinous habit of frequenting ale-houſes, ſeldom can they reſolve to forſake it. A great part of their earnings received on Saturday night, is ſquandered away there on *Sunday*. The wife and children are abandoned to hunger and nakedneſs, or are left to ſupply their neceſſities as well as they can by following profligate courſes!

VI. *Ale-houſes* have undoubtedly brought many families to want, infamy, and ruin.—As the improvidence of the people encourages theſe houſes, ſo do theſe houſes encourage that improvidence. Ale-houſes would not be ſo common as they are, if the keepers of them did not find their account in the improvidence of the people: nor would the people be ſo improvident as they are, if ale-houſes did not every where tempt them to drown their ſenſes, and waſte their time and money in them. But the loſs of ſenſe, time, and money, is not the worſt conſequence of frequenting theſe places. There is good reaſon to believe, that the prevailing corruption of morals in the common people has been very much owing to what is heard, ſeen, and practiſed in them. It is in theſe houſes that men, by falling into bad company, get the evil habits of idleneſs, blaſphemy, and drunkenneſs; which prepare them for the worſt crimes. The love of ſtrong drink acquired here drives numbers upon unlawful ways of making money: among which, from the high requeſt that *game* is held in, and from the little riſk attending the trade, *poaching* is very generally followed. To be a clever poacher is deemed a reputable accompliſhment in the country; and therefore parents take care to inſtruct their children betimes in

 this

this art; which brings them on gradually and regularly to pilfering and ſtealing. For poachers, in prowling about at night, if they miſs of game, properly ſo called, are ſometimes ſuſpected of ſeizing on their neighbours' poultry, and ſuch other things as they can find a vent for. By following theſe works of darkneſs, the loſs of ſleep and exceſſive drinking in time ruin their health. They get agues and other diſorders, which diſqualify them from either working or poaching; and then they and their families come on the pariſh. Every public-houſe, which is not abſolutely neceſſary, is certainly a nuiſance, and ought to be ſuppreſſed.

To the ſeveral cauſes and circumſtances pointed out in this and the preceding ſection, we muſt, I apprehend, aſcribe it, that multitudes of families, which about the middle of this century could with difficulty ſubſiſt without *any* help, do now require *ſome* help; and that multitudes of others, which then could not ſubſiſt without *ſome* help, do now require *more* help.

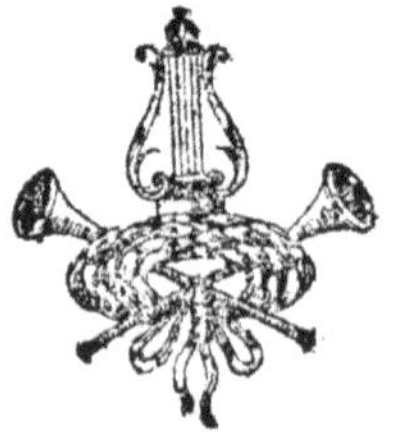

SECTION

SECTION IV.

TO THE FOREGOING CIRCUMSTANCES I WILL HERE ADD A FEW OTHERS, WHICH HAVE CONTRIBUTED TO INCREASE THE AMOUNT OF THE POOR-RATE DIRECTLY.

1ſt. THE *Negligence of Pariſhes in ſetting their Poor to work.*—If conſtant employment were found for the wives and children of labouring men, as well as for the men themſelves, the benefit public and private thence reſulting would be great. But from want of attention to this particular, the long winter evenings, and many intervals of ſpare time, are now wholly loſt or misſpent in moſt places. Many of the poor are extremely ignorant: having in youth been taught nothing but the common drudgery of the country within doors and without, they have afterwards no aptitude or inclination to learn any art whereby to earn a penny. Knitting and ſpinning are well calculated to fill up ſpare time; but from the incapacity of mothers to teach their children, theſe eaſy arts are now become quite unfaſhionable, even in cottages. Pariſhes are averſe to the purchaſing of wool, flax, and other materials and tools for their poor to work upon, both on account of the firſt expence, and alſo of the hazard of having goods left on their hands unfit for ſale. And the overſeers of the poor, having commonly buſineſs enough of their own to mind, (eſpecially in country places, ſince farms have been ſo much engroſſed) either

either cannot, or will not, give the time and attention neceſſary to the educating of the poor, and enforcing induſtry among them.—When the number of the poor was comparatively ſmall, this neglect in ſetting them to work might perhaps be of little conſequence: but now that their number is ſo prodigiouſly increaſed, it is become, evidently, a matter of very ſerious concern.

2dly. *Workhouſes* (contrary to what might have been expected) *have, in moſt places where they have been ſet up, increaſed the expence of maintaining the poor.*—It appears by the preceding accounts [ſee *Part* I. *Obſer.* 10.] that labouring families can maintain themſelves at their own houſes, and pay houſe-rent and every other neceſſary expence, for the ſmall ſum of five pounds four ſhillings *per* head. But by the accounts of ſeveral workhouſes it appears that the poor in them cannot be clothed and kept for leſs than ſeven pounds ſixteen ſhillings each, adults and children at an average. [See *Mr. Zouch's Remarks*, p. 55.]—If to this we add the *other* expences of a workhouſe, we may well reckon the whole at nine or ten pounds *per* head.—Experience has ſhewn, that but little work is done in theſe houſes, and that what is done, is ſo ill-executed, that the goods are ſcarcely ſaleable. For proof of this, and alſo of their ill effects on the *health and morals* of their inhabitants, ſee *the Tracts of Meſſrs. Zouch, Townſend, Howlett, and M'Farlan, relative to the Poor.*

3dly. *The frauds and abuſes, committed both by the poor and their overſeers, have augmented the rate.*—In populous pariſhes, where applications for relief are numerous, ſome undeſerving perſons will of courſe aſk aſſiſtance; and it is ſcarcely poſſible but that the overſeers, though honeſt men, muſt, from not knowing preciſely every one's circum-

circumſtances, and for want of time to examine narrowly into them, be ſometimes impoſed upon.—In great pariſhes too, where the poor-rates amount to many hundred pounds a year, overſeers of leſs ſcrupulous conſciences have frequent opportunities of abuſing their truſt, and ſometimes moſt iniquitouſly avail themſelves of them, either by embezzling the public money, or by partial indulgence to favourites.

It may be reaſonably ſuppoſed, that theſe circumſtances, jointly, have contributed in ſome degree to the augmentation of the poor-rate.

SECTION V.

A COMPARISON OF THE PRICES OF WHEAT AND OF MALT PER QUARTER AT WINDSOR MARKET, AT THREE DIFFERENT PERIODS OF THE PRESENT CENTURY.

THE Prices in the two former periods were extracted from the *Eton* Regifter: [See *Tracts on the Corn Trade*, or *Smith's Wealth of Nations*.] The prices in the laft period were, at my requeft, extracted from the books of the Dean and Canons of *Windfor*, by the *Rev. E. Wilfon*.

	Firft Period.							Second Period.							Third Period.					
Year.	Wheat.			Malt.			Year.	Wheat.			Malt.			Year.	Wheat.			Malt.		
	£.	s.	d.	£.	s.	d.		£.	s.	d.	£.	s.	d.		£.	s.	d.	£.	s.	d.
1701	2	0	0	1	11	4	1746	1	19	0	1	2	4	1783	3	8	0	2	12	0
1702	1	9	6	1	8	0	1747	1	14	10	1	2	8	1784	3	6	0	2	13	4
1703	1	16	0	1	3	4	1748	1	17	0	1	3	4	1785	2	16	0	2	10	8
1704	2	6	6	1	8	0	1749	1	17	0	1	5	4	1786	2	10	0	2	0	0
1705	1	10	0	1	6	0	1750	1	12	6	1	5	4	1787	2	6	0	2	8	0
1706	1	6	0	1	2	0	1751	1	18	6	1	6	0	1788	2	17	10	2	8	0
1707	1	8	6	1	3	4	1752	2	1	10	1	7	4	1789	3	3	0	2	6	0
1708	2	1	6	1	8	0	1753	2	4	8	1	7	4	1790	3	7	2	2	6	0
1709	3	18	6	1	13	4	1754	1	14	8	1	8	0	1791	3	0	6	2	8	0
1710	3	18	0	1	16	0	1755	1	13	10	1	5	4	1792	2	5	6	2	10	0
Aver.	2	3	5¼	1	7	11½	Ave.	1	17	4½	1	5	3½	Ave.	2	18	0	2	8	2½

Obfervation 1. The average price of wheat and of malt, refpectively, appears to have been a little lower in the fecond period, than it was in the firft. But the price of wheat in the third period is a full *third* higher than it was in the fecond. And the price of malt in the third period is *almoft double* what it was in the fecond.

Obf. 2. The prices of barley, beans, and peafe, (for feeding and fattening of animals) have been of late nearly, if not quite, double the prices which the fame articles bore refpectively, about the middle of this century.

A COMPARISON

A COMPARISON OF THE PRICES OF THE COMMON NECESSARIES OF LIFE ABOUT THE MIDDLE OF THIS CENTURY, WITH THE PRICES OF THE SAME FOR SOME YEARS PAST, TO 1794, IN THE COUNTY OF BERKS.

NOTE.—The prices in the former of theſe periods are given from the information of aged perſons of good memories, who have reſided all their life-time in or near this pariſh *(Barkham.)* And for the prices of late, I refer to the common experience of ſuch as have been houſekeepers the laſt ſeven years.

	Prices about the Middle of this Century.				Prices of late Years to 1794.			
	From		To		From		To	
	s.	*d.*	*s.*	*d.*	*s.*	*d.*	*s.*	*d.*
Flour *per* buſhel, or 56 lbs. *ſeconds* - -	3	4	4	0	6	8	8	4
Bread *per* half-peck loaf - - - -	0	7	0	8	0	11	1	2
Bacon *per* lb. in the flitch - - -	0	4	0	5	0	7	0	8
Bacon *per* ſingle pound - - - -	0	5	0	6	0	8	0	9
Beef *per* ſcore, 20 lb. - - - -	2	6	3	0	5	10	6	8
Beef and mutton, *per* lb. - - - -	0	3	0	3½	0	4½	0	5
Pork *per* lb. - - - - -	0	3½	0	4	0	4½	0	5
Veal *per* lb. - - - - -	0	3½	0	4	0	5	0	6
A ſheep's head - - - - -	0	6	0	6	0	10	1	0
Cheeſe *per* 112 lbs. at Reading fair - -	17	0	21	0	40	0	46	0
Cheeſe *per* lb. a good ſort - - -	0	3	0	3½	0	5½	0	6
Cheeſe *per* lb. an inferior ſort - - -	0	2½	0	3	0	4½	0	5
Malt *per* buſhel - - - - -	3	0	3	6	5	3	6	6
Freſh butter *per* lb. - - - -	0	5	0	6	0	10	1	0
Salt butter *per* lb. - - - - -	0	4	0	5	0	7	0	8
Common ſoft ſugar *per* lb. - - -	0	3	0	3	0	7	0	8
Soap and candles *per* lb. - - - -	0	5	0	6	0	8½	0	9
A pair of *men*'s ſtout ſhoes - - -	4	6	5	0	6	6	7	6
A pair of *women*'s ſtrong ſhoes - - -	2	6	3	0	4	0	4	6
Dowlaſs for ſhirting *per* ell - - -	1	0	1	0	1	4	1	6
Check for aprons - - - - -	0	0	1	0	1	4	0	0
Stuff for gowns *per* yard - - - -	0	9	0	9	1	0	0	0
A foul-weather coat, ready made for ſale -	11	0	12	0	21	0	24	0
Wool *per* todd, 28 lbs. - - - -	14	0	15	0	25	0	35	0

Obſervation.

Obſervation. It is manifeſt from inſpection, that the *retail* prices of the ſeveral articles contained in this liſt, eſpecially of ſuch as are, or ſhould be, daily uſed by poor families, have been of late *double*, or *nearly double*, the prices which the ſame articles bore, reſpectively, about the middle of the preſent century.

It is probable that the *proportion* between the prices, ſhewn by the foregoing ſtatements, will hold with reſpect to the whole kingdom. However, (keeping *much* within compaſs) we may certainly infer from them, that in the laſt forty or fifty years the advance has been, *generally*, a full *third* of the preſent prices.

But, in the ſame ſpace of time, what advance has taken place in the price of *day-labour?*—*Anſwer:* The advance has been, in ſome places, from *five* to *ſix* ſhillings, in others from *ſix* to *ſeven* ſhillings, a week; and, in ſome few places, a little more than this: that is, the advance has been *only* a *ſixth* or a *ſeventh* part of the preſent price. And even this ſmall advance is apparent, not real: for the additional ſhilling is not equivalent to certain advantages, which labouring people formerly enjoyed, but of which they have been gradually deprived; ſuch, for inſtance, as a meſs of milk or broth for breakfaſt; an allowance of ſmall beer; and the like.

SECTION VI.

APPLICATION OF THE CONTENTS OF SECTIONS II. AND III. TO ACCOUNT FOR THE LATE AUGMENTATION OF THE POOR-RATE.

	£
THE Poor-Rate about the year 1750, according to *H. Fielding*, was	1,000,000
Suppofe the prices of provifions and other neceffaries to have rifen (in confequence of the circumftances mentioned in Section II.) *one half* of what they were at that time: this rife (though the *number* of poor had remained the fame) will account for an addition to the rate, of - - - - - - - -	500,000
Suppofe alfo that in confequence of *that rife*, and of the feveral circumftances mentioned in Section III, the number of the poor depending on parifh relief has in the fame time increafed *one half*: this increafe muft have added to the rate,	
1. On account of that increafed number - £.500,000	
2. On account of the increafed expence of their maintenance - - - - - - - 250,000—	750,000
Therefore, taking thefe fuppofitions together, the amount of the Poor-Rate fhould be, and probably is, at this prefent time - -	*2,250,000

And if it be fuppofed farther, that the advance in the prices of provifion, &c. has been progreffive; and that the increafe of the number of dependent poor has gone on progreffively along with it; thefe confiderations will fufficiently explain that acceleration of the rate which is fhewn in Section I.

* To this fum may perhaps be added, on account of the circumftances mentioned in Section IV, about £.100,000.

SECTION VII.

THE RELATIVE PROPORTION BETWEEN LABOUR AND THE NECESSARIES OF LIFE AT DIFFERENT PERIODS.

I Have not thought it neceſſary to copy here the ſcanty materials from which the following ſketch has been drawn up: they may be found in Biſhop *Fleetwood*'s Chronicon, Dr. *Burn*'s Hiſtory of the Poor-Laws and Dr. *Price*'s work on Reverſionary Payments. Nor do I give this compariſon as quite exact; but I think it ſufficiently ſo to prove, that the condition of the day-labourer has been growing worſe continually from the middle of the fourteenth century to the preſent time.

Middle of Fourteenth Century.

Ordinary price of day-labour,	- - -	2*d*.
Price of the quarter of wheat	- - -	3*s*. 4*d*. to 4*s*.
Medium	- - - - - - -	3*s*. 8*d*.

22 days	- =	a quarter of wheat
20 days	- =	a fat hog, two years old
20 days	- =	clothing for a year of a common ſervant of huſbandry
6 days	- =	a quarter of beans or peaſe
5 days	- =	a quarter of barley
2 days	- =	a pair of ſhoes
1 day	- =	two gallons of ale.

Middle

Middle of Fifteenth Century.

Pay of a labourer per day - - - - - 3*d.*
Price of a quarter of wheat - - - - - 5*s.* to 5*s.* 6*d.*

20 to 22 days	=	a quarter of wheat
16 days -	=	a quarter of malt
16 days -	=	clothing for a year of a fervant
8 days -	=	a quarter of oats
7 days -	=	a flitch of bacon
4 days -	=	a yard of cloth for fhepherd
1 day -	=	two to three gallons of ale.

Former Part of Sixteenth Century.

Pay of a labourer per day - - - - - 3½*d.*
Price of a quarter of wheat about - - 7*s.* 6*d.*

26 days -	=	a quarter of wheat
13 or 14 days	=	a quarter of malt
7 days -	=	a quarter of oats
1 day -	=	eight or nine lbs. of beef, pork, veal
1 day -	=	feven lbs. of cheefe = four lbs. of butter.

About the Middle of Seventeenth Century.

In *Effex* the medium pay of a labourer *(rated)* was 13*d.*
Price of wheat (per *Fleetwood's Chronicon*, p. 106,) 40*s.* and of malt 24*s.* per quarter, as eftimated by the bifhop

37 days -	=	a quarter of wheat
22 days -	=	a quarter of malt
7 days -	=	a quarter of oats
4½ days -	=	two fhirts for a man, *made.*

Latter

Latter Part of Eighteenth Century.

Pay of a labourer per day - - - 14*d.*
Price of a quarter of wheat 48*s.*—of malt 42*s.* 6*d.*

41 days - -	=	a quarter of wheat
36½ days - -	=	a quarter of malt
96 days - -	=	a fat hog, fourteen ſcore, at 8*s.* per ſcore
27 or 28 days -	=	a quarter of beans or peaſe
20 or 21 days -	=	a quarter of barley
41 days - -	=	a flitch of bacon, ſix ſcore, at 8*s.*
9 days - -	=	a yard of cloth for ſervants
6 days - -	=	a pair of men's ſhoes
1 day - -	=	*leſs* than a gallon of ale
1 day - -	=	three lbs. ordinary cheeſe = 1½lb. butter
40 days - -	=	clothing for a year of a common ſervant of huſbandry.

I cannot forbear adding here, the following juſt and ſtriking obſervation by Dr. *Price.* [See *Rev. Paym.* vol. ii. p. 273.]

" The *nominal* price of day-labour is at preſent no more than about " *four* times, or at moſt *five* times higher than it was in 1514. But " the price of corn is *ſeven* times, and of fleſh meat and raiment about " *fifteen* times higher. So far therefore has the price of labour been " from advancing in proportion to the increaſe in the expences of " living, that it does not appear that it bears now *half* the proportion " to thoſe expences that it did bear formerly."

PART

PART THE THIRD.

MEANS OF RELIEF

PROPOSED.

PART III.

INTRODUCTION.

HAVING endeavoured in the preceding part to trace the Diſtreſſes and Vices of the Poor to the ſources in which they have originated, I come now in the laſt place to examine, *What are the proper means of removing thoſe Diſtreſſes, and curing thoſe Vices?*—This is a queſtion, which, as Sir *Joſiah Child* long ago remarked, " deſerves the moſt " deliberate conſideration of our wiſeſt counſellors: and if a whole " Seſſion of Parliament were employed upon this ſingular concern, " I think," ſays he, " it would be time ſpent as much to the glory " of GOD, and good of this Nation, as in any thing that noble and " worthy patriots can be engaged in."

Since he wrote, many very able men have employed their thoughts on this ſubject without much ſucceſs; which is, at once, a diſcouraging reflection to an enquirer of inferior judgment, and an argument that the queſtion itſelf is of difficult ſolution. But though the ſagacity of no one individual may be equal to ſo arduous a taſk, yet I am perſuaded, that the collective wiſdom of the legiſlature, aſſiſted by all the private information to be had in this country, may ſoon effect what has been ſo long wiſhed for.

Regarding our code of poor-laws as the Charter of the Poor, now well known and underſtood from the variety of caſes adjudged, and

 therefore

therefore too ſacred to be raſhly tampered with; and being alſo aware of the dangerous conſequences always to be apprehended from great changes and innovations in matters which concern the body of the people; I ſhall endeavour in the ſequel, keeping theſe conſiderations conſtantly in view, to ſpeak of ſuch meaſures only as have a tendency to improve the condition and morals of the poor, with the ſmalleſt alterations poſſible of the exiſting laws.

In forming new regulations, then, for the benefit of labouring families, the following appear to be the principal objects to which we ſhould direct our attention:

I. A reduction of the prices of certain neceſſary articles, as ſoon as this ſhall be practicable.

II. Providing *additional* employment for men and boys in winter, that they may loſe no time at that ſeaſon when they are uſually moſt diſtreſſed.

III. Providing *conſtant* employment for women and girls, to enable them to earn more than they commonly do.

IV. Correcting the improvidence of the lower people, and encouraging frugality among them.

V. Rating the wages of labourers according to the Statute 5 Eliz. cap. 4;—or,

VI. Regulating the price of day-labour by the price of bread, during the winter half year.

VII. Making a ſpecific proviſion out of the poor-rate for ſuch families as have more than three children unable to work.

SECTION

SECTION I.

A Reduction of the Prices of the Neceſſaries of Life, were it practicable, would be an effectual meaſure for relieving the poor. But it is to be feared, that in the preſent circumſtances of the nation, little or nothing can be done to eaſe them in this way. For the prices of neceſſaries having riſen unavoidably in conſequence of taxes, luxury, and other cauſes, this meaſure implies ſuch a reduction of taxes, and ſuch a reſtriction of luxury, as are at this time evidently impracticable.

1ſt. With regard to the taxes. The whole of the revenue being neceſſary, either for ſinking the principal and paying the intereſt of the national debt, or for carrying on the government and maintaining the dignity of the kingdom, it is in vain to expect that any ſpeedy reduction ſhould take place, ſince neither of theſe objects can be diſpenſed with. Nay; if our reſources would admit of it, it is much to be wiſhed that another million could be added, without farther diſtreſſing the lower claſſes, to the *ſinking fund* already provided, in order to accelerate its operation. For though the ſinking fund already provided will, if ſuffered to operate without interruption, certainly produce the effect expected from it in the long run; yet it operates ſo ſlowly at firſt as to create a prejudice againſt it in the minds of men ignorant of its powers, eſpecially when they reflect that poſterity, not themſelves, are to be benefited by this plan. It ſeems, therefore, that the prices of neceſſaries, ſo far as they have been enhanced by taxes, can no otherwiſe be lowered, than by transferring ſome of the heavieſt of theſe, at leaſt in part, from the neceſſaries of life daily uſed by the common people, to the luxuries conſumed by the higher ranks only.

2dly. This ſuppoſed transfer of taxes, if made, would alſo tend to reſtrain luxury, and to prevent the waſte occaſioned by it. But the misfortune is, that, if carried far enough to give relief to the poor, it might reſtrain luxury too much: for we muſt never forget that luxury feeds the revenue, the vaſt improvement of which, under the preſent adminiſtration, has been chiefly owing to the diffuſion of it. Our circumſtances require that luxury ſhould be gently treated. And of courſe ſuch a transfer of taxes can hardly be ſufficiently extenſive to produce any great beneficial effect to the poor, by diminiſhing the prices of the neceſſaries of life.

Some daring ſpirits have talked, very raſhly, of wiping out the National Debt with a *ſponge*, and ſo getting rid at once of half our taxes: and they would fain palliate this meaſure by comparing it to that of lopping off a limb in order to ſave life. But *firſt*, the probable conſequences of ſo iniquitous an act, which muſt ruin thouſands of innocent perſons, will doubtleſs prevent its being ever ſeriouſly propoſed; or, if propoſed, will influence the legiſlature and all good men indignantly to ſpurn the attempt. And were it practicable to carry this project into execution without overturning the government, which may well be queſtioned, it is likely, that ſuch a *ſudden* annihilation of taxes, inſtead of contributing to the relief of the inferior claſſes, would be followed by a more rapid increaſe of luxury in the higher

higher than we have yet ſeen; which would farther augment the prices of all things. *Secondly*, Though the National Debt has created many heavy taxes, ſeverely felt by the middle and lower claſſes of people; yet is the nation ſtill able to bear the burden, and actually does bear it without much diſcontent. There is therefore no abſolute neceſſity for having recourſe to the ſponge: and it is evidently the common intereſt of all perſons of property, to join in the moſt efficacious meaſures for preventing ſuch a neceſſity from ever ariſing.

When, by the operation of a ſinking fund, and other auxiliary means that may be adopted, the finances of this kingdom ſhall be in ſuch a ſtate as to admit of a gradual reduction or annihilation of taxes; the firſt ſtep to be taken for the benefit of the labouring people, is to *lower* the exciſe on *Malt*, in order to bring that article within their ability to purchaſe. *Malt* is now ſo dear, that the generality of poor families do not uſe a peck in a year. It would be not only a moſt popular, but alſo a moſt humane act, if the richer part of the nation would take *a conſiderable part* of this tax on themſelves in ſome ſhape or other, that poor people might be enabled to brew wholeſome drink at home. The other impoſts which preſs heavieſt on the poor, are, it is well known, thoſe on leather, ſoap, and candles; particularly the firſt, a pair of ſhoes now ſtanding a poor man in nearly a week's pay. Nor is it fit that, in ſo rich a nation as this, his wife and children ſhould be ſuffered to go barefoot in wet weather, much leſs in froſt and ſnow.

SECTION

SECTION II.

THE NEXT POINT IS THE PROVIDING ADDITIONAL EMPLOYMENT FOR MEN AND BOYS IN WINTER, THAT THEY MAY LOSE NO TIME AT THAT SEASON WHEN THEY ARE USUALLY MOST DISTRESSED.

IN a country like this, where ſo great a proportion of the land lies neglected, and almoſt uſeleſs, one would think it could be no difficult matter to find work for the induſtrious of every age all the year. It has been lately calculated that this iſland contains about twenty millions of acres capable of improvement, but remaining at preſent in an unimproved ſtate. Is all this land condemned, as it were, to perpetual ſterility? A great part of our waſtes might, it is ſaid, be eaſily converted into arable farms. And if "The improving a kingdom in "matter of huſbandry is better than conquering a new kingdom," as *Hartlib* has aſſerted, [*Legacy*, p. 42.]—"If the culture of the ſoil is the "greateſt of all manufactures, and the trueſt ſource of riches," as *Monteſquieu* has affirmed, [Eſpr. des Loix, l. xxi. c. 18:] "and if one "hundred pounds gained by a farmer, including the work of ſer-"vants, day-labourers, women, and children, employed by him, "bring more benefit to the community than three hundred, or twice "three hundred pounds acquired by the work of a ſingle artiſt oc-"cupied in things of mere ſuperfluity and ornament," as *Harte* has ſaid, faid, [Effays on Hufb. p. 30.] If thefe are indifputable truths, it is furely a matter of juft reproach to this wealthy nation, that almoft a third part of the land of the kingdom fhould be left in its prefent unprofitable ftate, when thoufands of families are ftarving for want of a few acres! The bringing into cultivation, and the improvement of twenty millions of acres would be much the fame thing as adding twenty-five new counties to the kingdom. And in what way can money be more ufefully expended? The expediency of bringing more land into tillage will be ftill more apparent, if we recollect a fact already mentioned, that this country has not of late produced a fufficient quantity of corn for the fubfiftence of its inhabitants, but has been obliged to pay annually large fums to foreigners for imported grain. Add to this, that we have at prefent a wide extent of dominions to protect; and it is well known that peafants make the the hardieft foldiers. This creation of additional employment would at once multiply this ufeful clafs of men, and keep them from degenerating. This meafure is therefore, in every view of the fubject, of the utmoft national importance.

But, befides the converfion of our waftes and commons into cornfields, judicious men have thought, that if hufbandry were as much attended to as it deferves, the land already in cultivation might be further improved beyond what the moft fkilful have any notion of: which would yield employment and fubfiftence to multitudes of people. The following inftance is given of what the perfection of agriculture can do:—The country poffeffed by the twelve tribes of *Ifrael* was only about one hundred and twenty miles in length, and eighty miles in breadth; that is, fomething more than fix millions of acres.

When

When *Joab* numbered the people, he found 1,300,000 fighting men; and as the fighting men of a nation are one-fourth of the whole, Paleſtine muſt then have contained about 5,200,000 inhabitants: which is at the rate of one perſon to a little more than one acre. But, ſuppoſing Great-Britain to contain ſixty-ſeven millions of acres, and its population to be ten millions, this gives the proportion of only one perſon to about ſix acres and a half. Here ſeems to be, therefore, great room for improvement. This comparatively much greater population of Paleſtine has been juſtly aſcribed to the following cauſes:—1ſt. The ſoil of that country was naturally ſomewhat more fertile than the ſoil of this country is.—2dly. The original diviſion of the land, as eſtabliſhed by *Joſhua*, was religiouſly preſerved, every particular family, of every tribe, having an intereſt in preſerving it; which prevented the exceſſive accumulation of landed property in few hands.—3dly. The laws concerning Uſury; on which ſir *J. Child* has this remark: "*Moſes* forbade the Jews to lend money to uſe to one another, but "permitted them to lend to ſtrangers. His laws concerning uſury "were ſufficient to make any barren land fruitful, and a fruitful land "an entire garden."—4thly. Theſe regulations diſpoſed the people to follow a ſimple life according to nature, friendly to marriage, and conſequently to population; and ſhut out luxury, the greateſt enemy of both. [*Harte.*]—*Laſtly*, They had but few horſes, and uſed oxen in huſbandry. With us the horſe is an expenſive ſervant, even when employed in tilling the ground.—Such was the policy of the wiſeſt of ancient nations, founded on laws of divine appointment. How different the policy of modern ſtates! and how thin the population attending it!

It

It will perhaps be ſaid, that numberleſs acts of incloſure have paſſed of late years; and that our agriculture has been continually advancing along with our other improvements. Let this be admitted: yet the fact more than once referred to, namely, our being now obliged to buy a great quantity of corn, whereas fifty years ago we uſed to ſell a great quantity, proves, unqueſtionably, that *tillage* has not advanced faſt enough by a great deal. It proves that ſufficient attention has not been given to the *grand manufacture*, the production of corn. And as to the numerous incloſures that have been made, I fear the acts themſelves will ſhew, that, in making them, too little regard has been paid to the encouragement and employment of labouring people. Care ſhould be taken to guard againſt this error in future.

I cannot forbear adding here, that were it even impoſſible to find additional employment of a *uſeful* kind, whereby men and boys might at all ſeaſons earn their living; yet it would be obviouſly better policy to ſet all ſuch perſons, as cannot otherwiſe be employed, on the *uſeleſs* work of building pyramids, than to let them ſtarve in ildeneſs, or become rogues, vagabonds, and beggars, to avoid ſtarving: becauſe by their being *conſtantly* employed in any work, which requires a great exertion of bodily ſtrength in the open air, ſloth would be diſcouraged, and the people kept from degenerating. But it is manifeſt, that we are far from being reduced to the neceſſity of recurring to ſuch an expedient as this; that abundance of the moſt uſeful work may eaſily be found; and that nothing is wanting to baniſh beggary from among us, but " the ſpirit to make a right uſe of our ſuperfluous wealth."

The waſte lands ſeem to be the grand reſource of the nation: and their gradual improvement, judiciouſly conducted, would afford employment and ſubſiſtence to multitudes of people. But on this head, as well as on other important points, the public has reaſon to expect a great deal of the moſt valuable information from the induſtry and zeal of the *Board of Agriculture*. And when, after full information obtained, the incloſure and improvement of theſe lands ſhall be reſolved upon, it is earneſtly to be wiſhed, that of the various meaſures which doubtleſs will then be propoſed, ſuch only may receive the ſanction of Parliament as ſhall appear the fitteſt for giving ſupport and encouragement to labouring families.

SECTION III.

ANOTHER ESSENTIAL IS THE PROVIDING CONSTANT EMPLOYMENT FOR WOMEN AND GIRLS, THEREBY TO ENABLE FAMILIES TO EARN MORE THAN THEY COMMONLY DO.

AT prefent the earnings of the wives and children of day-labourers are, in general, very fmall. Except what they earn in the time of hay-making, and at harveft, their earnings the reft of the year are infignificant. The greateft part of their time is unprofitably fpent, becaufe no care is taken to furnifh them with work. Were girls, in particular, inftructed betimes in knitting, fpinning, and in fuch other work as they are capable of, this would not only give them a habit of induftry, but alfo add greatly to their domeftic comfort as long as they lived.

One might fuppofe that workhoufes, and houfes of induftry, were calculated to anfwer this purpofe; but experience tells againft them. After a little time, thefe almoft always become mere receptacles of idle and vicious perfons; many of whom live better there at the public expence, than fome honeft people can do, who work hard to keep their families from the parifh. It has been found too, that the mortality in workhoufes is uncommonly great, particularly among the children.

Women and girls fhould be furnifhed with work to be done at their own homes. As a proof of what importance it is that they fhould be thus enabled to bring fomething into the common ftock, here follows an inftance of what may be gained by *fpinning*, where the mother

 has

has been well brought up herfelf, and is capable of inftructing her girls. It fhews, that, even in the prefent low condition of the poor, we may find here and there a *large* family making fhift to live without parifh relief, except on very preffing occafions; fuch as long ficknefs, fmall-pox, and the like. But this happens only where the man is expert at various kinds of work, or where the woman (as in this inftance) is more than ordinarily notable and induftrious.

WEEKLY EXPENCES OF A FAMILY,

Confifting of a Man, his Wife, and Five Children; the eldeft a boy aged twelve years; the next a boy aged nine; the third and fourth, girls aged feven and five; the youngeft, an infant.

(*This Account was taken at* EASTER 1787.)

	£.	s.	d.
ONE bufhel of flour, on an average, at 10*d.* per gallon - -	0	6	8
Yeaft and falt - - - - - - - - - - - -	0	0	3½
A fat hog bought, weight about fourteen fcore, at 7*s.* 6*d.* per fcore, 5*l.* 5*s.*—And *bacon* bought befide, about fix fcore, at 6½*d.* per lb. 3*l.* 5*s.*—Total 8*l.* 10*s.*——Per week - - - - - -	0	3	3½
Tea, 1½oz. 4*d.*—*Sugar,* ½lb. 4*d.*—*Butter,* ½lb. 4*d.* - - -	0	1	0
Brews a *peck of malt* once a fortnight, coft 1*s.* 4*d.*—Buys 1½ gall. of *hopfeed,* at 1*s.* 6*d.* which ferves all the year; a handful of this put into the beer makes it keep well enough for that fhort time	0	0	8¼
Soap, Candles, Worfted, &c. - - - - - - - - -	0	0	8
	£. 0	12	7

The good woman reckons *fmall beer and bread* a better and cheaper fupper, than *bread and cheefe and water*; and fays, that *cheefe* is the deareft article that a poor family can ufe.

Her general account was this: that the earnings of her hufband and the boys maintained the family in food; and that what fhe herfelf and the girls earnt by by ſpinning, and in harveſt, found them in clothes, linen, and other neceſſaries: with which the account of particulars agrees.

		£.	s.	d.
Twelve ſhillings and ſeven-pence per week, is per annum	- -	32	14	4
Add for rent, fuel, clothing, &c.	- - - - - - -	7	0	0
Amount of *expences* per annum	- £.	39	14	4

WEEKLY EARNINGS OF THE SAME FAMILY, (Easter, 1787.)

The huſband receives 8*s*. per week, throughout the year	- -	0	8	0
The eldeſt boy	- - - - - - - - - - -	0	2	6
The next boy	- - - - - - - - - - -	0	1	6
The *wife* was taught by her mother to *read* and *ſpin*, and ſhe teaches her girls the ſame. Before ſhe went into ſervice, ſhe uſed to ſpin a pair of coarſe ſheets every winter. When ſhe ſits cloſely to her wheel the whole day, ſhe can ſpin 2 lbs. of coarſe flax for ordinary ſheeting and toweling, at $2\frac{1}{2}$*d*. per lb; therefore, ſuppoſing the buſineſs of the family to take up two days in the week, the 8lbs. ſpun in the other four days comes to	- - - - - -	0	1	8
The *eldeſt girl* can earn 2*d*. per day, ſpinning near 1 lb. of ſuch flax; and ſuppoſing her alſo to loſe two days in the week in going of errands, tending the infant, &c. her earnings will be	- -	0	0	8
The *little girl*, aged five, can alſo ſpin adroitly; ſhe goes to the wheel when her ſiſter is otherwiſe employed, but is not kept cloſely to it, as that might hurt her health.				
This family earns ſomething extraordinary in harveſt; and as the *man* does not ſcruple working over-hours occaſionally, and looks after the ſtock on one of his employer's farms, they are allowed to live rent-free in the farm-houſe; all which together may be reckoned equal to	- - - - - - - - -	0	1	0
		0	15	4

Amount of *earnings* per annum	-	39	17	4
Amount of *expences* per annum	-	39	14	4
Surplus of earnings	- -	0	3	0

Obſervations on the preceding Account.

I. SUPPOSE the wife and girls *not* to have learnt to ſpin; then, inſtead of earning 2*s*. 4*d*. a-week, which comes to 5*l*. 17*s*. a-year, they would only earn, like the common run of women, about 1*l*. 10*s*.; and therefore, inſtead of a ſurplus at the year's end, there would be a deficiency of 4*l*. 4*s*. unleſs by living harder they curtailed their expences ſo much. It is owing to the money gained by ſpinning, that this family is enabled to keep out of debt, and to live ſo decently.

II. The whole annual expence of this family, (39*l*. 14*s*. 4*d*.) divided by 7, makes the average per head 5*l*. 13*s*. 6*d*.; and as the *extra* earnings of the mother and girls by ſpinning (as above reckoned) are about 4*l*. 7*s*. it is plain that ſpinning alone maintains *one* of the younger children.

III. The two boys together earn half as much as the father; and as the average expence per head is 5*l*. 13*s*. 6*d*. and the average earnings of the boys 5*l*. 4*s*. per annum each, it appears that between them they nearly get their living, the deficiency for each being only 9*s*. 6*d*. Therefore, allowing for this deficiency, we may put the two boys out of the queſtion and conſider the family as conſiſting of the remaining *five* perſons.

IV. The family then (excluſive of the two boys) conſiſting of the man, his wife, two girls, aged ſeven and five, and an infant, their earnings and expences will be as under:

From the earnings of the whole family - - -	39	17	4				
Deduct the earnings of the two boys - - - -	10	8	0				
				Rem.	29	9	4*
And from the expences of the whole family - -	39	14	4				
Deduct the expences of the two boys - - - -	11	7	0				
				Rem.	28	7	4
And from the former remainder deducting the latter, the ſurplus is -				£.	1	2	0

* See Obſervation 11, p. 24.

But if *ſpinning* were laid aſide, inſtead of this ſurplus there would be a deficiency of 3*l.* 5*s.*

V. Hence appears plainly the great importance of *ſpinning*, or of ſome other work at which women and girls may be conſtantly employed: for this circumſtance (accompanied with ſobriety and frugality) enables ſome families to live with credit, which muſt otherwiſe have come into difficulties, and in every difficulty have ſought help from their pariſhes.

But we have no reaſon to expect that ſuch induſtry as this will become general, unleſs ſome new meaſures are taken to encourage and enforce it. Let us then conſider what meaſures are proper to be adopted for that purpoſe.

1. The negligence of overſeers in ſetting the poor on work muſt be corrected. Good laws are but of little uſe, unleſs they are well executed. It concerns not only private families aud pariſhes, but the nation at large, that all ſuch perſons as are able and willing to work, ſhould have work. And therefore overſeers of the poor ſhould not be at liberty to neglect ſo important a part of their duty with impunity. Yet this is almoſt univerſally the caſe: for according to the returns made to parliament in 1786, the whole annual amount of the money expended in ſetting the poor on work, is under 16,000*l.* The penalty which the law threatens, being ſeldom inflicted, is by no means ſufficient to enforce obedience to its injunctions.

The churchwardens, and overſeers of the poor, have ample powers given them by 43 Eliz. cap. 2, to ſet all poor perſons on work, who want work. But in country places, farmers and tradeſmen are commonly appointed to thoſe offices; and theſe, having buſineſs enough of their

their own to mind, will not beſtow the neceſſary time and attention on the affairs of the poor and of their pariſh. To this negligence it is owing, that ſo many women are now quite ignorant of matters which all women ſhould underſtand, and wholly incapable of bringing up their children in uſeful and induſtrious habits. And to this it is alſo owing, that the ſad expedient of *farming* the poor is becoming every year more and more common.

In order, therefore, to *compel* overſeers of the poor to a better performance of their duty, I would propoſe that an *oath* be framed with that view, and that on their appointment they be ſworn faithfully to do what the law requires of them, to the beſt of their knowledge and ability. And that they may not plead ignorance of their duty, in excuſe for the non-performance of it, an abſtract of the poor-laws, carefully drawn up, ſhould at the ſame time be given them by the juſtices, for their direction, at leaſt in the moſt eſſential points.

To this I can ſee but one objection; namely, that being appointed for one year only, they are too ſhort a time in office to carry any plan, for ſetting the poor on work, effectually into execution. To obviate which, why may they not be appointed for *two*, *three*, or more years, inſtead of one? " A private bill paſſed, allowing the appointment of an " overſeer permanent in office, and on ſalary, to *Bradford* in *Wiltſhire*: " in conſequence of which, the poor have been better provided for, and " the poor-rates reduced from 3,300*l.* to 2,300*l.*" [See *Sir W. Young*'s Obſerv. Prelim. p. 64.]

And if appointed for a longer term than one year, they ſhould however be obliged yearly to verify their accounts on oath: which accounts ſhould be drawn up in a preſcribed form, and bear on the face of them,

in

in what manner the poor, capable of work, have been employed. And if provifion were made for the printing on a fheet of paper, and difperfing in each parifh, annual accounts of every difburfement and receipt of its officers, this would tend to check both the officers and the poor, and to inform and intereft the parifhioners with refpect to parifh concerns. [See *Franklin's* Tracts, p. 63.] Magiftrates too fhould not merely be authorifed, as now, to fwear the overfeers to their accounts on going out of office; but they fhould have, and be required to exercife, a controling power over them in this matter.

2. But, in the prefent ftate of things, it is not to be expected that thefe meafures alone will prove fufficient. Something further feems neceffary to be done, in order to ftimulate thofe, who have long been ufed to wafte time in idlenefs, to exert themfelves for the good of their families. To produce this effect, *encouragement* muft go along with coercion.

The following brief account of the means which were adopted with that view in the county of *Rutland*, in 1785 and 1786, furnifhes an example fit to be imitated in other places.

The juftices of the peace for the faid county having at their quarter feffions refolved to put in force the act of 43 Eliz. cap. 2, requiring overfeers of the poor " to fet on work all fuch perfons as have no " means to maintain them, and ufe no ordinary or daily trade,"

Ordered, " That the overfeers of the poor of each parifh within the county, do immediately provide fuch raw materials, as wool, yarn, hemp, and flax, as alfo wheels and other implements, for the employment of the poor of every denomination within their refpective parifhes, as fhall be neceffary to enable them to do fuch work as they are capable

 of

of performing. And that they ſhall meet together at leaſt once every month, in the church of their reſpective pariſhes, upon a Sunday immediately after divine ſervice, there to conſider of the beſt courſe and order to be taken and made in the employment of the ſaid poor."

Ordered alſo, " That no poor perſons be allowed any relief in money, until they have done ſuch work as they are capable of; nor allowed any relief on account of any child above *ſix* years of age, who ſhall not be able to knit; nor on account of any child above *nine* years of age, who ſhall not be able to ſpin either linen or woollen."

And to render the execution of the above act (43. Eliz. cap. 2.) more eaſy to the overſeers of the poor, and to encourage the induſtrious who ſhall be ſet to work agreeably to the ſame; it was unanimouſly reſolved at a general meeting of the county, " That a Fund be raiſed for giving them *premiums* according to their induſtry; and that a committee be appointed, and fully intruſted with the diſpoſal and management of the ſaid fund, in any ſuch manner as ſhall appear to them moſt conducive to the accompliſhment of the ſeveral purpoſes of the aſſociation."

The fund was raiſed by a ſubſcription from each pariſh that choſe to enter into the aſſociation, of *one per cent.* upon the poor-rate of the laſt year; by an annual ſubſcription from individuals of 5*s.* each; and by benefactions of the noblemen and gentlemen of the county.

The firſt committee appointed, having ſettled their mode of proceeding, came to ſeveral general reſolutions reſpecting the diſtribution of the money.—It was *reſolved,* " That when the number of ſubſcribing pariſhes ſhould be aſcertained, ſuch pariſhes ſhould be divided into *claſſes,* regard being had to neighbourhood, and the amount of the pariſh parifh rates. That it be recommended to the different parifhes to provide a convenient place as a fpinning-room, and a proper perfon as teacher. That *premiums,* confifting of clothing, be given to fuch children, of certain age and defcription, as in a *given time* fhall have produced the greateft quantity of *fpinning* or *knitting* of different kinds, and of the beft quality. That whenever any young perfon fhall go out to apprenticefhip or fervice, or fhall be married with the approbation of the committee, fuch young perfon fhall receive from the committee not lefs than 5l. nor more than 10l. if he or fhe fhall have received *three* of the annual premiums given by the committee; from *two* to *three* pounds, if fuch young perfon fhall have received *two* premiums; and from 30s. to 40s. if *one* premium. That premiums, at the difcretion of the committee, be given to thofe who bring up four children or more, born in wedlock, to the age of fourteen years, without relief from the parifh. And that premiums be alfo given, at the difcretion of the committee, to fuch overfeers of the poor as fhall diftinguifh themfelves in the due execution of the orders of the feffions relative to the employment of the poor."

Such is the outline of a plan, which in that county has been attended with the beft effects. The poor people, I am informed, fhewed the greateft willingnefs to profit by the encouragements held out to them. By their endeavours to obtain *premiums,* the fpinning in the county has been much improved as to the quality of the work. And the habits of induftry, which the people have acquired, though their earnings are fmall, have confiderably lowered the rates. But the principal benefit arifing from this inftitution, is the enabling the *juftices* to diftinguifh the deferving from the *idle* poor: for when a man applies for relief on account of a large family, the juſtice, to whom he applies, enquires of the overſeers whether his children earn as much as they might do by knitting or ſpinning: if they do, and, notwithſtanding that, he is in want, relief is of courſe granted him; but if his children are idle, and will not knit or ſpin, no relief is given, till they do ſpin or knit as they are able.

This inſtitution in the county of Rutland took its riſe from certain printed propoſals made by the Rev. *T. Foſter*, one of His Majeſty's juſtices of the peace for that county; which propoſals he was induced to bring forward by the ſucceſs that had attended an eſtabliſhment of the ſame kind in a part of the county of *Lincoln*.*

In every county ſome ſort of work might, doubtleſs, be found for the wives and children of labouring people, whereby they might be made to contribute largely towards their own maintenance, if the higher ranks would but ſet themſelves earneſtly to promote induſtry among them. Women and girls might ſoon be taught to manufacture coarſe linen and woollen ſtuffs for their own uſes. By means of ſchools of induſtry, encouraged by ſocieties of induſtry, (like thoſe juſt mentioned) the ſame induſtrious ſpirit might, in time, be univerſally diffuſed through the kingdom. And the advantage reſulting to the publick would, it is manifeſt, be very great, by training the riſing generation in a way to earn their bread, and by the multiplication of ſuch families as that which has given occaſion to theſe remarks.

I will add here, that it appears to be wholly owing to the want of proper care and attention in thoſe who direct and manage the buſineſs of

* See an excellent account of the Society for the promotion of Induſtry in Lincolnſhire, by the Rev. Mr. *Bower*, one of His Majeſty's juſtices of the peace for that county. Subjoined to that publication is the report of the Board of Trade in 1697, relative to the poor, drawn up by Mr. *Locke*, and which contains his plan of a ſchool of induſtry.

counties,

counties, that the unhappy perfons confined in our prifons are not made ufeful to the community. Dorchefter jail is an inftance which proves this. It appears by a printed account now before me, (communicated by my much refpected friend Mr. *Morton Pitt*) that the prifoners in that jail have, by being employed in fuch trades as they were capable of, and receiving the rewards due to their diligence, not only earned their own maintenance, but a confiderable furplus, over and above that, to be carried to the credit of the county. And, what is of much greater moment, the regulations there adopted have been productive of the moft falutary effects in amending the morals of the prifoners, and gradually leffening the number of offenders. And it is well known that His Majefty and the Royal Family, in a vifit to that jail in the fummer 1793, were highly pleafed with the induftry and orderly behaviour of the prifoners. The like good management has been attended with the like fuccefs in *Norfolk* and *Oxfordfhire*. And were it univerfally practifed, it would undoubtedly be everywhere productive of the fame benefits, by promoting induftry and good morals, and leffening parochial expences.

I cannot clofe this head without obferving farther, that fchools of induftry might, at a fmall additional charge, be made very ufeful as fchools of morals alfo. And what can be of greater importance, I will not fay to families and parifhes, but to the nation at large, than that the youth of both fexes fhould be trained up in habits of *piety*, as well as of *induftry*? If one or more fchools were fet up in every parifh with this two-fold intention, different days might be allotted for different purpofes: one day the children might be occupied in kitting or fpinning, another in making or mending their cloaths, and fo on: and fome part of each day they fhould be employed in learning to read, and getting by

rote

rote ufeful leffons. The fucceffion and variety of employments would prevent any one of them from becoming irkfome. And emulation might be excited in the fcholars by *premiums* fuited to their different degrees of proficiency in religious inftruction, in the fame manner as was done in the other cafe refpecting their fkill and dexterity at the feveral kinds of work.

We hear complaints every day made of the depraved manners of the common people: and we fee and feel that they are indeed depraved in a high degree. But let us candidly own that this depravity is not confined to them alone. Without doubt fome of their vices have defcended to them from above: for the lower-ranks are ever fond of apeing their fuperiors, particularly in vice and folly. The truth feems to be that *religion*, the principal engine in forming and preferving national manners, has loft much of that influence, which it always ought to have over the hearts and minds of *all* ranks of people. And hiftory tells, that wherever this has happened, the confequence has been, that human laws, deriving their chief authority from the divine, have loft much of their energy alfo. And when the joint power of both can no longer refift the torrent of vice and licentioufnefs, what fubftitutes can government employ, except the formidable ones of force and terror, for the prefervation of its own exiftence, and the maintenance of publick tranquillity? *Religion* may with great juftice and propriety be faid to be the only folid foundation of good laws, mild government, and genuine liberty.

The firft neceffary ftep towards *restoring the influence of religion*, is the making a permanent provifion for the *religious education* of poor children. Is the expence an objection? Yet in *Scotland* and *Switzerland*,

poorer

poorer countries than this, the importance of the religious education of the poor is ſo well underſtood, that due proviſion has been there made for that purpoſe. In Scotland, in particular, no pariſh is without a ſchool. [See Mr. *Howard*'s State of Priſons, p. 124, 196.] We profeſs to believe that it is our duty as *Christians*, to feed the hungry, clothe the naked, comfort the afflicted, and *instruct the ignorant*. Our laws have provided that all theſe duties ſhould be tolerably performed, except the laſt; with reſpect to which they are plainly deficient. And the conſequence is but too viſible in the ill manners and bad morals of the lower ſort of people. Of this we are conſtantly complaining, without once reſolving to apply the proper remedy.

Will it be ſaid, that it is a principal part of the buſineſs of the clergy, to inſtruct young perſons? Without doubt it is: nor can any thing more uſeful be conceived, than the appointment of this order of men, for keeping up a ſenſe of religion in the minds of the people. But the defect lies here, that the children of the poor are not ſufficiently inſtructed *beforehand*, for receiving with profit the further inſtructions of the clergy. And to this want of preparatory education we ought to attribute, in a great meaſure, that ſuppoſed inefficacy of the labours of the clergy, for which they have been, ſo often, unreaſonably cenſured.

Will it be ſaid, that the neceſſity of making a publick proviſion for this purpoſe has been ſuperſeded by the numerous charity ſchools and Sunday ſchools exiſting in this kingdom? Far be it from me to depreciate theſe inſtitutions. The benevolence of their founders and ſupporters will receive its reward in heaven. *Charity ſchools*, however, take in but a ſmall number, comparatively, of the children of the poor; in *England* and *Wales* about 30,000 only. *Sunday ſchools*, indeed, are calculated

culated to reſcue a far greater number from total ignorance; but they reſt on the precarious foundation of voluntary charity, and conſequently are very ſubject to fail. Mr. *Morton Pitt*'s plan for ſecuring their *permanency* has been ſome years before the publick: and it is much to be regretted that it has hitherto been no-where carried into execution, except in a part of Dorſetſhire under his own inſpection. More *certain* proviſion ſhould be made for the education of poor children, which might be beſt attained by making ſchools of induſtry ſchools of morals alſo.

The number of the living from 6 to 10 years of age (both incluſive) is about a *tenth* of the whole number of the living of all ages. Therefore ſuppoſing the inhabitants of *England* and *Wales* to be 8,000,000, the number of children from 6 to 10 will be 800,000. *Three-fourths* of theſe, or 600,000, belong probably to poor parents; ſome of whom, however, manage ſo as to give their children a little ſchooling, Let it be ſuppoſed,

That the number of thoſe educated at the expence of their parents is	20,000
The number admitted into *Charity ſchools* is known to be about	30,000
Suppoſe the *Sunday ſchools* to receive - - - - - - - - - - -	150,000
Total educated - -	200,000

Therefore the number of thoſe uneducated is 400,000; that is to ſay, *two-thirds* of the children of the poor receive not the ſmalleſt degree of ſchooling. The ſchooling of theſe, at 10s. each per ann. would amount to 200,000l. If this ſum were to be raiſed by a pariſh rate, it would, ſurely, be money well laid out, the importance of the object conſidered. But if a plan of this kind were once fully carried into execution, there can be no doubt but it would ſupport itſelf; for theſe children might

with

with common care and pains be made to earn, one with another, 20s. a year each, or double the expence of their ſchooling. [See Mr. *Bower*'s publication referred to in p. 92.

I have dwelt the longer on this point from the fulleſt conviction of its importance. Moſt unfortunately, the inordinate love of pleaſure and amuſement in the higher ranks ſeems to yield but ſlowly, if at all, to ſober and ſerious reflection, to a practical ſenſe of religion and piety: yet in theſe, licentiouſneſs is kept within ſome bounds, by a regard to character, and the value of a good name. But when the low and uneducated part of mankind come to adopt the looſe principles of the infidel and the atheiſt, the moſt dreadful conſequences to ſociety are juſtly to be apprehended. Reflect on this, ye rich and great! and if every worthier motive has no weight with you, let a ſenſe of *intereſt* influence you to reſpect religion: certainly you will gain nothing by its deſtruction.

SECTION IV.

ANOTHER IMPORTANT POINT IS TO DEVISE MEANS FOR CORRECTING THE IMPROVIDENCE OF WORKING PEOPLE, AND ENCOURAGING FRUGALITY AMONG THEM.

THIS may perhaps be attained, 1ſt. By removing the cauſe of their too great reliance on pariſh relief: 2dly, By inſtructing them how to ſecure and improve ſuch ſavings as they might make out of their pay: and, 3dly, By holding out to them a probable proſpect of bettering their condition in conſequence of ſuch frugality.

In the firſt place, young perſons in ſervice, and day-labouring men, might, while ſingle, ſave more money than they uſually do ſave. But the misfortune is, that our poor-laws, by making an indiſcriminate proviſion for *all* in want, have rendered them very careleſs in this reſpect. And this careleſſneſs has been much encouraged by that ſpirit of diſſipation, which has deſcended from the higher to the middling, and from the middling to the lower ranks of people. This prevailing turn to expence ſeems, indeed, to be one principal cauſe, that there have been of late ſo many more executions in the houſes of the rich, ſo many more bankruptcies among merchants and tradeſmen, and ſo much more beggary among the poor, than were ever known before. So far as this improvidence in the lower ranks has proceeded from the like diſpoſition in the higher, it may not perhaps admit of a cure; ſince it is not to be expected that the richer part of a luxurious nation ſhould be induced by by prudential motives to practiſe frugality for the ſake of example. But ſo far as this improvidence has ariſen from a too great reliance on parochial relief, it may ſurely be remedied by removing the cauſe of that reliance. The obvious cauſe of that reliance is the indiſcriminate proviſion made by law for all in want. Draw a line of ſeparation, therefore, between ſuch as are deſerving, and ſuch as are undeſerving of parochial aſſiſtance. Suppoſe, for inſtance, (the pay of labourers being firſt ſettled on a right foot, and overſeers compelled to ſet families to work) it were then enacted, that no ſingle perſons of either ſex, if able to earn their living; and that no family having only three young children at home; ſhall be entitled, except in ſome extraordinary ſpecified caſes, to receive relief out of the poor-rate. This excluſion might perhaps oblige ſervants and day-labourers to take more care in future to huſband well their earnings. And if from a regulation of this kind ſome hardſhip ſhould caſually be felt by particular families or individuals, the removal of that hardſhip might ſafely be left to their charitable neighbours, who, knowing their circumſtances, would not fail to relieve them if deſerving relief.

But, then, on the other hand, as it would be manifeſtly unjuſt that any perſon willing to work ſhould be ſuffered to ſtarve for want of work, let employers be required to do their part. In order to this, let it be provided that every *man*, who has not been able, at the time of receiving his wages on Saturday evening, to obtain of the ſame employer work for himſelf and his boys the enſuing week; and who having, at the pariſh-church on the Sunday immediately following, applied for work to the churchwardens and overſeers of the poor, or any one of them there preſent, without obtaining any; or who, if none of thefe officers were there prefent, has made the like application at the houfe of one or more of them without fuccefs; I fay, let every man, who, having complied with thefe directions, is neverthelefs fuffered to lofe his time without any fault of his own, be by law entitled to two-thirds of a day's wages, to be paid out of the poor-rate for every day that he fhall fo remain unemployed; and in a reafonable proportion for boys above the age of twelve years. It is furely fufficient that labouring people fhould offer themfelves to do fuch work as they are capable of: it is the duty of their fuperiors to find them fuch work; which they will be moft careful to do, when they fhall be obliged to pay for idle time.

2dly. Notwithftanding the encouragement given to wafteful expence both by our poor-laws, and alfo by the wide fpread luxury of the age we live in; yet there are no doubt many fervants and others, who would fave a part of their earnings againft a time of need, if they knew how to fecure and improve their favings. Their ignorance in this refpect, there is reafon to think, renders many of them lefs thrifty than they would otherwife be. Few of the lower fort of people know any thing of the nature of the public funds; and if they knew more than they do, ten or a dozen guineas faved make too trifling a fum to carry to the Stock Exchange. And if the owner lays them up in a corner of his box, in the hope of adding more to them, it is odds but fome temptation comes in the way, and the money vanifhes. Another circumftance which has difcouraged many from faving any thing is this: they have lif-tened to the melancholy tales of fome of their acquaintance, who having unfortunately placed the little money they had got in fervice in the hands of fome plaufible tradefman, have by his failure loft it all; or to

the

the equally melancholy tales of others, who had experienced the like in ſome of thoſe irregular box-clubs ſome years ago common in this kingdom, in which, when the contributions had amounted to a large ſum, the whole was, for the ſake of intereſt, lent to ſome knave and loſt. It is therefore a matter of conſequence to teach ſuch people as earn more money than they need ſpend, how to ſecure and improve ſuch ſmall ſums as they may be diſpoſed to ſave, that they may reap the full benefit of their parſimony, when they come to ſettle in the world.

Now there are two methods of doing this, more eſpecially ſuited to the circumſtances of the people in queſtion: 1ſt. By engaging in a *friendly ſociety for mutual relief*, as now regulated by act of parliament; and 2dly, By engaging in one of thoſe *provident ſocieties* which have been lately ſet up in ſeveral towns. By becoming members of a friendly ſociety, ſuch perſons as are deſirous of keeping themſelves free from the ſhame and miſery of being burdenſome to their pariſh, have it in their power to make for themſelves a proviſion againſt ſickneſs, accident, or old age; and that without the hazard to which ſome clubs of this kind were heretofore ſubject, whoſe ſchemes, having been arbitrarily formed, were of courſe fraught with miſchievous conſequences. Theſe ſocieties the rich would do well to encourage by liberal ſubſcriptions. By becoming members of a provident ſociety, ſuch perſons as are deſirous of placing a part of their preſent wages in a fund to be improved for the benefit of the contributors, with the view of receiving back the ſame ſo improved at the end of a ſhort term of years, have an opportunity of doing ſo. And as the bankers and principal tradeſmen in thoſe towns, where theſe ſocieties have been ſet up, are the truſtees and managers of the funds ſo raiſed, the riſk to the members muſt here

alſo

alſo be inconſiderable. They who may wiſh for further information reſpecting friendly ſocieties, may peruſe the act paſſed in 1789 with the ſcheme annexed. See alſo a ſcheme of the ſame kind at the end of a publication in 1787, intitled a Narrative of the Proceedings tending towards a National Reformation, &c. by a Country Magiſtrate. At the end of Mr. Baron *Maſeres'* excellent work on the Principles of Life-Annuities, there is a copy of a bill, with the requiſite tables, (which paſſed the Houſe of Commons, but was rejected by the Lords) being the firſt plan of this kind formed on juſt principles for the uſe of the common people. See another plan for the uſe of the *poor* in Dr. *Price's* work on Reverſionary Payments, vol. i. p. 140, *note*. And with reſpect to the ſeveral Provident Societies, it is ſufficient to refer to the plans of thoſe ſocieties, which may be had of the ſecretaries.

3dly. *Hold out to the induſtrious and frugal a probable proſpect of bettering their condition.* If it be reaſonable that idleneſs and improvidence ſhould be diſcouraged and puniſhed, it is without doubt equally ſo that induſtry and parſimony ſhould receive their proper reward. Inſtead, therefore, of driving poor people to deſpondency and deſpair, by making it impoſſible for them to riſe even a ſingle ſtep from their preſent low condition, you ſhould cheriſh in their breaſts the hope of advancing themſelves to more comfortable circumſtances, which is aſſuredly the beſt preſervative from vice and beggary. *Hope* is a cordial, of which the poor man has eſpecially much need, to cheer his heart in the toilſome journey through life. And the fatal conſequence of that policy, which deprives labouring people of the expectation of poſſeſſing any property in the ſoil, muſt be the extinction of every generous principle in their minds. Therefore, 1ſt. Allow to the cottager a little land about

about his dwelling; for keeping a cow, for planting potatoes, for raiſing flax or hemp. 2dly, Convert the waſte lands of the kingdom into *ſmall* arable farms, a certain quantity every year, to be let on favourable terms to induſtrious families. 3dly, Reſtrain the engroſſment and over-enlargement of farms. The propriety of theſe meaſures cannot, I think, be queſtioned. For ſince the deſtruction of ſmall farms, and of cottages having land about them, has ſo greatly contributed to bring the lower peaſantry into the ſtarving condition in which we now ſee them, the moſt effectual means ſhould be taken without delay for checking this practice, and counteracting the miſchief it has already done. The miſchief is univerſally felt. For whilſt this practice has been reducing the generality of ſmall farmers into day-labourers, and the great body of day-labourers into beggars, and has been multiplying and impoveriſhing even beggars themſelves, it has perhaps elevated the body of farmers above their proper level, enabling many of them not only to tyrannize over their inferiors, but even to vie with their landlords in diſſipation and expence.

For full and rational information on each of the foregoing heads, I cannot do better than refer the reader to Mr. *Kent's Hints to Gentlemen of Landed Property*. Yet I will here mention ſome few particulars which ſeem to merit attention.

1ſt. As to cottagers, I could name ſome worthy perſons now living, who, by giving to their labouring people a ſmall quantity of land contiguous to their dwellings, have thereby rendered their condition far more comfortable than it was before. Their example therefore deſerves imitation. In many country pariſhes there is abundance of common and waſte land, which in its preſent ſtate is of very little value: but if

a ſmall

a ſmall part of it were incloſed for the uſe of the poor, and tilled at the expence of the reſpective pariſhes, this would greatly help many families. No gentleman ſhould be permitted to pull down a cottage, until he had firſt erected another, upon one of Mr. *Kent*'s plans, either on ſome convenient part of the waſte, or on his own eſtate, with a certain quantity of land annexed. In the 30th *Eliz.* it was enacted, that no cottage ſhould be erected in country places without four acres of land about it, that poor people might ſecure for themſelves a maintenance, and not be obliged on the loſs of a few days labour to come to the pariſh. If ſome regulations of this kind were now adopted, they would be at once an encouragement to the poor, and a great check on the increaſe of the rates.

2dly. Convert gradually the waſte lands of the kingdom into ſmall arable farms. For the encouragement of induſtrious perſons there ſhould be a much greater number of ſuch farms than there is at preſent, and a gradation as to ſize and rent. The advantages, public and private, likely to reſult from ſuch a meaſure are well deſcribed by Mr. *Kent* in the work before-mentioned. At preſent ſmall farms, on account of the great demand there is for them, let at ſuch exorbitant rents, that it is ſcarcely poſſible for poor families to get a livelihood on them. Were the number of ſuch farms increaſed, beſides the encouragement thence ariſing to the lower peaſantry, this further benefit would flow from it to the poorer cottagers. The occupiers of theſe ſmall farms, as well as the occupiers of Mr. *Kent*'s larger cottages, would not think much of retailing to their poorer neighbours a little corn or a little milk, as they might want, which the poor can now ſeldom have at all, and never but as a great favour from the rich farmers.

3dly. Reſtrain

3dly, Reſtrain the engroſſment and over-enlargement of farms. If this ſyſtem goes on much longer, landlords may be obliged to let their lands to the great farmers on almoſt their own terms. Some proprietors of lands have complained that this is too much the caſe already.

Bacon, in his Hiſtory of Henry VIIth, praiſes the policy of that reign, in which it was enacted, in order to promote tillage and prevent a decay of people, " that all houſes of huſbandry with twenty acres of ground to them ſhould be kept up for ever, together with a competent proportion of land to be occupied with them, and in no wiſe to be ſevered from them. By theſe means the houſes being kept up, did of neceſſity enforce a dweller; and the proportion of land for occupation being alſo kept up, did of neceſſity enforce that dweller not to be a beggar." Lord *Bacon*'s Works, vol. iii. p. 431.

And touching the engroſſment of farms, in the 25th Hen. VIIIth, it is ſet forth, " that many farms, and great plenty of cattle, particularly ſheep, had been gathered into few hands, whereby paſturage had been increaſed exceſſively, and tillage was very much decayed; the old rate of rents ſo raiſed, that farmers of ſmall ſubſtance could not meddle with them; churches and towns pulled down; the price of proviſions exceſſively enhanced; and a marvellous number of people rendered incapable of maintaining themſelves and families: and therefore it was enacted, that no perſon ſhould keep above 2000 ſheep, nor hold more than *two* farms."

All this ſeems now to be a dead letter. Nor do I mean to recommend the ſtrict revival of theſe regulations. I only mention them, that people may turn their thoughts to theſe matters, and deviſe ſome reſtraints on the evils complained of.

 The

The laſt-mentioned regulation, however, that no perſon ſhould hold more than two [moderate] farms, is plainly founded in good ſenſe and good policy.

SECTION V.

RATING THE WAGES OF LABOURERS ACCORDING TO THE STATUTE 5th ELIZABETH, CAP. 4.

THE meaſures already propoſed, though they were forthwith adopted, can only be carried into execution gradually and ſlowly, except thoſe contained in Section III. But it appears that the diſtreſſes of our lower peaſantry are ſuch as call for *immediate* relief. And the moſt effectual meaſure for giving them immediate relief is, *To raiſe the price of day-labour.*

It is obviouſly reaſonable and right that the pay of the labourer ſhould keep pace with the general advance in the prices of thoſe things which are neceſſary for his ſupport. If the juſt proportion which ſhould conſtantly ſubſiſt between the one and the other be any how deſtroyed, proper means ſhould be taken for reſtoring that proportion as ſoon as poſſible. Delays in a matter of this moment, which deeply concerns the great body of a people, muſt be dangerous.

It is a miſtake to ſay, as ſome eminent writers have ſaid, that the price of labour muſt unavoidably advance in proportion with the ad-

vanced

vanced prices of neceſſaries. This, however plauſible it may be in theory, is contradicted by experience. In fact, the price of labour is but *one* article; and the ſlow advance that uſually takes place in this one, in countries that have been long ſettled, ſeldom compenſates the *ſum* of the advances in all thoſe articles which are accounted neceſſaries. The propoſition may be true with reſpect to freſh *acceſſions of money* to a country, which, gradually getting into the hands of *all*, give to all a greater ability to purchaſe what they want: " though, even in this " caſe, the day-labourer, having nothing to ſubſiſt on but his daily " work, muſt ever be behind-hand in advancing the price of his labour." But it will not hold with reſpect to luxury and taxes, the former of which raiſes prices without adding to the ability to purchaſe; and the latter, whilſt they enhance prices, often diminiſh that ability. Owing to various cauſes, the plenty of working hands may be ſuch as, by their competition to prevent wages from riſing faſt enough, (if they riſe at all) to anſwer the increaſed expence of living.

The prices of the neceſſaries of life are, from the nature of things, fluctuating and variable, depending on accidents which it is impoſſible for human laws to fix or regulate. But it is a matter eaſily practicable to adapt the price of labour to the plenty or ſcarcity of the times. Our anceſtors were ſo ſenſible of this, that they made ſeveral laws for *the rating of wages*; the ſubſtance of which is compriſed in the ſtat. 5 Eliz. c. 4. And though this ſtatute has been long diſregarded in practice, it is probable that enforcing the execution of it would be attended at this time with the moſt ſalutary conſequences. Only it may be proper that ſome few alterations ſhould be made in it, to ſuit it to our preſent circumſtances.

 As

As the prices of neceſſaries vary in different counties, it is plain, that none can be competent for the rating of wages, but ſuch as are reſident upon the ſpot, or near it. Therefore, the ſtatute 5 Eliz. c. 4, directs,

1. That the juſtices of every ſhire, riding, and liberty, or the more part of them, being then reſiant within the ſame, and the ſheriff, if he conveniently may, and every mayor and other head officer within any city or town corporate, wherein is any juſtice of the peace within the limits of the ſaid city or town corporate, and of the ſaid corporation, ſhall yearly, in *Eaſter ſeſſions*, or within ſix weeks next after, aſſemble, and call unto them ſuch diſcreet and grave perſons as they ſhall think meet; and having reſpect to the plenty or ſcarcity of the time, and other circumſtances, ſhall have authority to limit, rate, and appoint the wages of all ſuch labourers, artificers, workmen, or apprentices of huſbandry, as they ſhall think meet, by their diſcretions, to be rated, limited, or appointed, by the year, or by the day, week, month, or otherwiſe; with meat and drink, or without meat and drink; and what wages every workman or labourer ſhall take by the great, for mowing, reaping, or threſhing of corn and grain, or for mowing or making of hay; or for ditching, paving, railing, or hedging, by the rod, perch, lugg, yard, pole, rope, or foot, and for any other kind of reaſonable labour or ſervice. 5 Eliz. c. 4, §. 15.

And by 1 Jac. c. 6, the juſtices, or the more part of them, reſiant in any riding, liberty, or diviſion, where the ſeſſions are ſeverally kept, ſhall have power to rate the wages within ſuch diviſion, as if the ſame were done in the general ſeſſions for the county: §. 5. And by the ſaid ſtatute 1 Jac. c. 6, the ſaid act of 5 Eliz. ſhall extend to the rating of wages of all labourers, weavers, ſpinſters, and workmen or work-

women

women whatſoever, either working by the day, week, month, year, or taking any work by the great, or otherwiſe: §. 3.

And if any juſtice reſiant within the county, or mayor, ſhall be abſent at the rating of wages, and not hindered by ſickneſs or other lawful cauſe, to be allowed by the juſtices then aſſembled for rating wages, upon the oath and affidavit of ſome creditable perſon, he ſhall forfeit to the King 10l. to be recovered in the ſeſſions or other court of record, by indictment or otherwiſe. 5 Eliz. c. 4. §. 17. And the juſtices ſhall yearly, between September 29 and December 25, and between March 25 and June 24, make ſpecial and diligent enquiry of the good execution of this ſtatute, and puniſh defaulters; and ſhall have for every day that they ſit about the execution thereof (not exceeding three days at a time) 5s. each, out of the forfeitures due to the King: §. 37, 38.

2. By the ſaid act, 5 Eliz. c. 4, the rates were to be certified into the the chancery; but by the 1 Jac. c. 6, they need not to be certified into the chancery, but ſhall be kept amongſt the records of the county or town corporate. §. 8. And after the ſaid rates are made and engroſſed in parchment, under the hands and ſeals of the perſons having authority to rate the ſame, the ſheriff, or mayor, may cauſe proclamation thereof to be made in ſo many places as to them ſhall ſeem convenient, and every perſon ſhall be bound to obſerve the ſame. §. 6.

3. If any perſon, upon the proclamation publiſhed, ſhall directly or indirectly retain or keep any ſervant, workman, or labourer, or ſhall give any *more or greater wages*, or other commodity, than ſhall be ſo appointed in the ſaid proclamation, he ſhall, on conviction before any of the juſtices or other head officers abovementioned, be impriſoned for ten days without bail, and ſhall forfeit 5l. half to the king, and half to him

him that ſhall ſue before the ſaid juſtices in their ſeſſions: 5 Eliz. c. 4, §. 18. And any perſon that ſhall be ſo retained, and take wages contrary to the ſaid ſtatute of the 5 Eliz. or to the ſaid proclamation, and ſhall be thereof convicted before the juſtices aforeſaid, or any two of them, or before the mayor or other head-officers aforeſaid, ſhall be impriſoned for 21 days, without bail. §. 19. And every retainer, promiſe, gift, or payment of wages, or other thing, contrary to the ſaid act, and every writing and bond to be made for that purpoſe, ſhall be void. §. 20.

And by 1 Jac. c. 6, if any clothier, or other, ſhall refuſe to pay ſo much wages to their weavers, ſpinſters, workmen or workwomen, as be rated; and ſhall be convicted thereof by confeſſion, or oath of two witneſſes, at the aſſizes, or ſeſſions, or before any two juſtices (1 Q.) he ſhall forfeit 10s. to the party grieved, to be levied by diſtreſs and ſale. §. 7.

So ſtands the law concerning the *rating of wages*, [ſee *Burn's Juſtice*, title, *ſervants*, §. 2.] which I have here copied for the ſake of making the following obſervations: viz.

Obſ. 1. In the ſtatutes enacted for this purpoſe, before the reign of Elizabeth, the object of the legiſlature appears to have been, as to this matter, to keep wages moderately low, many perſons, on account of the ſcarcity of hands, being not willing to ſerve without *exceſſive* wages. But this ſtatute of Eliz. repeals the ſaid former laws, becauſe they could not, without the great grief and burden of the poor labourer and hired man, be put in due and good execution, on account of the rated wages being in divers places *too ſmall*, reſpecting the advancement of neceſſaries; and directs the rating of wages in the manner ſet forth above, with

with the view of yielding unto the hired perſon, both in the time of ſcarcity and in the time of plenty, a *convenient proportion* of wages. So that the declared deſign of this ſtatute is to effect the very thing which is at preſent neceſſary to be done.

Obſ. 2. The laws antecedent to the reign of Elizabeth limit the *higheſt wages*, which were allowed to be given to, or taken by, perſons of different occupations; and that very properly, becauſe their aim was to reſtrain workmen from demanding exceſſive wages. But this act of Elizabeth, though propoſing to remedy this grievance of hired people, in being compelled to take too ſmall wages, has, neverthelefs, very improperly copied them in this particular. To adapt this law to the circumſtances of the preſent time and the neceſſities of the poor, it would be more fit to ſpecify the *loweſt wages* to be given or taken, allowing the more induſtrious and ſkilful workmen to take greater if they can get greater. It was requiſite *formerly* to prevent labourers and others from taking advantage of the neceſſities of maſters, and demanding too great wages; and therefore it was right then to fix the *maximum*. What is wanted *now* is to prevent maſters from taking advantage of the numbers and neceſſities of the poor, and allowing them too ſmall wages; and therefore it is proper now to fix the *minimum*.

Obſ. 3. If the *minimum* of wages were ſettled, it would free this meaſure from the only plauſible objection that has been urged againſt it, namely, " that if all perſons, in the ſame kind of work, were to receive equal wages, there would be no emulation."* For in that caſe all perſons being not compellable to take equal wages, the beſt workmen would

* Burn's Hiſt. of Poor Laws, p. 130.

of

of courſe be both more ſure of employment, and would alſo get better wages, than inferior ones. And conſequently this meaſure, inſtead of diſcouraging, would tend to promote emulation.

Obſ. 4. This ſtat. of Eliz. directs the rating of wages in the general ſeſſions for the county. The ſubſequent act of 1 Jac. c. 6, (which alſo extends the rating of wages to ſuch as could not be rated by the ſaid act of Eliz.) empowers the major part of the juſtices reſiant in any riding, liberty, or diviſion, where the ſeſſions are ſeverally kept, to rate the wages within ſuch diviſion. This two-fold authority given to the juſtices, to rate wages in either of theſe two ways at their diſcretion, was probably one cauſe of its not being done at all. If the practice ſhould be revived, it will be proper to aboliſh one of theſe methods, and to enforce the other. The rating of wages in the general ſeſſions of the county, *for the whole county*, ſeems to deſerve the preference. The penalty for non-attendance at the rating of wages ſhould be made much heavier than it is at preſent.

Obſ. 5. This ſtatute of Eliz. directs the rating of wages to be at the *Easter* ſeſſions, or within ſix weeks after; that is, before the commencement of ſummer, when, on account of the plenty of work to be had, and the great demand for hands, wages do uſually riſe. At preſent, it would be obviouſly better, if this were directed to be done at the *Michaelmas* ſeſſions, when, the harveſt being gathered in, it is known whether the crop of corn has been plentiful or ſcarce, both in our own and in other countries; and of courſe, whether bread the following winter is likely to be cheap or dear;—a very eſſential piece of information for guiding the juſtices in ſettling the price of labour. Or, the juſtices may have authority to rate wages at any quarter-ſeſſions, or any ad-

journment

journment thereof, notice of fuch intention being advertifed fifteen days before.

Obf. 6. It does not feem neceffary now to meddle with the pay of artificers, handicraftfmen, or hired fervants, thefe, as fettled by cuftom, being fufficiently high, though not exceffive. Nor need the price of work done by the great be difturbed, the poor being content with the pay which they ufually receive in that way. The pay of manufacturers too is generally thought to be fufficiently high, though probably, all things confidered, it is not too high. The only thing wanted is to raife the pay of the day-labouring peafant, who, not receiving the value of his labour, cannot fubfift a moderate family.

Obf. 7. Proclamation of the rated wages fhould be made in every parifh church as foon as conveniently may be after the rating: and a paper, pafted on a board, containing the rated wages, fhould be put up in every church, there to remain for the information of all perfons concerned, till the next rating takes place.

But, the propriety of this meafure being admitted, it may be afked, *By what ftandard fhall the price of labour be regulated?* In order to anfwer this queftion, let it be obferved, that a *fingle man* having full employment might at prefent, with frugality, fave a third part at leaft of his earnings, though inftead of doing this he too commonly fpends it in the ale-houfe. With refpect therefore to *fingle men*, wages may be faid to be already too high. But labouring men do not long remain fingle; they marry and beget children; and then, what was before a too ample provifion for *one*, comes to be an infufficient provifion for *many*. Every ftate is defirous of advancing population; which can only be done by encouraging marriage among the lower claffes of people, cottages being the chief nurſeries of men. For theſe reaſons every labouring man ſhould be enabled to earn a ſubſiſtence for a certain number of perſons, beſides himſelf. The queſtion therefore comes to this: *What is the preciſe number of perſons which a labouring man's wages ſhould be calculated to maintain?* To determine this I cannot conceive any plainer or juſter way of proceeding, than by having regard to the *average* number of perſons in a family, and ſettling the proportion accordingly. The average number of perſons in a family, taking in all ranks, has been found to be rather under five; but in the lower claſſes of people, eſpecially that of labourers in huſbandry, it is at leaſt five. Therefore the average earnings of *a family* ſhould be ſufficient for the neceſſary maintenance of five perſons. Now it appears by the accounts in the firſt part, that the ſum neceſſary for the annual maintenance of a family, conſiſting of a man and his wife, and three children, in *Berkſhire*, and therefore in all the ſouthern counties, is not leſs than 26*l.** per annum, or 10*s.* a week. And if the wife and children earn between them, on an average, 1*s.* a week, (which I believe is above the mark;) ſince this 1*s.* is only ſufficient to maintain an infant, it follows that the man alone ought to earn by his labour as much as will ſuffice for the maintenance of himſelf, his wife, and *two* children; he ought to earn at leaſt 9*s* a week. According to the principle I have aſſumed, then, 9*s.* a week is the *loweſt proportion* of wages which a grown man ſhould receive for a week's labour, in thoſe counties wherein wheaten bread is commonly eaten. In the ſame manner the proper wages may be found for *any* particular place or county.

* Be it remembered that this ſum ſhould be 30*l.* if labouring families were to drink ſmall-beer in common.

SECTION

SECTION VI.

REGULATING THE PRICE OF DAY-LABOUR BY THE PRICE OF BREAD.

THOUGH I can ſee no valid objection againſt the foregoing method of ſettling wages, yet it may be proper to give another, by which the ſame end may be attained. And as this which I am going to explain is very ſimple in itſelf, and capable of being eaſily put in practice, it may perhaps on that account be thought by ſome to deſerve the preference over the former.

As *bread* is the principal part of the food of labouring people, making full two-thirds of the whole in value wherever wheaten bread is in common uſe, *I think the price of bread might with great propriety be made to regulate the price of labour.* And bread being the ſtaff of life, the price of it ever varying, and the variations ſometimes conſiderable, the chief point to be attended to is plainly this, to guard the poor againſt the diſtreſs which an exceſſive price of this article never fails to bring on them.

For this purpoſe, nothing more is requiſite than that the average number of perſons in a family, the quantity of bread eaten by them weekly, and the weekly amount of their other expences, ſhould be aſcertained. This being done, a ſcale of day-wages might be calculated, and ſo adapted to the table of the price of bread as to ſhew at ſight the wages correſponding to any particular price.

For inſtance; let it be ſuppoſed, that the expences of a family of five perſons, the mean number, in ſuch parts of this kingdom where

wheaten

wheaten bread is in common ufe, amount to 26*l.* a year, or 10*s.* a week. On looking at the abftract of accounts, p. 18, we find that the bread alone of fuch a family requires a trifle more than 4*s.*; confequently, all the other articles taken together, including the *annual outgoings*, require the remaining 6*s.* But we may regard the amount of thefe other articles as *a given fum*, that will not vary much in many years: for the fum of the annual expences for houfe-rent, fuel, clothing, and contingencies, will probably remain for many years much the fame as at prefent; and the prices of bacon, tea and fugar, foap, candles, &c. may likewife be looked upon as tolerably fteady. Allow therefore 6*s.* a week to anfwer all the wants of the family, bread excepted.

1. Suppofe now, *firft*, that in any particular town or place, the certified price of wheat is 4*s.* per bufhel, *Winchefter* meafure; the allowance to the baker for baking, 1*s.*; both together, 5*s.* In the table of the price of bread (ftat. 31 G. II. cap. 29.) the price of the half-peck loaf, houfehold, correfponding to 5*s.* is 8½*d.* The average expence in bread of our fix families of labourers is one half-peck loaf per head, as may be feen by the abftract fo often referred to. A family of five perfons therefore will require five fuch loaves weekly, the value of which is 3*s.* 6½*d.* Add this to the *given amount* of all other articles, 6*s.* and the whole weekly expence comes to 9*s.* 6½*d.* This fum, then, the family ought to earn among them. Suppofe the wife and children to earn 1*s.* a week; then the hufband, it is plain, ought to receive in this cafe for his week's labour 8*s.* 6½*d.*; which divided by 6, the number of workdays in a week, gives 1*s.* 5*d.* per day.

2. For a *fecond* example, let the price of the bufhel of wheat with the allowance for baking be 6*s.*; the correfponding price of the half-peck loaf

loaf is 10¼*d.* and of five loaves 4*s.* 3¼*d.* which added to 6*s.* the given ſum of all other neceſſary outgoings, makes 10*s.* 3¼*d.*; and deducting 1*s.* for the ſuppoſed earnings of the wife and children, there remains 9*s.* 3¼*d.* which the man ought to get weekly, or 1*s.* 6½*d.* per day.

3. For a *third* inſtance, ſuppoſe the price of the buſhel of wheat with the allowance to the baker to be 7*s.*; then the correſponding price of the half-peck loaf will be 1*s.* and of five loaves 5*s.*; and this added to the *given ſum* of 6*s.* makes the total 11*s.*; from which deducting 1*s.* for the earnings of the wife and children, the man ought to receive 10*s.* a week, or 1*s.* 8*d.* per day.

4. *Laſtly,* Let the price of the buſhel of wheat with the allowance be 8*s.*; the correſponding price of the half-peck loaf is 1*s.* 1¾*d.* and the price of five loaves is 5*s.* 9*d.*; which added, as before, to 6*s.* makes the whole weekly expence of the family 11*s.* 9*d.*; out of which deducting 1*s.* for the earnings of the wife and children, there remains the man's wages 10*s.* 9*d.* weekly, or 1*s.* 9½*d.* a day.

In the like manner the wages may be calculated for other variations of the price of corn and bread, and for any other grain beſides wheat. But this method of regulating wages will perhaps appear more plain, if we place the foregoing examples in columns, as follows:

Examples.	Price of the buſhel of wheat with allowance for baking.		Weight of the penny-loaf houſehold.		Price of the half-peck loaf houſehold.		Correſponding price of labour per day.	
	s.	*d.*	*oz.*	*dr.*	*s.*	*d.*	*s.*	*d.*
1	5	0	16	6	0	8½	1	5
2	6	0	13	9	0	10¼	1	6½
3	7	0	11	9	1	0	1	8
4	8	0	10	2	1	1¾	1	9½

Obſ.

Obſ. Whoever caſts his eye over this ſhort table muſt be ſtruck with aſtoniſhment at ſeeing how deficient the preſent pay of day-labour is, when compared with the price of corn for many years paſt.

Where fuel is ſcarce and dear, poor people find it cheaper to buy their bread of the baker, than to bake for themſelves; and therefore the baker's allowance is added to the price of the buſhel of corn in the above inſtances. But where fuel abounds, and coſts only the trouble of cutting and carrying home, there they may ſave ſomething by baking their own bread.

By this regulation the common people would be effectually ſecured from wanting the abſolute neceſſaries of life, provided they were always employed. Nor could the farmers reaſonably object againſt paying their labourers higher wages as the price of grain advanced; becauſe by that very advance they would be abundantly enabled to do this. And for the ground-work of ſuch a regulation, nothing more is required than to continue to enforce the due execution of the ſtatutes for certifying the prices of grain, meal, and flour, and for ſetting the aſſize and declaring the price of bread.

Perhaps it might be ſufficient, if the price of bread were made to regulate the price of labour for that half of the year only in which labouring people are moſt diſtreſſed, namely, from *Michaelmas* to *Lady-day*, or rather from the 1ſt of *November* to the 1ſt of *May*, leaving things to go on as at preſent for the other half year.

SECTION

SECTION VII.

SUPPLYING THE DEFICIENCY OF THE EARNINGS OF LARGE FAMILIES OUT OF THE POOR-RATE.

THE price of day-labour, ſettled in either of the foregoing methods, is calculated for the neceſſary ſupport of ſuch families only as conſiſt of not more than five perſons. But there are many families which conſiſt of a greater number, and in which none of the children are capable of earning a livelihood. It remains that we conſider of a due proviſion for the relief of theſe. And I think the propereſt way of making up the deficiency of their earnings, is by an allowance out of the poor-rate.

For the propoſed meaſure of raiſing wages is not meant to ſuperſede a poor-rate, but only ſo to reduce it's magnitude, as to exclude the many evils attending it in it's preſent extent. There muſt ſtill be a rate in every pariſh, in order not only that large families may not ſtarve for want of that bread which they cannot fully earn, but alſo that ſuch leſſer families, as cannot find conſtant employment, may, when unemployed, receive due aſſiſtance; in ſhort, that all neceſſitous and infirm perſons may be taken proper care of, and none be left to periſh through want in a *christian* country.

With reſpect to ſuch families as conſiſt of more than five perſons, all the children being incapable of work, and the mother of courſe earning very little, there are two methods of making up the deficiency of their earnings

earnings out of the rate; either, *first*, by entitling them to demand a certain *weekly stipend* out of that fund, ſufficient for the maintenance of all the children above three in number; or, *ſecondly*, which appears to be the better way, by allowing to them *wholly*, or *in part*, what I have called the *annual outgoings*, out of the ſame fund; that is to ſay, where there are five children unable to work, the family ſhould receive the *whole* amount of thoſe annual outgoings, or about 7*l.* per ann.; and where there are four ſuch children, the family ſhould be allowed the *half* of that ſum; not in money, but in rent, fuel, clothing, &c.

And with reſpect to ſuch large families, wherein one or two of the children earn ſomething, but cannot earn their whole living; theſe might be privileged to demand a leſſer ſtipend weekly, or to have a ſpecified part of the annual outgoings allowed them, in proportion as the earnings of the family fell ſhort of their maintenance.

A regulation of this kind might induce pariſhes and their officers to exert themſelves in eaſing poor families of ſupernumerary children, by apprenticing ſome, and placing others out in ſervice, as ſoon as they came to be of a fit age.

In theſe caſes families ſhould have a *legal* claim to ſuch pariſh allowances, not only on account of the heavy expence and trouble of bringing up a numerous brood of children; but alſo for having ſo meritoriouſly contributed to the population of the kingdom at a time when celibacy in the higher ranks is become ſo faſhionable as to bear taxation. I think there would be good ſenſe in appropriating the tax on batchelors to the better ſupport of families of the above deſcription.

It ſeems proper too, that proviſion ſhould be made by law, in more definite terms than has yet been done, that *all* poor families ſhould,

whilſt

whilſt out of work, in ſickneſs, ſmall-pox, and on the like extraordinary occaſions, receive due relief out of the rate, until the cauſe of their diſtreſs ceaſes.

But, in all common caſes, ſuch families as have not more than *three* children unable to work may, I think, be thrown off the rate, and left to ſhift for themſelves, their pay being ſufficient to maintain them. And *ſingle men*, who can earn much more than they need ſpend on themſelves, ſhould by no means have any claim on the rate, for this obvious reaſon; namely, that they may reſolve in youth and health to be more ſaving of their money, and be induced to enter into *friendly* and *provident* ſocieties for that purpoſe.

If ſome ſuch regulations as theſe here propoſed, with ſuch others as have been already ſuggeſted for the employment and encouragement of induſtrious families, were to accompany the meaſure of raiſing wages, the following good conſequences would probably reſult from their joint operation:

1. As the poor-rate would be no longer a partial ſubſtitute for wages, the ſums of money paſſing through the hands of the overſeers of the poor would be, on this account, much leſs than they are now: conſequently the frauds, impoſitions, and abuſes now complained of, could not then be practiſed in any alarming degree.

2. The overſeers of the poor, being obliged by their oath on admiſſion into the office, either to ſet poor families on work, or to pay them at a certain rate for idle time; pariſhes would ſoon come to ſee the neceſſity of requiring from thoſe officers the ſtrict performance of their duty in the former of theſe reſpects.

 3. Men

3. Men having more in family than the average number of five perſons, as they would then be ſecure from the apprehenſion of wanting neceſſaries, would ſeldom be tempted to deſert their families and leave them upon their pariſh, which is now frequently done.

4. And men having fewer than the average number, would become more provident, ſober, induſtrious, and frugal, as knowing themſelves not to be entitled to any aid from their pariſhes, except on certain occaſions particularly ſpecified. And for the ſame reaſon their wives would perhaps exert themſelves more than they now do, to add ſomething to their huſbands' earnings, and ſo contribute to the ſupport of their families: a point, as we have ſeen, of no ſmall importance.

5. Single men, having nothing but their wages to depend on, would be more careful to make proviſion againſt accidents; and when they reſolved to marry, would look out for ſuch *notable* wives as could earn money by knitting, ſpinning, ſewing, and the like. And as ſuch women would be then more courted than the ignorant and unſkilful, this might induce the women in general to learn theſe eaſy and uſeful arts: and having learnt them, they would know their value, and teach their children the ſame.

6. Thus ſufficient wages being given to day-labourers; idleneſs, improvidence, and vice checked and diſcouraged; induſtry, ſobriety, and frugality, countenanced and promoted; the opportunities for frauds, impoſitions, and abuſes, in a great meaſure, taken away; the poor-rate would of courſe be reduced, and all thoſe who pay to it would be relieved from a great part of that burden which they now conſider as a heavy grievance.

7. The

7. The *charitable* and *humane* might then exercife their benevolence, without the hazard of giving their alms improperly, towards fuch families and individuals as were excluded from a legal provifion, and fhould accidentally fall into diftrefs: for, it is well known that oftentimes what is now apparently given to the poor, is in reality a mere donation to the rich.

8. Offenders againft the *game-laws* might then be punifhed rigoroufly with fome fhew of juftice; becaufe the plea of *neceffity* could not be alledged in mitigation of the offence; their only motive in purfuing game could then be merely to procure money to be fpent in drink.

9. *Laftly*; Juftices of the peace would in a little time be eafed of a great part of the trouble which they are now obliged to take in fettling difputes concerning the poor.

SECTION

SECTION VIII.

A SUPPOSED OBJECTION AGAINST THE MEASURE OF RAISING WAGES, ANSWERED.

CONCLUSION.

HAVING ſtated, as plainly as I could, all that has occurred to my mind, with reſpect to labourers in huſbandry, as highly deſerving the public attention, I will only add a few ſhort obſervations, and conclude.

Of the meaſures which have been here propoſed for the relief of labouring families, thoſe which appear moſt neceſſary to be immediately adopted, are the two following; viz. that of *raiſing wages*, and that of *providing employment for women and girls*. Theſe two meaſures ſhould go together. The laws in being enjoin the doing of both theſe things; but there is a lamentable defect in the execution. It is on the enacting of a *ſupplementary law* for enforcing theſe two meaſures, that we are to look for an amendment of the condition of labouring families, and for a ſalutary reduction of the poor-rates.

I am not aware that any ſolid objection can be urged againſt the immediate adoption of theſe two meaſures, and therefore I truſt that they will ſpeedily attract the notice of the legiſlature; and, if after examination, they are approved, be digeſted into a proper form for receiving their ſanction. Juſtice, ſound policy, and religion, ſeem all to require that *ſomething* ſhould be done forthwith in favour of that denomination of people, whoſe diſtreſſed caſe we have been contemplating.

I am

I am convinced that the meaſure of raiſing wages muſt, from neceſſity, be very ſoon adopted. Indeed that opinion becomes every day more and more prevalent. But as it will probably, for ſome time to come, be diſliked by many, I will here ſay a few words more on this head. If any one ſhould object that this meaſure will injure the farmer, *who feeds us all*; and ſhould think that he ought to be left at liberty to get labour as cheap as he can; I anſwer, *first*, that however valuable the farmer may be, and confeſſedly is, as a member of the community, yet the day-labourer muſt be acknowledged to be *equally* valuable. The great body of farmers are indeed the principal employers of the far greater body of day-labourers; but what could the former do without the latter? "*The head cannot ſay to the feet, I have* "*no need of you.*" As theſe together conſtitute the greater part of the nation, ſo the proſperity of the one, and the comfortable ſituation of the other, are equally eſſential to the national happineſs. All orders of men are much intereſted in the well-being of all thoſe who are occupied in the cultivation of the ſoil. This will hardly be denied.

I anſwer, *ſecondly*, that when the meaſure of raiſing wages is carried into execution, the farmer will *probably* find at the year's end, that he has ſaved more in poor-rates than the advance in pay has taken from him. This muſt be the caſe if this meaſure be accompanied, as it ought to be, by that for enforcing the law for ſetting the poor to work. However, were it otherwiſe, yet the day-labourer muſt be enabled to ſubſiſt his family. And as the land-owner ſhould not oppreſs the farmer, by exacting an exceſſive rent; ſo neither ſhould the farmer oppreſs the day-labourer, by giving him for his work leſs than its value: for "*the labourer is worthy of his hire.*" If the land-owner has

in

in ſome inſtances, by raiſing the rent too high, forced the farmer to ſqueeze the day-labourer, he has been thereby guilty of a *double* oppreſſion. The truth is, the price of every article of the produce of land has been riſing continually for a long time paſt; and *this* has both enriched the farmer, and enabled the landlord to raiſe his rents. But on the other hand, this has alſo contributed greatly to impoveriſh and diſtreſs the day labourer. Therefore, though the meaſure of raiſing wages ſhould take ſome ſmall matter out of the pockets of the farmer and land-owner; yet it is evident that, even on this ſuppoſition, neither of them will have any reaſonable ground of complaint.

That ſpirit of humanity, which, pervading all ranks, eminently characterizes this nation, and which has been ever ready to relieve the private diſtreſs of the ſtranger, the fatherleſs, and the widow, as ſoon as it was made known, encourages me in hoping that this feeble attempt to repreſent faithfully the miſerable ſtate of the great body of our peaſantry, will meet with a candid, and even generous reception from thoſe who have the power of removing the grievance.

Gratitude obliges me to ſay, that this little work would never have ſeen the light, had it not been for the aſſiſtance kindly given me by a moſt valuable *friend*, whoſe zeal in the cauſe of the induſtrious poor firſt ſuggeſted the idea of an enquiry into their circumſtances; who alſo furniſhed me with ſeveral hints and obſervations whilſt I was employed in writing theſe ſheets; and through whoſe hands I received moſt of the papers contained in the following Appendix.

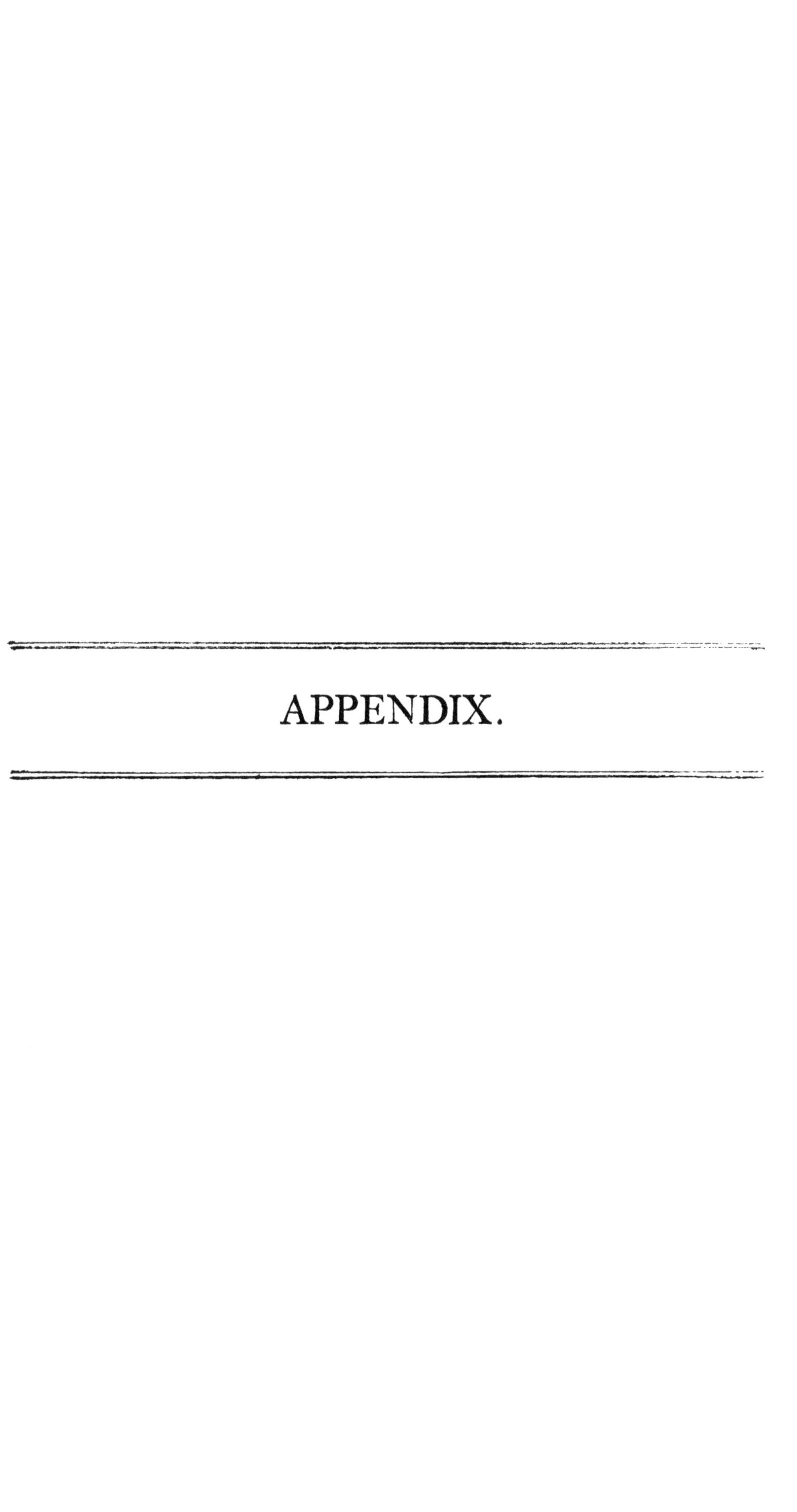

APPENDIX.

APPENDIX;

CONTAINING

A COLLECTION OF ACCOUNTS,

SHEWING

THE EARNINGS AND EXPENCES OF LABOURING FAMILIES IN DIFFERENT PARTS OF THE KINGDOM.

PAUPER UBIQUE JACET!" *Queen Elizabeth's Exclamation, in her Progress through the Kingdom.*——See RUGGLES's Hist. of the Poor, vol. i. p. 186.

THE *firſt* paper in this collection is that which was circulated for the purpoſe of obtaining information. It is here reprinted juſt as it was originally drawn up, becauſe ſome of the following papers refer to it in *that* ſtate; but as the *annual expences*, eſpecially the articles of *rent and clothing*, have ſince appeared to me to be eſtimated too low in *this* account, I have made *them* more correct in that which is given in Part I, p. 18. This collection contains *all* the accounts that have come to my hands in conſequence of the diſtribution of the *Barkham* paper. In the *Table of Contents* prefixed, I have thought it neceſſary to give ſome *ſhort notes* on the accounts.

D. D.

A LIST of the ACCOUNTS

CONTAINED IN

THIS APPENDIX,

WITH SHORT NOTES ON THEM.

COUNTIES.	PARISHES.	NOTES.
Berks.	BARKHAM.	The *annual outgoings* are made more correct in Part I, p. 18.
	PANGBOURN.	A man's *extra* earnings in harvest may be reckoned at 1l.; which, if added to the earnings in these accounts, would make the deficiency in each so much less. The *annual expences* are here, very properly, stated at 7l. nearly.
Cornwall.	ANTONY SAINT JACOB.	*Barley bread.* The *annual outgoings* are stated very low. *No beer. No cheese.*
	ST. AUSTEL.	No beer. No cheese.
	ST. MICHAEL PENKEVIL.	No beer. No cheese.
Derbyshire.	KEDDLESTONE.	In the *annual expences* rent and fuel only are accounted for. Nothing for clothing, lying-in, &c. The harvest gains are not, probably, included in the earnings: about 1l. each family.

COUNTIES.	PARISHES.	NOTES.
Dorſetſhire.	Aff-Piddle.	The pariſh pays the rent of Nos. 1, 3, 4, 6: No. 6 allowed fuel too. The allowance for clothing very ſmall. If the *annual expences* were completed by the addition of rent, fuel, and a more competent ſum for clothing, there would then be great deficiencies at the foot of *all* theſe accounts.
	Bishop's-Caundle.	Perhaps in theſe accounts the *extra* gains in harveſt ſhould be added to the earnings; which would of courſe leſſen the deficiencies ſo much.
	Town of Sherborne.	In theſe accounts the charge for clothing is very low. Nothing for caſualties. No beer. If a proper ſum of expenditure were allowed for each family, there would then be deficiencies where we now ſee exceedings. On the other hand the *extra* earnings in harveſt ſeem to be omitted.
	Stinsford.	Rent and fuel paid for by the pariſh: if theſe were added to the expences, there would be deficiencies in *all* theſe accounts, except perhaps in No. 4 of four perſons.
Durham.	Auckland-Castle.	The article of clothing ſeems high; but warm clothes are neceſſary in the Northern counties.

COUNTIES.	PARISHES.	NOTES.
	TANFIELD.	Rye and maslin flour, and some wheat flour, used here. *Annual expences* the same as in the Barkham account. Several families (Mr. Whitelocke observes) live comfortably on 7s. *per week*, or 18l. 4s. *per annum.*
Gloucestershire.	NEWENT.	If these families were obliged to buy their fuel, the deficiencies at the bottom of their accounts would be so much greater than they are stated at.
Hampshire.	CRAWLEY.	These families *have* beer and cheese. The parish pays the rent of Nos. 2 and 5: if the rent were added to the expences, there would be a deficiency in *all* these accounts.
	LONG PARISH.	Some of these families *have* beer, and some cheese. The *annual expences* are stated very properly at 7l.
	MONK-SHERBORNE and BASING.	No *tea* in any of these accounts. Rent not included in the expences of Nos. 1, 2, 3.
Lancashire.	ST. MICHAEL, PRESTON, GARSTANG.	Oat-meal bread and potatoes. No cheese. By this account it appears that a family of five persons may subsist here on the present wages.
	WINWICK.	Meal, flour, and potatoes, 6s. for seven persons. The *annual expences* of this family seem *very* high.

COUNTIES.	PARISHES.	NOTES.
Norfolk.	Marsham.	The Poor-Rate amazingly high.
Northamptonshire.	Brington.	Of thefe accounts No. 2 of fix perfons is moft deferving of regard; the others are families of an uncommon defcription.
	Castor.	Thefe accounts feem complete
Somerfetfhire.	Holwell.	None of the *annual expences* are brought to account, except clothing: if *thefe* were completed, the deficiencies would be 4l. or 5l. greater than they are fet down at.
Surry.	Sidlesham.	In Nos. 2, 3, 4, the parifh allowance of 1s. per week is reckoned in the earnings. No other *annual expences* are accounted for, but rent and fuel. No. 2, no fuel. No. 3, no rent. The price of malt and hops not included in the expences. It is plain, therefore, that if the parifh allowance of 1s. per week were deducted from the earnings, and the expences made complete, there would be a confiderable deficiency at the bottom of all thefe accounts, except perhaps in No. 2.
Suffex & Surry.	Tuntington and Sidlesham.	In five of thefe accounts there *appears* to be a confiderable furplus; but the expences are not complete: if they were made fo, there would be a deficiency at the foot of them all, except perhaps in No. 1 of three perfons.

COUNTIES.	PARISHES.	NOTES.
Westmorland.	MARTON.	The food of day-labouring families is rye and barley bread, potatoes, milk and bread, oatmeal porridge. *No meat.* No beer. Yet the deficiencies are great.
Yorkshire.	THORNER, AND CHAPEL-ALLERTON, *near Leeds.*	Thefe accounts feem complete. The half-peck loaf is here reckoned at 1s. which perhaps may now be regarded as the *mean* price. It is remarkable that the two families of four perfons have great deficiencies.
Wales.		
DENBIGHSHIRE.	LLANDEGLA.	Barley and oatmeal bread. No beer.
MERIONETH.	LLANFAWR.	Ditto.
Scotland.		
ABERDEENSHIRE, E. LOTHIAN, SUTHERLAND.		Thefe accounts furnifh wonderful inftances of good œconomy. The penury in which the people live, will perhaps account for a remarkable fact mentioned by Dr. A. Smith in his Wealth of Nations, viz. That in the Highlands it is not uncommon for a woman who has borne twenty children, not to have *two* alive! It will account alfo for the emigrations from that country.

PARISH OF BARKHAM, BERKS.

COLLECTED AT EASTER 1787, FIRST PRINTED IN JUNE 1788.

Expences and Earnings of six Families of Labourers, by the Week, and by the Year.

	No. 1. 7 Persons.			No. 2. 7 Persons.			No. 3. 6 Persons.			No. 4. 5 Persons.			No. 5. 5 Persons.			No. 6. 4 Persons.		
Expences per Week.	£.	s.	d.	£.	s.	d.	£.	s.	d.	£.	s.	d.	£.	s.	d.	£.	s.	d.
Bread or Flour - - - -	0	6	3	0	5	5	0	5	0	0	2	6	0	3	9	0	4	2
Yeast and Salt - - - -	0	0	4	0	0	3½	0	0	3½	0	0	2½	0	0	3	0	0	3
Bacon or other Meat - -	0	0	8	0	1	4	0	0	8	0	1	9	0	1	8	0	1	0
Tea, Sugar, Butter - - -	0	1	0	0	1	0	0	1	0	0	1	2¼	0	1	0	0	0	10
Cheese (seldom any) - -	0	0	0	0	0	0	0	0	0	0	0	2½	0	0	0	0	0	0
Beer (seldom any) - - -	0	0	0	0	0	0	0	0	0	0	0	5	0	0	0	0	0	0
Soap, Starch, Blue, - - -	0	0	2¼	0	0	2½	0	0	2¼	0	0	3	0	0	6	0	0	2¼
Candles - - - - - - -	0	0	3	0	0	3	0	0	3	0	0	3	0	0	3	0	0	3
Thread, Thrum, Worsted -	0	0	3	0	0	3	0	0	3	0	0	2	0	0	3	0	0	3
Total	0	8	11¼	0	8	9	0	7	7¾	0	6	11¼	0	7	8	0	6	11¼
Amount *per annum*	23	4	9	22	15	0	19	17	7	18	0	9	19	18	8	18	0	9
Earnings per Week.	£.	s.	d.	£.	s.	d.	£.	s.	d.	£.	s.	d.	£.	s.	d.	£.	s.	d.
The Man earns at a medium	0	8	0	Parish pay	5	0	0	8	0	0	8	4	0	8	0	0	8	0
The Woman - - - - -	0	0	6	0	1	0	0	0	6	0	0	8	0	1	0	0	0	6
The Children - - - -	0	0	0	0	3	0	0	0	0	0	0	0	0	0	0	0	0	0
Total	0	8	6	0	9	0	0	8	6	0	9	0	0	9	0	0	8	6
Amount *per annum*	22	2	0	23	8	0	22	2	0	23	8	0	23	8	0	22	2	0
	£.	s.	d.	£.	s.	d.	£.	s.	d.	£.	s.	d.	£.	s.	d.	£.	s.	d.
To the above Amount of Expences *per annum* -	23	4	9	22	15	0	19	17	7	18	0	9	19	18	8	18	0	9
Add Rent, Fuel, Clothes, Lying-in, &c. - - -	6	0	0	6	0	0	6	0	0	6	0	0	6	0	0	6	0	0
Total of Expences *per annum*	29	4	9	28	15	0	25	17	7	24	0	9	25	18	8	24	0	9
Total of Earnings *per annum*	22	2	0	23	8	0	22	2	0	23	8	0	23	8	0	22	2	0
Deficiency of Earnings - -	7	2	9	5	7	0	3	15	7	0	12	9	2	10	8	1	18	9

PARISH OF BARKHAM.

ACCOUNT OF THE FAMILIES.

No. 1. A man, his wife, and five children, the eldeſt eight years of age, the youngeſt an infant.

No. 2. A woman, whoſe huſband is run away, and ſix children; the eldeſt a boy of ſixteen years of age, the next a boy aged thirteen, the youngeſt five: four of the children too young to earn any thing.

No. 3. A man, his wife, and four ſmall children, the eldeſt under ſix years of age, the youngeſt an infant.

No. 4. A man, his wife, and three ſmall children, the eldeſt not quite five years old, the youngeſt an infant.

No. 5. A man, his wife, and three young children, the eldeſt ſix years of age, the youngeſt an infant.

No. 6. A man, his wife, and two young children, the eldeſt ſeven years of age, the youngeſt four.

	£.	s.	d.
Price of the half-peck loaf of wheaten bread - - - -	0	0	11½
—— of the gallon of flour -	0	0	10
—— of a week's labour in winter	0	7	0
—— of a week's labour, where the labourer is employed conſtantly, all weather, the year through - - - - - -	0	8	0

ANNUAL EXPENCES.

	£.	s.	d.
Rent of a cottage and garden, from 1l. 5s. to 2l. 2s. ſay - - - - - - - - - -	1	10	0
Fuel, if bought, coſts 12s. but reckoned here at a week's wages, becauſe a man can in a week cut turf enough on the common to ſerve the year, and the farmers give the carriage for the aſhes - - - - - -	0	8	0
Clothing.—The Man's: wear of a ſuit per annum 5s.; wear of a working jacket and breeches 4s.; two ſhirts 8s.; one pair of ſtout ſhoes nailed 7s.; two pair of ſtockings 4s.; hat, handkerchief, &c. 2s.:—ſum 1l. 10s. ——The Woman's: wear of gown and petticoats 4s.; one ſhift 3s. 6d.; one pair of ſtrong ſhoes 4s.; one pair of ſtockings 1s. 6d.; two aprons 3s.; handkerchiefs, caps, &c. 4s.:—ſum 1l.——But as few poor people can every year beſtow on themſelves the ſums here ſuppoſed, let the children's clothing (partly made up of the parents' old clothes, partly bought at ſecond-hand) be included, and the whole eſtimated at - -	2	10	0
Lying-in, ſickneſs and loſs of time thereby; burials, and loſs of time by extreme bad weather; eſtimated one year with another at	1	12	0
	£.6	0	0

Rent, fuel, clothing, lying-in, &c. are ſet down in the columns at 6l. to *every* family alike, becauſe it is the *leaſt* ſum at which thoſe articles can well be reckoned.

The tea uſed per family is from 1 to 1½ oz. per week, at 2d. per oz.

Soft ſugar, ½lb. at 7d. to 8d. per lb.

Salt butter, or lard, ½lb. at 7½d. to 8d. per lb.

Poor people reckon cheeſe the deareſt article they can buy.

Malt is ſo dear, they ſeldom brew any ſmall beer, except againſt a lying-in or a chriſtening.

To eke out ſoap, they burn *green* fern, and knead the aſhes into balls, with which they make a lye for waſhing.

In No. 5, the woman waſhes for one or two ſingle labourers, for which reaſon 6d. is charged for ſoap.

In No. 4, the charge for bread is conſiderably leſs than in the others; becauſe that family, by buying a whole hog at once, has for the ſame money almoſt double the quantity of meat, which the others get who buy by retail; and that greater quantity of meat, with greens and potatoes, makes the bread go farther.

PANGBOURN, BERKS.

[COMMUNICATED BY THE REV. W. ROMAINE, JUN. IN FEB. 1790.]

EXPENCES AND EARNINGS OF SIX FAMILIES OF LABOURERS, BY THE WEEK, AND BY THE YEAR.

	No. 1. 5 Persons.			No. 2. 7 Persons.			No. 3. 3 Persons.			No. 4. 8 Persons.				
Expences per Week.	£.	s.	d.	£.	s.	d.	£.	s.	d.	£.	s.	d.		
Bread - - - - - - - -	0	4	6	0	8	0	0	4	0	0	7	10½		
Salt - - - - - - - -	0	0	2	0	0	2	0	0	2	0	0	1		
Meat, chiefly Bacon - -	0	1	6	0	1	0	0	1	0	0	0	0		
Tea, Sugar, Salt, Butter -	0	1	0	0	1	2	0	1	0	0	1	10½		
Cheese - - - - - - -	0	0	4½	0	0	0	0	0	2¼	0	0	2¼		
Beer - - - - - - - -	0	0	0	0	0	0	0	0	5	0	0	0		
Soap, &c. - - - - - -	0	0	4	0	0	2¼	0	0	2	0	0	3		
Candles - - - - - - -	0	0	4	0	0	4	0	0	3	0	0	4		
Thread, &c. - - - - - -	0	0	3	0	0	2	0	0	3	0	0	3		
Total	0	8	5½	0	11	0¼	0	7	5¼	0	10	10¼		
Earnings per Week.	£.	s.	d.	£.	s.	d.	£.	s.	d.	£.	s.	d.		
The Man earns at a medium	0	7	0	0	8	0	0	6	0	0	7	0		
The Woman - - - -	0	0	8	0	0	0	0	1	6	0	1	6		
The Children - - - -	0	0	0	0	2	0	0	0	6	0	0	0		
Total	0	7	8	0	10	0	0	8	0	0	8	6		
Amount *per annum*	19	18	8	26	0	0	20	16	0	22	2	0		
	£.	s.	d.	£.	s.	d.	£.	s.	d.	£.	s.	d.		
To the above Amount of Expences *per annum* -	21	19	10	28	13	1	19	6	9	28	4	5		
Add Rent, Fuel, Clothes, &c. - - - - - - -	6	19	0	8	12	0	6	19	0	6	19	0		
Total Expences *per annum* -	28	18	10	37	5	1	26	5	9	35	3	5		
Total Earnings *per annum* -	19	18	8	26	18	8	20	16	0	22	2	0		
Deficiency	9	0	2	10	6	5	5	9	9	13	1	5		

EXPENCES AND EARNINGS OF SIX FAMILIES OF LABOURERS, BY THE WEEK, AND BY THE YEAR.

The above is as accurate a ſtatement as a perſonal enquiry could afford me from the different families. The harveſt additional earnings are not, but ought to be included.

PANGBOURN, BERKS.

ACCOUNT OF THE FAMILIES.

No. 1. A man, (being a widower) woman, (the wife's mother) 3 children, the eldeſt aged ten, the youngeſt five.

No. 2. A man, wife, and five children, the eldeſt twelve, the youngeſt two years old.

No. 3. A man, wife, and one daughter aged twelve.

No. 4. A man, wife, and ſix children, the eldeſt aged eleven years and a half, the youngeſt one year and a half.

	£.	s.	d.
Price of the half-peck loaf, wheaten	0	1	$1\frac{1}{2}$
Flour per buſhel - - - - -	0	8	0

ANNUAL EX PENCES.

	£	s.	d.
Rents* of Cottages and Gardens, on average, each - - - - . - - - - -	2	2	0
Fuel;†—one load of beech - - - - -	0	15	0
Clothing, as per printed eſtimate for Barkham	2	10	0
Lying-in, ſickneſs, &c. as per ditto - -	1	12	0
	£.6	19	0

No. 1. Four half-peck loaves; $\frac{1}{2}$lb. ſalt butter; 2 oz. tea; 1lb. cheeſe; $\frac{1}{2}$lb. ſoap; $\frac{1}{2}$lb. candles; per week.

No. 2. Bake at home a buſhel of flour per week: $\frac{1}{2}$lb. butter; 2 oz. tea; $\frac{1}{2}$lb. ſugar; $\frac{1}{2}$lb. candles; thread, &c. per week 2d. Some of their flour ſerves inſtead of ſtarch. The woman earns nothing, having a ſick child, beſides the other children, to attend, and being herſelf infirm.

No. 3. Flour, half a buſhel; bacon $1\frac{1}{2}$lb. more or leſs; tea 2 oz.; ſugar $\frac{1}{2}$lb.; butter $\frac{1}{2}$lb.; beer 1 quart.

No. 4. Seven gallon loaves; tea 2 oz. at $2\frac{1}{4}$d.; 1lb. ſugar, at 7d.; butter and dripping 10d.; cheeſe $\frac{1}{2}$lb.

* The houſe-rent of No. 2 is £2 10 0 per annum.

† The fuel of No. 2 is £2 0 0—ſuppoſed ſo on account of the continued illneſs of one of the children, as the man's account varies ſo much from the reſt: perhaps the hedge-rows ſupply ſome of the others with what may be wanted over the above allowance of a ſingle load.

PARISH OF ANTONY IN THE EAST, OTHERWISE ANTONY ST. JACOB, IN THE COUNTY OF CORNWALL.

[COMMUNICATED BY P. CAREW, ESQ; 1789.]

EXPENCES AND EARNINGS OF SIX FAMILIES OF LABOURERS, BY THE WEEK, AND BY THE YEAR.

	No. 1. 7 Persons.			No. 2. 6 Persons.			No. 3. 6 Persons.			No. 4. 5 Persons.			No. 5. 4 Persons.			No. 6. 4 Persons.		
Expences per Week.	£.	s.	d.	£.	s.	d.	£.	s.	d.	£.	s.	d.	£.	s.	d.	£.	s.	d.
Bread and Flour - - -	0	3	6	0	3	2	0	3	0	0	3	4	0	3	0	0	3	6
Yeast and Salt - - - -	0	0	3	0	0	2½	0	0	2½	0	0	2½	0	0	2½	0	0	3
Bacon or other Meat - -	0	1	9	0	1	6	0	1	6	0	1	0	0	1	6	0	1	9
Tea, Milk, and Sugar - -	0	0	8	0	0	6	0	1	8	0	1	0	0	0	6	0	0	8
Cheese (never any) - -	0	0	0	0	0	0	0	0	0	0	0	0	0	0	0	0	0	0
Beer (never any) - - -	0	0	0	0	0	0	0	0	0	0	0	0	0	0	0	0	0	0
Soap, Starch, and Blue, -	0	0	3	0	0	2¼	0	0	2	0	0	2½	0	0	2	0	0	3
Candles - - - - - - -	0	0	3	0	0	3	0	0	3	0	0	3	0	0	3	0	0	2
Thread, Yarn, and Worsted	0	0	2	0	0	1½	0	0	1½	0	0	1½	0	0	2	0	0	1
Total	0	6	10	0	5	11¼	0	5	11	0	6	1½	0	5	9½	0	6	8
Amount *per annum*	17	15	4	15	8	9	15	7	8	15	18	6	15	1	2	17	6	8
Earnings per Week.	£.	s.	d.	£.	s.	d.	£.	s.	d.	£.	s.	d.	£.	s.	d.	£.	s.	d.
The Man at a medium -	0	7	0	0	7	0	0	7	0	0	7	0	0	6	6	0	6	6
The Woman, - - - -	0	0	6	0	0	8	0	0	10	0	1	0	0	0	10	0	1	6
The Children - - - -	0	0	9	0	0	6	0	0	6	0	0	0	0	0	0	0	0	0
Total	0	8	3	0	8	2	0	8	4	0	8	0	0	7	4	0	8	0
Amount *per annum*	21	9	0	21	4	8	21	13	4	20	16	0	19	1	4	20	16	0
	£.	s.	d.	£.	s.	d.	£.	s.	d.	£.	s.	d.	£.	s.	d.	£.	s.	d.
To the above Amount of Expences *per annum* -	17	15	4	15	8	9	15	7	8	15	18	6	15	1	2	17	6	8
Add Rent, Fuel, Clothing, Lying-in, &c. - -	5	12	6	5	12	6	5	12	6	5	12	6	5	12	6	5	12	6
Total Expences *per annum* -	23	7	10	21	1	3	21	0	2	21	11	0	20	13	8	22	19	2
Total Earnings *per annum* -	21	9	0	21	4	8	21	13	4	20	16	0	19	1	4	20	16	0
Deficiency of Earnings (Except No. 2, which faves 3s. 5d.; and No. 3, which faves 13s. 2d. *per ann.*	1	18	10	0	3	5 Surplus.	0	13	2 Surplus.	0	15	0	1	12	4	2	3	2

PARISH OF ANTONY IN THE EAST, CORNWALL.

ACCOUNT OF THE FAMILIES.

No. 1. A man, his wife, and five children, the eldeft nine years of age, the youngeft an infant.

No. 2. A man, his wife, and four children, the eldeft eight years of age, the youngeft an infant.

No. 3. A man, his wife, and four children, the eldeft eight years of age, the youngeft an infant.

No. 4. A man, his wife, and three children, the eldeft feven years of age, the youngeft two years.

No. 5. A man, his wife, and two children, the eldeft three years of age, the youngeft one year old.

No. 6. A man, his wife, and two children, the eldeft four years of age, the youngeft two years.

	£.	s.	d.
Price of the half-peck loaf of wheaten bread - - - -	0	0	11
—— of a gallon of flour - -	0	0	9½
—— of eight gallons of barley (being the chief article for making bread for the poor) -	0	2	9

Price of a week's labour, where the labourer is employed conftantly, all weather, the year through—fome 7s., others 6s. 6d.

ANNUAL EXPENCES.

	£.	s.	d.
Rent of a cottage, at a medium - - - -	1	10	0
Part of the fuel fuppofed to be bought (the remainder thereof they gather or pick up by the cliffs, and from the farmers' fields and hedges) - - - - - - - - -	0	12	0
Clothing.—The Man's: wear of a fuit per annum 4s.; wear of a working jacket and breeches 3s.; two fhirts 7s.; one pair of fhoes, foled and nailed, 7s. 6d.; two pair of ftockings 3s. 6d.; hat, handkerchief, &c. 2s. 6d.;—fum 1l. 7s. 6d.——The Woman's: wear of gown and petticoats 4s.; fhift 3s. 6d.; one pair of fhoes, nailed, &c. 4s.; one pair of ftockings 1s. 6d.; two aprons 3s.; handkerchiefs, caps, &c. 3s.;—fum 19s.——The Children's clothing (over and above their parents' old clothes which is made up for them) 10s.	2	16	6
Lying-in, ficknefs, and lofs of time thereby, burials, and lofs of time by extreme bad weather, eftimated one year with another at	0	14	0
	£.5	12	6

Rent, fuel, clothing, lying-in, &c. are fet down in the columns at 5l. 12s. 6d. to every family alike, becaufe it is the leaft fum at which thofe articles can well be reckoned.

Tea commonly fold at 1½d. per ounce.

Soft fugar from 6d. to 7d. per pound.

Poor people reckon cheefe the deareft article they can buy.

Malt is fo dear, they feldom brew any beer, except againft a lying-in or a chriftening.

Price of eight gallons of wheat 6s. of which the poor in general ufe very little.

PARISH OF ST. AUSTEL, CORNWALL;

REV. RICHARD HENNAH, VICAR.

[COMMUNICATED BY MRS. LEVESON GOWER.]

EXPENCES AND EARNINGS OF SIX FAMILIES OF LABOURERS, BY THE WEEK, AND BY THE YEAR.

	No. 1. 7 Persons.			No. 2. 7 Persons.			No. 3. 6 Persons.			No. 4. 5 Persons.			No. 5. 5 Persons.			No. 6. 4 Persons.		
Expences per Week.	£.	s.	d.	£.	s.	d.	£.	s.	d.	£.	s.	d.	£.	s.	d.	£.	s.	d.
Bread or Flour* - - - -	0	7	3½	0	7	0	0	6	5	0	5	6½	0	5	6½	0	4	8
Yeast and Salt - - - -	0	0	3	0	0	3	0	0	3	0	0	2½	0	0	2½	0	0	2
Bacon or other Meat - -	0	1	0	0	1	0	0	0	8	0	1	0	0	1	0	0	1	0
Tea, Sugar, Butter - - -	0	1	0	0	1	0	0	1	0	0	1	0	0	1	0	0	0	10
Cheese (seldom any) - -	0	0	0	0	0	0	0	0	0	0	0	0	0	0	0	0	0	0
Beer (seldom any) - - -	0	0	0	0	0	0	0	0	0	0	0	0	0	0	0	0	0	0
Soap, Starch, Blue - - -	0	0	2½	0	0	2½	0	0	2½	0	0	2½	0	0	6	0	0	2½
Candles - - - - - - -	0	0	3	0	0	3	0	0	3	0	0	3	0	0	3	0	0	3
Thread, Thrum, Worsted -	0	0	3	0	0	3	0	0	3	0	0	3	0	0	3	0	0	3
Total	0	10	3	0	9	11½	0	9	0½	0	8	5½	0	8	9	0	7	4½
Amount *per annum*	26	13	0	25	17	10	23	10	2	21	19	10	22	15	0	19	3	6
Earnings per Week.	£.	s.	d.	£.	s.	d.	£.	s.	d.	£.	s.	d.	£.	s.	d.	£.	s.	d.
The Man earns at a medium	0	6	0	Parish pay }	4	0	0	6	0	0	6	0	0	6	0	0	6	0
The Woman - - - - -	0	0	6	0	0	6	0	0	6	0	0	8	0	0	8	0	1	0
The Children - - - -	0	0	6	0	5	0	0	0	0	0	0	0	0	0	0	0	0	0
Total	0	7	0	0	9	6	0	6	6	0	6	8	0	6	8	0	7	0
Amount *per annum*	18	4	0	24	14	0	16	18	0	17	6	8	17	6	8	18	4	0
	£.	s.	d.	£.	s.	d.	£.	s.	d.	£.	s.	d.	£.	s.	d.	£.	s.	d.
To the above Amount of Expences *per annum* -	26	13	0	25	17	10	23	10	2	21	19	10	22	15	0	19	3	6
Add Rent, Fuel, Clothes, Lying-in, &c. - - -	6	0	0	6	0	0	6	0	0	6	0	0	6	0	0	6	0	0
Total Expences *per annum* -	32	13	0	31	17	10	29	10	2	27	19	10	28	15	0	25	3	6
Total Earnings *per annum* -	18	4	0	24	14	0	16	18	0	17	6	8	17	6	8	18	4	0
Deficiency of Earnings - -	14	9	0	7	3	10	12	12	2	10	13	2	11	8	4	6	19	6

* The charge of bread or flour to each individual of a family per day is as under: Labourer 3d.—Wife 2d.—Child 1½d.

PARISH OF ST. AUSTEL, CORNWALL.

ACCOUNT OF THE FAMILIES.

No. 1. A man, his wife, and five children, the eldeſt eight years of age, the youngeſt an infant.

No. 2. A woman, whoſe huſband is run away, and ſix children; the eldeſt a boy of ſixteen years of age, the next a boy aged thirteen, the youngeſt five: four of the children too young to earn any thing.

No. 3. A man, his wife, and four ſmall children, the eldeſt under ſix years of age, the youngeſt an infant.

No. 4. A man, his wife, and three ſmall children, the eldeſt not quite five years old, the youngeſt an infant.

No. 5. A man, his wife, and three young children, the eldeſt ſix years of age, the youngeſt an infant.

No. 6. A man, his wife, and two young children, the eldeſt ſeven years of age, the youngeſt four.

	£.	s.	d.
Price of the half-peck loaf of wheaten bread - - - -	0	1	1
—— of the gallon of flour -	0	0	9
—— of a week's labour in winter	0	6	0
—— of a week's labour, where the labourer is employed conſtantly, all weather, the year through - - - - - - -	0	6	0

ANNUAL EXPENCES.

	£.	s.	d.
Rent of a cottage and garden, from 1l. 5s. to 2l. 2s. ſay - - - - - - - - - -	1	10	0
Fuel, if bought, coſts 12s. but reckoned here at a week's wages, becauſe a man can in a week cut turf enough on the common to ſerve the year, and the farmers give the carriage for the aſhes - - - - - - -	0	8	0
Clothing.—The Man's: wear of a ſuit per annum 5s.; wear of a jacket and breeches 4s.; two ſhirts 8s.; a pair of ſtout ſhoes nailed 7s.; two pair of ſtockings 4s.; hat, handkerchief, &c. 2s.:—ſum 1l. 10s. ——The Woman's: wear of gown and petticoats 4s.; one ſhift 3s. 6d.; one pair of ſtrong ſhoes 4s.; one pair of ſtockings 1s. 6d.; two aprons 3s.; handkerchiefs, caps, &c. 4s.:—ſum 1l.——But as few poor people can every year beſtow on themſelves the ſums here ſuppoſed, let the children's clothing (partly made up of the parents' old clothes, partly bought at ſecond-hand) be included, and the whole eſtimated at - -	2	10	0
Lying-in, ſickneſs and loſs of time thereby; burials, and loſs of time by extreme bad weather; eſtimated one year with another at	1	12	0
	£.6	0	0

Rent, fuel, clothing, lying-in, &c. are ſet down in the columns at 6l. to *every* family alike, becauſe it is the *leaſt* ſum at which thoſe articles can well be reckoned.

The tea uſed per family is from 1 to 1½ oz. per week, at 2d. per oz.

Soft ſugar, ½lb. at 7d. to 8d. per lb.

Salt butter, or lard, ½lb. at 7½d. per lb.

Poor people reckon cheeſe the deareſt article they can buy.

Malt is ſo dear, they ſeldom brew any ſmall beer, except againſt a lying-in or a chriſtening.

To eke out ſoap, they burn *green* fern, and knead the aſhes into balls, with which they make a lye for waſhing.

In No. 5, the woman waſhes for one or two ſingle labourers, for which reaſon 6d. is charged for ſoap.

No. 4. This caſe, I may venture to ſay, ſeldom or never occurs in this neighbourhood.

PARISH OF ST. MICHAEL PENKEVILL, CORNWALL.

[COMMUNICATED BY LORD VISCOUNT FALMOUTH, IN 1790.]

EXPENCES AND EARNINGS OF SIX FAMILIES OF LABOURERS, BY THE WEEK, AND BY THE YEAR.

	No. 1. 7 Persons.			No. 2. 5 Persons.			No. 3. 6 Persons.			No. 4. 3 Persons.			No. 5. 3 Persons.			No. 6. 3 Persons.		
Expences per Week.	£.	s.	d.	£.	s.	d.	£.	s.	d.	£.	s.	d.	£.	s.	d.	£.	s.	d.
Bread or Flour - - - -	0	4	6	0	4	0	0	4	6	0	2	3	0	2	6	0	2	3
Yeast and Salt - - - -	0	0	3	0	0	3	0	0	3	0	0	1½	0	0	1½	0	0	1½
Bacon or other Meat - -	0	1	9	0	1	9	0	1	9	0	1	0	0	1	3	0	1	0
Tea, Sugar, and Butter - -	0	1	6	0	1	6	0	1	6	0	0	9	0	1	0	0	0	9
Soap, Starch, and Blue - -	0	0	6	0	0	6	0	0	6	0	0	3	0	0	3	0	0	3
Candles - - - - - - -	0	0	3	0	0	3	0	0	3	0	0	3	0	0	3	0	0	3
Thread and Worsted - -	0	0	3	0	0	3	0	0	3	0	0	1½	0	0	1½	0	0	1½
Total	0	9	0	0	8	6	0	9	0	0	4	9	0	5	6	0	4	9
Amount *per annum*	23	8	0	22	2	0	23	8	0	12	7	0	14	6	0	12	7	0
Earnings per Week.	£.	s.	d.	£.	s.	d.	£.	s.	d.	£.	s.	d.	£.	s.	d.	£.	s.	d.
The Man earns at a medium	0	6	6	0	5	0	0	7	0	0	7	0	0	6	0	0	7	0
The Woman - - - -	0	1	0	0	1	0	0	1	0	0	0	0	0	0	0	0	0	0
The Children - - - -	0	1	6	0	1	6	0	1	6	0	0	0	0	0	6	0	0	0
Total	0	9	0	0	7	6	0	9	6	0	7	0	0	6	6	0	7	0
Amount *per annum*	23	8	0	19	10	0	24	14	0	18	4	0	16	18	0	18	4	0
	£.	s.	d.	£.	s.	d.	£.	s.	d.	£.	s.	d.	£.	s.	d.	£.	s.	d.
To the above Amount of Expences *per annum* -	23	8	0	22	2	0	23	8	0	12	7	0	14	6	0	12	7	0
Add Rent, Fuel, Clothes, Lying-in, &c. - -	6	0	0	6	0	0	6	4	0	6	0	0	6	0	0	6	0	0
Total Expences *per annum* -	29	8	0	28	2	0	29	8	0	18	7	0	20	6	0	18	7	0
Total Earnings *per annum* -	23	8	0	19	10	0	24	14	0	18	4	0	16	18	0	18	4	0
Deficiency of Earnings	6	0	0	8	12	0	4	14	0	0	3	0	3	8	0	0	3	0

PARISH OF ST. MICHAEL PENKEVILL, CORNWALL.

ACCOUNT OF THE FAMILIES.

No. 1. A man, his wife, and five children, the eldeſt a boy thirteen years of age, the youngeſt two years of age.

No. 2. A man, his wife, one daughter (an idiot and cripple) twenty-one years of age, and two other children, the eldeſt ſixteen years of age, and the youngeſt eleven years.

No. 3. A man, his wife, and four children; one of them an idiot aged twenty-two years, (likely never to earn any thing) the eldeſt of the others eighteen years of age, and the youngeſt eleven years of age.

No. 4. A man, his wife, and one child an infant.

No. 5. A man, his wife, and one child, a girl twelve years of age.

No. 6. A man, his wife, and one child, an infant.

ANNUAL EXPENCES.

	£.	s.	d.
Rent of a cottage and garden	1	0	0
Fuel - - - - - - - -	0	12	0
Clothing:—the Man's -	1	10	0
——— —the Woman's -	1	0	0
Lying-in, ſickneſs, burials, loſs of time by bad weather, &c. - - - - - -	1	18	0

Price of wheat per buſhel -	0	5	6
A week's labour, the year through - - - - -	0	6	0

In No. 1, the man's wages are charged 6s. 6d. on account of extra wages in harveſt; and in Nos. 3, 4, and 6, are charged 7s. on account of being employed in carrying ſea ſand for manure, &c.

The poor people buy corn, and get it ground for bread.

KEDDLESTONE, NEAR DERBY.

BY CAPTAIN, NOW ADMIRAL COLPOYS, SEPT. 1788.

[COMMUNICATED BY VISCOUNTESS CREMORNE.]

EXPENCES AND EARNINGS OF THREE FAMILIES OF LABOURERS, BY THE WEEK, AND BY THE YEAR.

	No. 1. 7 Persons.			No. 2. 6 Persons.			No. 3. 5 Persons.											
Expences per Week.	£.	s.	d.	£.	s.	d.	£.	s.	d.									
Bread, Flour, and Oatmeal	0	3	6	0	4	2	0	2	0									
Yeast and Salt - - - -	0	0	3	0	0	2	0	0	6									
Bacon and other Meat - -	0	1	6	0	1	6	0	1	0									
Milk - - - - - - - -	0	0	7	0	1	2	0	0	0									
Cheese - - - - - - -	0	0	10	0	0	10	0	0	10									
Butter - - - - - - -	0	0	4	0	0	8	0	0	0									
Candles, Soap, Starch, Thread,	0	0	6	0	0	6	0	0	10									
Tea, Sugar, and Butter -	0	0	0	0	0	0	0	1	0									
Beer - - - - - - - -	0	0	0	0	0	0	0	0	2									
Total	0	7	6	0	9	0	0	6	4									
Amount *per annum*	19	10	0	23	8	0	16	9	4									
Earnings per Week.	£.	s.	d.	£.	s.	d.	£.	s.	d.									
The Man earns at a medium	0	4	8	0	7	8	0	5	0									
The Woman - - - -	0	0	0	0	0	0	0	0	0									
The Children - - - -	0	0	0	0	0	0	0	0	0									
Total	0	4	8	0	7	8	0	5	0									
Amount *per annum*	12	2	8	19	18	8	13	0	0									
	£.	s.	d.	£.	s.	d.	£.	s.	d.	£.	s.	d.	£.	s.	d.	£.	s.	d.
To the above Amount of Expences *per annum* -	19	10	0	23	8	0	16	9	4									
Add Rent and Fuel for Nos. 1, 2, and Fuel only for No. 3. -	1	11	0	1	11	0	2	0	0	A.			B.			C.		
Total Expences *per annum* -	21	1	0	24	19	0	18	9	4	21	1	0	24	19	0	16	9	4
Total Earnings *per annum* -	12	2	8	19	18	8	13	0	0	19	18	8	19	18	8	20	16	0
Deficiency of Earnings	8	18	4	5	0	4	5	9	4	1	2	4	5	0	4	4	6	8 Surplus.

KEDDLESTONE, NEAR DERBY.

ACCOUNT OF THE FAMILIES.

No. 1. A man, wife, and five children at home; the firft, a boy nine years of age; the fecond and third, a boy and girl, twins, fix years of age; the fourth, a boy three years of age; and the fifth, a boy one year.

No. 2. A man, wife, and four children at home; the firft, a daughter nineteen years of age, ill, and not able to go to fervice, but fhe goes out fometimes to work; the fecond, a fon ten years of age, has had his arm broke, and could not go out; the third, a fon fix years of age; the fourth, a fon, three years old.

No. 3. A man, wife, and three children at home; the firft, a girl twelve years old, affifts her mother at home, but earns nothing abroad; the fecond, a girl eight years old; and the third, a boy four years.

Note. In No. 1, the man earns 6s. per week for four months, and 4s. per week the reft of the year, and has his victuals of his employer.——In No. 2, the man earns 9s. per week for four months, and 7s. the reft of the year, but eats at home.——In No. 3, the man earns 7s. per week for four months, and 4s. the reft of the year, and has his victuals of his employer.

The wives, it feems, earn nothing; their employment being to look after the children, and make and mend for their families. But in No. 2, the eldeft daughter earns *fomething*, which is not brought to account.

ANNUAL EXPENCES.

	£.	s.	d.
No. 1. Rent, an acknowledgment of - - - - - - - - -	0	1	0
Fuel - - - - - - - - - -	1	10	0
No. 2. The fame - - - -	1	11	0
No. 3. Rent, with other payments, amount to 5l. per annum; but this is repaid by lodgers.			
Fuel - - - - - - - - - -	2	0	0

Neither of thefe families could fay how much they laid out in clothing, &c.

PRICES OF SUNDRY ARTICLES IN DERBY TOWN.

Flour, beft fort, 2s. per ftone of 14lbs. common fort 1s. 9d. ditto.

Bread is fold by the fhilling and fix-penny loaf; the weight fixed by the Corporation.

Oatmeal 1s. per peck. Potatoes 6d. ditto. Bacon 7½d. per lb. Beef and mutton 4½d. Butter from 9d. to 11d. per lb. Cheefe 4d. Coals 5½d. per 112lbs.; in winter fometimes 8d.

NOTES.

In No. 1, a boy fourteen years of age, and a girl of eleven, though in fervice, are of fome expence to the parents. The man makes bee-hives at home of nights, and earns fomething, or (he fays) his family would be ftarved.

If the man's victuals in Nos. 1 and 3 be be reckoned at 3s. per week each, and this be added to their weekly earnings, the accounts will then ftand as in columns A, B, C.

AFF-PIDDLE PARISH, IN THE COUNTY OF DORSET.

[COMMUNICATED BY THE REV. MR. ETTERICK, 1789.]

EXPENCES AND EARNINGS OF SIX FAMILIES OF LABOURERS, BY THE WEEK, AND BY THE YEAR.

	No. 1. 6 Persons.			No. 2. 4 Persons.			No. 3. 5 Persons.			No. 4. 9 Persons.			No. 5. 8 Persons.			No. 6. 5 Persons.		
Expences per Week.	£.	s.	d.	£.	s.	d.	£.	s.	d.	£.	s.	d.	£.	s.	d.	£.	s.	d.
Bread and Flour - - -	0	6	0	0	3	2	0	4	6	0	7	7	0	6	0	0	6	6
Yeast and Salt - - - -	0	0	2	0	0	2	0	0	4	0	0	4	0	0	3	0	0	1
Bacon or other Meat - -	0	0	8	0	0	0	0	0	8	0	0	4	0	0	0	0	0	4
Tea, Sugar, Butter, Cream	0	0	10	0	1	4	0	0	11	0	1	2	0	1	4	0	0	6
Cheese - - - - - - -	0	0	3	0	0	7	0	0	7	0	0	0	0	0	8	0	0	0
Beer - - - - - - - -	0	0	2	0	0	0	0	0	0	0	0	0	0	0	2	0	0	0
Soap, Starch, and Blue, -	0	0	1	0	0	2½	0	0	2½	0	0	2½	0	0	2½	0	0	2½
Candles - - - - - - -	0	0	2½	0	0	3	0	0	3	0	0	3	0	0	2½	0	0	4½
Thread, &c. - - - - - -	0	0	0¾	0	0	2	0	0	2	0	0	3	0	0	2	0	0	3
Potatoes and Barley - -	0	0	2	0	0	6¾	0	0	0	0	0	0	0	0	6¾	0	0	0
Total	0	8	7½	0	6	5¼	0	7	7½	0	10	1½	0	9	6¾	0	8	3
Amount *per annum*	22	7	5	16	14	9	19	16	6	26	6	6	24	17	3	21	9	0
Earnings per Week.	£.	s.	d.	£.	s.	d.	£.	s.	d.	£.	s.	d.	£.	s.	d.	£.	s.	d.
The Man earns } Throwing in harveſt work and Summer labour. -	0	8	0	0	7	0	0	7	0	0	7	0	0	8	0	0	0	0
The Woman -	0	0	6	0	0	3	0	0	0	0	1	0	0	0	1	0	0	1
The Children -	0	1	6	0	0	0	0	0	0	0	1	0	0	1	3	0	6	3
																Pariſh	2	6
Total	0	10	0	0	7	3	0	7	0	0	9	0	0	9	4	0	8	10
Amount *per annum*	26	0	0	18	17	0	18	4	0	23	8	0	24	5	4	22	19	4
	£.	s.	d.	£.	s.	d.	£.	s.	d.	£.	s.	d.	£.	s.	d.	£.	s.	d.
Annual Sum of Expences -	22	0	5	16	14	9	19	16	6	26	6	6	24	17	3	21	9	0
Expence of Rent, Fuel, &c.	3	13	0	7	11	0	1	18	0	5	6	4	7	3	1½	1	15	3
Total Expences *per annum* -	26	0	5	24	5	9	21	14	6	31	12	10	32	0	4½	23	4	3
Total Earnings *per annum* -	26	0	0	18	17	0	18	4	0	23	8	0	24	5	4	22	19	4
Deficiency of Earnings	0	0	5	5	8	9	3	10	6	8	4	10	7	15	0½	0	4	11

AFF-PIDDLE PARISH, DORSET.

ACCOUNT OF THE FAMILIES.

No. 1. Robert and Martha Miller, and four children at home, the eldeſt fifteen years of age, the youngeſt ſix.

No. 2. George and Mary Houſe, and two children, the one four years of age, the other an infant.

No. 3. Matthew and Ann Lawrence, and three children, the eldeſt ſix years of age, the youngeſt an infant.

No. 4. Francis and Lydia Harvey, and ſeven children, the eldeſt ſeventeen years of age, the youngeſt one.

No. 5. William and Jane Reaſon, and ſix children, the eldeſt eleven years of age, the youngeſt an infant.

No. 6. Mary Chilcott, a widow, with four children, the eldeſt nineteen years of age, the youngeſt ſix.

ANNUAL EXPENCES.

Rent of a cottage and garden from £.1 5 0 to £.2 5 0.

Fuel coſts a week's labour. In caſe of conſtant work with a farmer, it is brought home gratis, otherwiſe at 2s. or 2s. 6d. the load.

The prices of the neceſſaries of life are the ſame as in the Barkham account.

PROBABLE CAUSES OF THE DISTRESSES OF THE POOR ARE,

The riſe of the price of neceſſaries, the buying them at the deareſt hand, the low and unproportionate price of labour, the increaſing ſcarcity of employment for the poor, and their own want of induſtry, having no encouragement given them. Many working men breakfaſt and dine on dry bread alone, without either cheeſe or drink of any kind; their meal is ſupper, and that generally no better than unpealed potatoes and ſalt, or barley-cake fried, and water. Clothes they get as they can, and the children go nearly naked. There is little work now for lads, and that at a reduced price; two-pence or three-pence a day, inſtead of four-pence or five-pence, which it was formerly. With all this the weight upon the pariſh is almoſt inſupportable, a ſmall property of 5l. per annum yielding ſometimes only 20s. clear of rates and taxes; and if ſmaller property ſtill, the owner is worſe off than thoſe that have none, but receive pariſh pay.

REMARKS.

No. 1. The charge for ſoap is very low, for they are almoſt naked; and thread, &c. low charged for the ſame reaſon. They have a garden, but do not grow potatoes enough for their uſe. The wife and children knit at home. Milk or cream I find often a weekly article in very poor families, though ſome have none, nor any ſugar. The pariſh allows the rent here in this family, and gives them help about 8s. one year with another in loſs of employment, &c. They cut the fuel, and pay 2s. for carriage home. Sum: fuel 10s.; clothes 15s.; lying-in 6s.; loſs of work at a medium about four weeks 2l. 2s.;—in all 3l. 13s.

No. 2.

No. 2. They keep a pig, and the beſt of its food barley) is uſed in the family, and the charge thrown in with *the article potatoes* at a very low calculation, for they grow potatoes enough. The pig coſts about 1l. 5s. Sum: fuel 8s; clothes (very neat, and whole, and clean) 2l. 10s.; lying-in and burials and loſt time, at a medium, 1l. 15s.; rent 1l. 13s. Sum 6l. 6s.; add the pig and it is 7l. 11s.

No. 3. The pariſh pays rent here, and allows 3s. a week when out of work, which has been hitherto one quarter of the year at a medium, but now he has thrown himſelf on the pariſh, and they either pay him 6s. or find him work. He will not acknowledge any expence for clothes of any kind; and this charge muſt indeed be very low, ſay 1l. 1s. Burials, &c. paid by the pariſh. Fuel 7s. or a week's labour, but coſts 2s. 6d. the load carriage; five loads, one given by the pariſh, = 7s. + 10s.—17s. Caſualties the pariſh ſupplies.

No. 4. The pariſh pays rent. They keep a pig. The barley is thrown in with the flour here. Pigs coſt at a medium (being bought ſmall) 14s. Of clothes they can give little account, as they buy none, and have had ſome ſmall help by deaths. Let the wear of clothes, and ſhoes, and mending, &c. be ſet down at 2l. 14s. 4d. (children's included;) loſs of work by ſickneſs and other caſualties at 1l. 10s. fuel at 8s.;—ſum 5l. 6s. 4d.

No. 5. They keep a pig which coſt 14s. Rent 2l. Clothes, with ſheeting and repairs of all kinds, with allowance for help, and a good ſtock to begin withl but now quite reduced, 2l. 6s. 1½d. Lying-in 10s. (being 20s. every other year.) Schooling for two children beſt part of the year 10s. Loſt work and other caſualties 10s. Pariſh help little or none, ſay 5s. per annum. Fuel 8s. Sum 7l. 3s. 1½d.

No. 6. She earns nothing, except in harveſt. Fuel and 2s. 6d. a week allowed by the pariſh, with houſe-rent, but no garden, which is a hard circumſtance. She has been uſed to the ſpinning of harn, (the refuſe of flax) for which there is no call here, and ſhe cannot ſpin worſtead. To the flour alſo is added what barley ſhe conſumes. Clothes ſhe cannot afford to buy; the children have had the father's, and the pariſh has promiſed further aſſiſtance in linen, ſo this charge muſt be ſet very low, ſay 15s. The boys' loſs of work and ſickneſs, at a medium three weeks, 1l. 0s. 3d. Sum 1l. 15s. 3d.

BISHOP's-CAUNDLE, DORSETSHIRE.

ACCOUNT OF THE FAMILIES.

No. 1. A man, his wife, and ſeven children, the eldeſt twelve years of age, the youngeſt an infant.

No. 2. A man, his wife, and ſix children, the eldeſt eighteen years of age, the youngeſt one year and a half old.

No. 3. A man, his wife, and three children, the eldeſt nine years of age, the youngeſt an infant.

ANNUAL EXPENCES.

	£.	s.	d.
Rent - - - - - - - - -	1	12	0
Fuel - - - - - - - - -	0	10	0
Clothes, &c. - - - - - -	2	10	0
Loſs of time by ſickneſs, extreme bad weather, &c.	2	0	0
	£.6	12	0

	£.	s.	d.
Price of the half-peck loaf of wheaten bread - - - -	0	1	2

BISHOP's-CAUNDLE, DORSETSHIRE.

BY THE REV. MR. BRISTED, OCT. 1789.

EXPENCES AND EARNINGS OF THREE FAMILIES OF LABOURERS, BY THE WEEK, AND BY THE YEAR.

	No. 1. 9 Persons.			No. 2. 8 Persons.			No. 3. 5 Persons.					
Expences per Week.	£.	s.	d.	£.	s.	d.	£.	s.	d.			
Bread - - - - - - - -	0	8	2	0	7	0	0	4	0			
Salt, Soap, Candles, Starch	0	0	0	0	1	0	0	1	0			
Thread and Worsted - -	0	1	6	0	0	3	0	0	2			
Meat, Bacon, or Pork - -	0	0	8	0	2	0	0	1	0			
Tea—no Sugar or Butter -	0	0	3¼	0	1	0	0	0	3			
Cheese - - - - - - -	0	0	6	0	2	0	0	2	0			
Beer or Cyder - - - -	0	0	0	0	1	6	0	0	0			
Total	0	11	1¼	0	14	9	0	8	5			
Amount *per annum*	28	17	5	38	7	0	21	17	8			
Earnings per Week.	£.	s.	d.	£.	s.	d.	£.	s.	d.			
The Man earns at a medium	0	6	0	0	8	0	0	5	6			
The Woman - - - -	0	1	0	0	0	0	0	1	3			
The Children - - - -	0	2	6	0	7	0	0	0	6			
Total	0	9	6	0	15	0	0	7	3			
Amount *per annum*	24	14	0	39	0	0	18	17	0			
	£.	s.	d.	£.	s.	d.	£.	s.	d.			
To the above Amount of Expences *per annum* -	28	17	5	38	7	0	21	17	8			
Add Rent, Fuel, Clothes, Lying-in, &c. - -	6	12	0	6	0	0	6	0	0			
Total Expences *per annum* -	35	9	5	44	7	0	27	17	8			
Total Earnings *per annum* -	24	14	0	39	0	0	18	17	0			
Deficiency of Earnings	10	15	5	5	7	0	9	0	8			

TOWN OF SHERBORNE, COUNTY OF DORSET.

MAY 1789.

[COMMUNICATED BY W. TOOGOOD, ESQ.]

EXPENCES AND EARNINGS OF SIX FAMILIES OF LABOURERS, BY THE WEEK, AND BY THE YEAR.

	No. 1. 7 Persons.			No. 2. 6 Persons			No. 3. 5 Persons.			No. 4. 4 Persons.			No. 5. 5 Persons.			No. 6. 4 Persons.		
Expences per Week.	£.	s.	d.	£.	s.	d.	£.	s.	d.	£.	s.	d.	£.	s.	d.	£.	s.	d.
Bread - - - - - - -	0	4	0	0	5	0	0	3	0	0	3	0	0	3	6	0	3	6
Salt - - - - - - - -	0	0	1½	0	0	1	0	0	1½	0	0	1	0	0	1	0	0	1
Meat - - - - - - - -	0	0	0	0	1	0	0	0	8	0	0	8	0	1	0	0	0	8
Tea, &c. - - - - - - -	0	0	3	0	0	5	0	0	1½	0	0	0	0	0	6	0	0	5
Cheese - - - - - - -	0	0	8	0	0	4	0	0	7	0	1	3	0	0	4	0	0	7½
Milk - - - - - - - -	0	0	0	0	0	3½	0	0	4	0	0	1	0	0	3½	0	0	2
Soap - - - - - - - -	0	0	2	0	0	7	0	0	2½	0	0	3	0	0	2½	0	0	3
Candles - - - - - - -	0	0	4	0	0	4	0	0	6	0	0	3	0	0	4	0	0	2
Thread, &c. - - - -	0	0	3	0	0	2	0	0	1	0	0	3	0	0	1½	0	0	1
Total	0	5	9½	0	8	2½	0	5	8	0	5	10	0	6	4½	0	5	11½
Amount *per annum*	15	1	2	21	6	10	14	14	8	15	3	4	16	11	6	15	9	10
Earnings per Week.	£.	s.	d.	£.	s.	d.	£.	s.	d.	£.	s.	d.	£.	s.	d.	£.	s.	d.
The Man earns at a medium	Pariſh pay	2	6	0	6	6	0	6	0	0	6	0	0	5	6	0	6	0
The Woman - - - - -	0	2	0	0	1	6	0	2	6	0	0	6	0	1	0	0	1	6
The Children - - - -	0	2	9	0	0	0	0	0	0	0	2	0	0	0	0	0	0	0
Total	0	7	3	0	8	0	0	8	6	0	8	6	0	6	6	0	7	6
Amount *per annum*	18	17	0	20	16	0	22	2	0	22	2	0	16	18	0	19	10	0
	£.	s.	d.	£.	s.	d.	£.	s.	d.	£.	s.	d.	£.	s.	d.	£.	s.	d.
To the above Amount of Expences *per annum* -	15	1	2	21	6	10	14	14	8	15	3	4	16	11	6	15	9	10
Add Rent, Fuel, Clothes, &c.	4	13	4	3	7	0	6	18	0	5	19	0	2	0	0	3	3	0
Total Expences *per annum* -	19	14	6	24	13	10	21	12	8	21	2	4	18	11	6	18	12	10
Total Earnings *per annum* -	18	17	0	20	16	0	22	2	0	22	2	0	16	18	0	19	10	0
Deficiencies of Earnings	0	17	6	3	17	10	0	0	0	0	0	0	1	13	6	0	0	0
Exceedings							0	9	4	0	19	8				0	17	2

TOWN OF SHERBORNE, COUNTY OF DORSET.

ACCOUNT OF THE FAMILIES.	ANNUAL EXPENCES.		£.	s.	d.
No. 1. A widow and ſix children, the eldeſt twelve years of age, the youngeſt two years of age.	No. 1.	Rent - - - -	1	14	4
		Fuel - - - - - -	1	19	0
		Clothes, &c. - -	1	0	0
			4	13	4
No. 2. A man, his wife, and four children, the eldeſt nine years of age, the youngeſt one year.	No. 2.	Rent - - - - - -	1	17	0
		Fuel - - - - - -	0	0	0
		Clothes, &c. - -	1	10	0
			3	7	0
No. 3. A man, his wife, and three children, the eldeſt nine years of age, the youngeſt three years.	No. 3.	Rent - - - - - -	2	0	0
		Fuel - - - - - -	3	18	0
		Clothes, &c. - -	1	0	0
			6	18	0
No. 4. A man, his wife, and two children, the eldeſt eleven years of age, the youngeſt ſix years.	No. 4.	Rent - - - - - -	2	10	0
		Fuel - - - - - -	1	19	0
		Clothes, &c. - -	1	10	0
			5	19	0
No. 5. A man, his wife, and three children, the eldeſt ſix years of age, the youngeſt an infant.	No. 5.	Rent - - - - - -	1	10	0
		Fuel - - - - - -	0	0	0
		Clothes, &c. - -	0	10	0
			2	0	0
No. 6. A man, his wife, and two children, the eldeſt five years of age, the youngeſt one year.	No. 6.	Rent - - - - - -	1	10	0
		Fuel - - - - - -	0	13	0
		Clothes, &c. - -	1	0	0
			3	3	0

STINSFORD, DORSET.

[COMMUNICATED BY W. MORTON PITT, ESQ. M. P. 1789.]

EXPENCES AND EARNINGS OF FIVE FAMILIES OF LABOURERS, BY THE WEEK, AND BY THE YEAR.

	No. 1. 4 Persons.			No. 2. 7 Persons.			No. 3. 4 Persons.			No. 4. 4 Persons.			No. 5. 6 Persons.		
Expences per Week.	£.	s.	d.	£.	s.	d.	£.	s.	d.	£.	s.	d.	£.	s.	d.
Wheat - - - - - - -	0	4	6	0	4	6	0	3	9	0	3	0	0	4	6
Yeast and Salt - - - - -	0	0	5	0	0	5	0	0	5	0	0	5	0	0	4½
Bacon - - - - - - - -	0	2	6	0	2	6	0	0	10½	0	1	10½	0	1	3
Tea and Sugar - - - -	0	0	6	0	0	6	0	0	8	0	0	10	0	0	3
Cheese - - - - - - -	0	0	11¼	0	1	1½	0	0	2¼	0	0	6¾	0	1	0
Soap and Candles - - - -	0	0	8	0	0	8	0	0	8	0	0	8	0	0	8
Thread, Worsted, &c. - -	0	0	3	0	0	3	0	0	3	0	0	1½	0	0	3
Total	0	9	9¼	0	9	11½	0	6	9^3	0	7	5¾	0	8	3½
Amount *per annum*	25	8	1	25	17	10	17	15	3	19	8	11	21	11	2
Earnings per Week.	£.	s.	d.	£.	s.	d.	£.	s.	d.	£.	s.	d.	£.	s.	d.
The Man - - - - -	0	6	6	0	6	6	0	6	6	0	6	6	0	7	6
The Woman - - - -	0	0	0	0	0	8	0	0	3	0	0	6	0	0	0
The Children - - - -	0	5	0	0	4	6	0	1	0	0	3	0	0	0	0
Total	0	11	6	0	11	8	0	7	9	0	10	0	0	7	6
Amount *per annum*	29	18	0	30	6	8	20	3	0	26	0	0	19	10	0
	£.	s.	d.	£.	s.	d.	£.	s.	d.	£.	s.	d.	£.	s.	d.
To the above Amount of Expences *per annum* -	25	8	1	25	17	10	17	15	3	19	8	11	21	11	2
Add Clothing, &c. - -	4	0	0	4	0	0	4	0	0	4	0	0	4	0	0
Total Expences *per annum* -	29	8	1	29	17	10	21	15	3	23	8	11	25	11	2
Total Earnings *per annum* -	29	18	0	30	6	8	20	3	0	26	0	0	19	10	0
Deficiency of Earnings	0	0	0	0	0	0	1	12	3	0	0	0	6	1	2
Exceediugs	0	9	11	0	8	10	0	0	0	2	11	1	0	0	0

STINSFORD, DORSET.

ACCOUNT OF THE FAMILIES.

No. 1. A widower with three children, a boy fourteen years of age, another boy twelve years of age, and a girl feventeen.

No. 2. A man, his wife, and five children, viz. a girl feventeen years of age, a boy fifteen, a girl thirteen, a girl ten, and a girl eight.

No. 3. A man, his wife, and two children, viz. a girl fourteen years of age, and a girl ten.

No. 4. A man, his wife, and two children, viz. a girl fourteen years of age, and a boy twelve.

No. 5. A man, his wife, and four fmall children, viz. a boy fix years of age, a girl five, a girl three, and a girl one year and an half.

ANNUAL EXPENCES.

	£.	s.	d.
Rent - - - - - - - -	0	0	0
Fuel - - - - - - - -	0	0	0

N. B. Rent and Fuel allowed in confideration of the low price of labour.

Clothing and cafual expences by computation, about -	4	0	0

Wheat 6s. per bufhel, always fold at that price to the parifh poor.

Labour all the year 6s. per week, except in harveft, when they work piece-work.

Labourers often accept of 1l. 1s. extra for harveft, in lieu of advanced wages.

Tea 2s. per lb. Sugar 8d. per lb. Cheefe, made of fkimmed milk, 2¼d. per lb. Bacon 7½d. per lb.

N. B. No. 5, is an exceeding good workman, and a very induftrious man, and, in confideration of his hard family, is (when it is poffible) fupplied with piece-work, fuch as hedging, &c. in the winter whilft the weather is open; mowing and reaping, &c. in fummer.

The exceedings in No. 1, 2, and 4, are only owing to the age of the children, which enables them to contribute fo much to the family ftock, and to the care taken to fupply them with conftant employment.

AUCKLAND, COUNTY OF DURHAM.

ESTIMATE MADE BY WM. EMM, Esq. STEWARD AT AUCKLAND-CASTLE, 1789.

[COMMUNICATED BY THE REV. A. CROMLEHOLME.]

EXPENCES AND EARNINGS OF THREE FAMILIES OF LABOURERS, BY THE WEEK, AND BY THE YEAR.

	No. 1. 7 Persons.			No. 2. 6 Persons.			No. 3. 5 Persons.				
Expences per Week.	£.	s.	d.	£.	s.	d.	£.	s.	d.		
Bread or Flour - - - -	0	4	2	0	3	6	0	3	0		
Salt - - - - - - - -	0	0	1½	0	0	1½	0	0	1½		
Potatoes - - - - - -	0	0	6	0	0	6	0	0	4		
Flesh Meat - - - - -	0	2	0	0	1	6	0	1	6		
Tea, and Sugar - - - -	0	0	10	0	0	9	0	0	9		
Milk - - - - - - - -	0	1	6	0	1	3	0	1	0		
Soap, Starch, and Blue, -	0	0	6	0	0	4½	0	0	4½		
Candles - - - - - -	0	0	3½	0	0	3½	0	0	3½		
Thread, Worsted, &c. - -	0	0	3	0	0	3	0	0	2½		
Total	0	10	2	0	8	6½	0	7	7		
Amount *per annum*	26	8	8	22	4	2	19	14	4		
Earnings per Week.	£.	s.	d.	£.	s.	d.	£.	s.	d.		
The Man earns at a medium	0	6	0	0	6	0	0	6	0		
The Woman - - - - - -	0	2	0	0	2	0	0	2	0		
The Children - - - -	0	1	6	0	1	8	0	0	0		
Total	0	9	6	0	9	8	0	8	0		
Amount *per annum*	24	14	0	25	2	8	20	16	0		
	£.	s.	d.	£.	s.	d.	£.	s.	d.		
To the above Amount of Expences *per annum* -	26	8	8	22	4	2	19	14	4		
Add Rent, Fuel, Clothes, Lying-in, &c. - -	9	2	5½	9	2	5½	9	2	5½		
Total Expences *per annum* -	35	11	1½	31	6	7½	28	16	9½		
Total Earnings *per annum* -	24	14	0	25	2	8	20	16	0		
Deficiencies of Earnings	10	17	1½	6	3	11½	8	0	9½		

AUCKLAND, COUNTY OF DURHAM.

ACCOUNT OF THE FAMILIES.

No. 1. A man, his wife, and five children, the eldeſt eight years of age, and the youngeſt an infant.

No. 2. A man, his wife, and four ſmall children, the eldeſt eleven years of age, the youngeſt three years.

No. 3. A man, his wife, and three young children, the eldeſt ſix years of age, the youngeſt an infant.

ANNUAL EXPENCES.

	£.	s.	d.
Rent of a cottage - - - -	1	5	0
Fuel, reckoning two horſe-loads of coals a week in winter, and one load in ſummer - - - - - - -	1	6	0
Clothing, as in the Barkham Paper, I think may do, for the man 1l. 10s.; for the woman, a gown 6s.; one petticoat 3s. 3d.; two ſhifts 4s. 8d.; ſhoes and mending 5s.; two pair ſtockings 2s. 6d.; two aprons 3s.; two handkerchiefs 2s. 8d.; caps 1s. 8½d.—1l. 8s. 9½d. For the children, ſhoes 14s.; ſtockings, one pair each, 3s.; coats or gown, one each, 9s.; petticoats, one each, 4s.; ſhirts, one each, 4s. 8d.—1l. 14s. 8d.			
Total Clothing - - - -	4	13	5½
Lying-in, ſickneſs, and loſs of time thereby, burials, and loſs of time by extreme bad weather, one year with another - - - - - -	1	18	0
	£. 9	2	5½

Flour reckoned at 1s. 6d. per ſtone. Fuel cannot be got cheaper in this county, as coals only are uſed.

Pitmen, miners, and keelmen, will earn ſometimes fourteen ſhillings per week; but they are generally ſo extravagant, that their ſavings for their families come to little or nothing.

PAROCHIAL CHAPELRY OF TANFIELD, COUNTY OF DURHAM.

NOVEMBER 20, 1789.

[COMMUNICATED BY MR. ROBERT WHITELOCK.]

EXPENCES AND EARNINGS OF FIVE FAMILIES OF LABOURERS, BY THE WEEK, AND BY THE YEAR.

	No. 1. 7 Persons.			No. 2. 7 Persons.			No. 3. 6 Persons.			No. 4. 5 Persons.			No. 5 5 Persons.		
Expences per Week.	£.	s.	d.	£.	s.	d.	£.	s.	d.	£.	s.	d.	£.	s.	d.
Rye or Maslin Flour - -	0	2	0	0	2	0	0	1	6	0	1	0	0	1	0
Wheat Flour - - - - -	0	1	0	0	1	0	0	1	0	0	1	0	0	1	0
Oatmeal - - - - - -	0	0	4	0	0	4	0	0	3	0	0	3	0	0	3
Milk - - - - - - -	0	1	2	0	1	2	0	1	0	0	0	9	0	0	9
Potatoes - - - - - -	0	0	4	0	0	4	0	0	4	0	0	3	0	0	3
Butcher's Meat - - - -	0	0	8	0	0	8	0	0	8	0	1	0	0	1	0
Soap, Salt, and Candles - -	0	0	3	0	0	3	0	0	3	0	0	3	0	0	3
Tea, Sugar, and Butter - -	0	0	8	0	0	8	0	0	8	0	0	8	0	0	8
Cheese (old milk) - - -	0	0	5	0	0	5	0	0	5	0	0	5	0	0	5
Thread, and Worsted - -	0	0	2	0	0	2	0	0	2	0	0	2	0	0	2
Total	0	7	0	0	7	0	0	6	3	0	5	9	0	5	9
Amount *per annum*	18	4	0	18	4	0	16	5	0	14	19	0	14	19	0
Earnings per Week.	£.	s.	d.	£.	s.	d.	£.	s.	d.	£.	s.	d.	£.	s.	d.
The Man earns at a medium	0	7	0	Pariſh	3	0	0	7	0	0	7	0	0	7	0
Women & young Children -	0	0	0	0	1	0	0	0	0	0	0	0	0	0	0
The eldest Children - - -	0	0	6	0	6	0	0	0	6	0	0	0	0	0	6
Total	0	7	6	0	10	0	0	7	6	0	7	0	0	7	6
Amount *per annum*	19	10	0	26	0	0	19	10	0	18	4	0	19	10	0
	£.	s.	d.	£.	s.	d.	£.	s.	d.	£.	s.	d.	£.	s.	d.
Annual Sum of Expences -	18	4	0	18	4	0	16	5	0	14	19		14	19	0
Rent, Fuel, Clothes, &c. -	6	0	0	6	0	0	6	0	0	6	0	0	6	0	0
Total Expences *per annum* -	24	4	0	24	4	0	22	5	0	20	19	0	20	19	0
Total Earnings *per annum* -	19	10	0	26	0	0	19	10	0	18	4	0	19	10	0
Deficiency of Earnings	4	14	0	0	0	0	2	15	0	2	15	0	1	9	0
Exceedings				1	16	0									

TANFIELD, COUNTY OF DURHAM.

ACCOUNT OF THE FAMILIES.

No. 1. A man, his wife, and five children, the eldeſt eight years of age, the youngeſt an infant.

No. 2. A woman, whoſe huſband is dead, and ſix children, the eldeſt a boy ſixteen years of age, the next a boy thirteen years of age, and the youngeſt five years.

No. 3. A man, his wife, and four ſmall children, the eldeſt ſix years of age, the youngeſt an infant.

No. 4. A man, his wife, and three ſmall children, the eldeſt not quite five years old, the youngeſt an infant.

No. 5. A man, his wife, and three young children, the eldeſt ſix years of age, the youngeſt an infant.

The above families were all living when this report was made, and are now [Oct. 4th, 1790] nearly in the ſame way.

ANNUAL EXPENCES.

	£.	s.	d.
Rent of houſe, fuel, clothing, lying-in, &c. I ſuppoſe the ſame as in the printed ſheet for Barkham	6	0	0

REMARKS.

In Nos. 1, 3, 4, 5, the woman can earn nothing, as ſhe will have enough to do to keep the family clean, and clothes whole: the youngeſt, being infants, will live moſtly on breaſt milk.

No. 2, in my opinion, ſhould live the beſt. They may all, except the youngeſt, clean weed, and do other little jobs. In this country we never pay more than 9d. per week for each perſon out of a work-houſe.

Alſo in No. 2, one muſt ſuppoſe two of the eldeſt of the four younger, children will be above ſeven years of age; if they be in health, the pariſh will give them nothing; this is ſeldom looked at except the parent be idle.

The man in time of cutting graſs earns more than ſeven ſhillings per week. The loſt time, by bad weather and incidental misfortunes, may run that out.

I know many families who are induſtrious, pay their credit, and live comfortably on ſeven ſhillings per week.

Rye, 8s. 6d. per boll, or two Wincheſter [buſhels.
Barley 6s. per ditto.
Oats 3s. 6d. per ditto.

NEWENT, GLOUCESTERSHIRE.

A LARGE PARISH WITH A SMALL MARKET, NO TRADE, NO MANUFACTURE.

[COMMUNICATED BY THE REV. J. FOLEY, NEWENT, 1789.]

EXPENCES AND EARNINGS OF SIX FAMILIES OF LABOURERS, BY THE WEEK, AND BY THE YEAR.

	No. 1. 7 Persons.			No. 2. 7 Persons.			No. 3. 6 Persons.			No. 4. 5 Persons.			No. 5. 5 Persons.			No. 6. 4 Persons.		
Expences per Week.	£.	s.	d.	£.	s.	d.	£.	s.	d.	£.	s.	d.	£.	s.	d.	£.	s.	d.
Bread, Flour, Yeast, & Baking	0	4	9	0	4	9	0	4	0	0	3	6	0	3	6	0	3	0
Salt - - - - - - - -	0	0	$2\frac{1}{4}$	0	0	$2\frac{1}{4}$	0	0	$2\frac{1}{4}$	0	0	2	0	0	2	0	0	2
Tea, Sugar, and Butter -	0	0	$8\frac{3}{4}$	0	0	$8\frac{3}{4}$	0	0	$8\frac{3}{4}$	0	0	7	0	0	7	0	0	7
Cheese - - - - - - -	0	0	$1\frac{1}{2}$	0	0	$1\frac{1}{2}$	0	0	$1\frac{1}{2}$	0	0	$1\frac{1}{2}$	0	0	$1\frac{1}{2}$	0	0	$1\frac{1}{2}$
Bacon - - - - - - - -	0	0	$3\frac{1}{2}$	0	0	$3\frac{1}{2}$	0	0	$3\frac{1}{2}$	0	0	$2\frac{3}{4}$	0	0	$2\frac{3}{4}$	0	0	$2\frac{3}{4}$
Soap, Starch, Blue (if used)	0	0	$2\frac{1}{2}$	0	0	$2\frac{1}{2}$	0	0	$2\frac{1}{2}$	0	0	$2\frac{1}{2}$	0	0	$2\frac{1}{2}$	0	0	$2\frac{1}{2}$
Candles, or rather rush-lights	0	0	2	0	0	2	0	0	2	0	0	2	0	0	2	0	0	2
Thread, Worsted, Pins, &c.	0	0	2	0	0	2	0	0	2	0	0	$1\frac{1}{2}$	0	0	$1\frac{1}{2}$	0	0	1
Milk - - - - - - - -	0	0	6	0	0	6	0	0	6	0	0	3	0	0	3	0	0	2
Total	0	7	$1\frac{1}{2}$	0	7	$1\frac{1}{2}$	0	6	$4\frac{1}{2}$	0	5	$4\frac{1}{4}$	0	5	$4\frac{1}{4}$	0	4	$8\frac{3}{4}$
Deduct Labourer's Bread, Cheese, & Bacon, for four weeks in wheat harvest, Amount per annum for the other 48 weeks	18	3	10	18	0	10	16	4	10	13	12	0	13	12	0	11	19	6
Earnings per Week.	£.	s.	d.	£.	s.	d.	£.	s.	d.	£.	s.	d.	£.	s.	d.	£.	s.	d.
The Man earns for 44 weeks	0	4	6	P. P. 6 weeks	4	0	0	4	6	0	4	6	0	4	6	0	4	6
And 8 weeks in harvest	0	6	0	0	4	0	0	6	0	0	6	0	0	6	0	0	6	0
The Woman earns 39 weeks	0	0	6	0	0	6	0	0	6	0	0	6	0	0	6	0	0	6
And *in toto* for the other 13 w.	2	11	6	2	11	6	2	11	6	2	11	6	2	11	6	2	11	6
The Boys in No. 2, 46 weeks				0	2	6												
Total Amount *per annum*	15	17	0	20	18	0	15	17	0	15	17	0	15	17	0	15	17	0
	£.	s.	d.	£.	s.	d.	£.	s.	d.	£.	s.	d.	£.	s.	d.	£.	s.	d.
To the above Amount of Expences *per annum* -	18	3	10	18	0	10	16	4	10	13	12	0	13	12	0	11	19	6
Add Rent, &c. except in No. 2, where is no lying-in, &c.	5	14	0	4	12	0	5	14	0	5	14	0	5	14	0	5	14	0
Total Expences *per annum* -	23	17	10	22	12	10	21	18	10	19	6	0	19	6	0	17	13	6
Total Earnings *per annum* -	15	17	0	20	18	0	15	17	0	15	17	0	15	17	0	15	17	0
Deficiency of Earnings	8	0	10	1	14	10	6	1	10	3	9	0	3	9	0	1	16	6

NEWENT, GLOUCESTERSHIRE.

ACCOUNT OF THE FAMILIES.

The ſame as in the printed ſchedule for Barkham, and this eſtimate is formed partly from the accounts given by the labourers, and partly from the ſhopkeepers' books. My calculations of Bread are according to the following proportion, which is ſufficient with potatoes:

A labouring man, I ſuppoſe, will eat weekly 15 pennyworth.

A woman with a child at her breaſt, 12 pennyworth.

A woman without one, 9 pennyworth.

A lad of ſixteen years of age, 15 pennyworth.

A lad between thirteen and ſeven years of age, 9 pennyworth.

A lad under ſeven years of age, 6 pennyworth.

And as additional food for a ſucking child, if a quarter old, I allow for flour 3d.

A pound of bacon will laſt, if bought, a fortnight or three weeks: little cheeſe is uſed; and in the wheat harveſt I deduct bacon, cheeſe, and the man's bread, as for that month he has his whole maintenance. Where the man, as in No. 2, is run away, we do not willingly allow the woman any pariſh relief, till the two eldeſt children are put out, as lads of that age are ſeldom governable by a mother; however, I have here ſuppoſed them at home, and contributing their labour to the common ſupport. Many poor families uſe not any ſoap, ſtarch, or blue.

ANNUAL EXPENCES.

	£.	s.	d.
Rent of a cottage and garden - -	1	10	0
Clothing - - - - - -	2	10	0
Lying-in, ſickneſs, bad weather, &c.	1	12	0
Statute duty on the highway - -	0	2	0
Fuel - - - - - - - - -	0	0	0
	£. 5	14	0

I take the eſtimate in the Barkham ſchedule for the 2d and 3d articles, not being able to form a proper judgment.

Rent varies from 20s. to 50s. according to ſituation, whether in the town or country, and according to the goodneſs of the garden. If it be extenſive, it ſupplies the family with potatoes, the great article of their food, eſpecially for the younger part, and enables them to nurſe up a ſmall pig: towards Michaelmas the children flock under every oak, to collect acorns to feed him, and *at the laſt*, three or four buſhels of peaſe are procured him to make his fat more ſolid. No poor man here can muſter up money enough to buy a whole fat pig: where they are unable to nurſe up one, they have recourſe to the retail ſhops.

I allow nothing for fuel. Mr. A. Foley has an annual fall of coppice, and gives the poor all the browſe gratis. The woods are between two and three miles diſtant. A burden, if ſold, will bring about 3d. the poor man's fire is generally backed with tan, which the tanners ſuffer them to take away after it is come out of the pits.

Earnings of a man who works by the great: for 44 weeks, he will get 1s. per day; for four weeks in wheat-harveſt, he will get 18d. a day, and all his maintenance; for four weeks in mowing, and lent-grain harveſt, he will get 18d. a day without his maintenance.

NEWENT, GLOUCESTERSHIRE.

Taking in this latter calculation, the Expences and Earnings of the Families will ſtand thus:

	No. 1.			No. 2.			No. 3.			No. 4.			No. 5.			No. 6.		
	£.	s.	d.	£.	s.	d.	£.	s.	d.	£.	s.	d.	£.	s.	d.	£.	s.	d.
Total Expences *per ann.*	23	17	10	22	12	10	21	18	10	19	6	0	19	6	0	17	13	6
Total Earnings *per ann.*	20	7	6	20	18	0	20	7	6	20	7	6	20	7	6	20	7	6
Deficiency of Earnings	3	10	4	1	14	10	1	11	4									
Surplus -										1	1	6	1	1	6	2	14	0

The ſtanding wages of the common day-labourer, in this pariſh and ſome adjoining ones, are 4s. 6d. per week, with one meal of victuals weekly, and a gallon of drink *per diem.* In other of the neighbouring pariſhes it is 5s. weekly: but the induſtrious labourer chooſes to be employed by the great—to threſh by the buſhel, to hedge and ditch by the perch, to raiſe and break ſtone by the ton;—and this man will in the winter time get 6s. or 7s. in the week. I have ſtated it at the loweſt in the calculations. In harveſt, the worſt man will get his ſhilling a day; and in wheat-harveſt, he has three meals a day, and drink unlimited; nor is it uncommon for a man to drink eight or ten quarts in the day. I ſuppoſe the wheat-harveſt to laſt four weeks, and have for this time deducted out of the expences the man's 15d. for bread, and alſo the cheeſe and bacon, it being the man that chiefly conſumes them. The woman for 39 weeks will get at leaſt 6d. per week, be her family what it will, by ſpinning, &c. the remaining weeks will, I think, produce her 2l. 11s. 6d. in the whole, which I thus make out:

	£.	s.	d.
Bean or peaſe ſetting, for 3 weeks, at 7d. per day - - - - -	0	10	6
Fruit-picking, 2 weeks, at 4d. -	0	4	0
Hay-making, 2 weeks, at 4d. -	0	4	0
Gleaning or leaſing 6 buſhels at 5s. 6d. per buſhel - - - -	1	13	0
	£. 2	11	6

It ſhould be obſerved, that the labouring part of the family, for obvious reaſons, require more victuals in ſummer than in winter; the garden is cultivated either on rainy days, or elſe previous to the hours of working. I have known a labourer work four *extra* hours in the day, occaſionally.—So much depends upon œconomy, prudent management, induſtry, health, and even the appetites of different perſons, that no calculation can perhaps be thoroughly depended upon.

I have known a numerous family ſubſiſting without relief, whilſt another family, apparently in ſimilar ſituations, but with two or three children leſs, have perpetually been applying

plying to the pariſh. One criterion has particularly ſtruck me:—Cleanlineſs about the houſe is almoſt a ſure indication of the family not wanting parochial aſſiſtance.

In general, I fear the wages of the labourer are not adequate to his maintenance, ſuppoſing him to have three or four children. How then is the deficiency to be made up? if you ſay—by *poor-rates*; I anſwer, that the legiſlature ſeems rather originally to have conſidered the infirm, the impotent, and the old, and not to have had ſo much in view the able and the induſtrious. If you ſay, *the charity of the rich* is to ſupply the deficiency of the earnings of the poor, I cannot help thinking this to be reſting the matter upon an improper foundation. It ſeems to me, that every man who labours in ſociety has a juſt claim upon the laws of that ſociety to allow him a ſufficient return for that labour—a return fully adequate to maintain himſelf and his family, though ever ſo numerous.

Labour on one hand, and the neceſſaries of life on the other, ſeem to be as reciprocal terms as protection and obedience. The labourer has a legal right, a right from the laws of nature, to an adequate maintenance. Charity, I ſhould think, ought to ſupply the comforts rather than the neceſſaries of life, and ſeems more adapted for the ſick, infirm, and aged, than for the healthy and the ſtrong.

In ſome of the inferior trades, the weekly wages are ſettled by law; and it is well known that in the great trading towns, ſuch as Mancheſter, Sheffield, Birmingham, &c. four days work in the week amply ſupply the diſſolute and the drunken. Why might not the magiſtrates exert the power lodged in them, by the ſtat. of Q. Eliz. and raiſe the price of labour in proportion to the exigencies of the times?

Should a ſociety ever be formed for the purpoſe of protecting the lower claſs, perhaps the following objects might not be undeſerving their notice:—1. To reſcue them from the harpy claws of pettyfogging attornies, who are perpetually harraſſing them in county courts, and plundering them with impunity. 2. To adjuſt the weights and meaſures of the little retail ſhops, which are too often ſcandalouſly deficient. 3. To extend to the country that great advantage obtained in London by fixing the aſſize of bread. 4. To diſperſe ſmall tracts containing uſeful knowledge with reſpect to little profits, which may be in their power to attain, and to cheap articles of diet. By the former I mean keeping of bees, raiſing turnip-ſeed, and the like. As to the latter, Mr. *Pennant* ſays that in *Ila*, heath is ſubſtituted partly for malt:—in Shrewſbury, treacle is uſed for the ſame purpoſe. What more nutritious than ſalep, common in all our fields: the root of the ſagittaria is almoſt equally ſo.

CRAWLEY

CRAWLEY PARISH, IN HAMPSHIRE.

EXPENCES AND EARNINGS OF SIX FAMILIES OF LABOURERS, BY THE WEEK, AND BY THE YEAR.

	No. 1. 8 Persons.			No. 2. 6 Persons.			No. 3. 7 Persons.			No. 4. 6 Persons.			No. 5. 7 Persons.			No. 6. 6 Persons.		
Expences per Week.	£.	s.	d.	£.	s.	d.	£.	s.	d.	£.	s.	d.	£.	s.	d.	£.	s.	d.
Bread or Flour - - - -	0	6	5	0	5	10	0	5	10	0	4	2	0	5	10	0	5	10
Salt - - - - - - - -	0	0	2	0	0	1	0	0	1	0	0	1	0	0	1	0	0	1½
Bacon - - - - - - - -	0	1	6	0	0	8	0	1	10	0	1	6	0	1	0	0	0	4
Tea, Sugar, and Butter -	0	0	6	0	0	9	0	0	9	0	0	9	0	1	5	0	1	10
Cheese - - - - - - -	0	1	0	0	0	4	0	0	3	0	0	4½	0	0	2	0	0	4
Beer - - - - - - - -	0	0	9	0	0	8	0	0	6½	0	0	5½	0	0	3	0	0	2
Soap, Starch, and Blue - -	0	0	2¾	0	0	2½	0	0	3	0	0	3	0	0	2¼	0	0	2¼
Candles - - - - - - -	0	0	3	0	0	2	0	0	3	0	0	3	0	0	2¼	0	0	2¼
Thread and Worsted - -	0	0	2	0	0	0½	0	0	2	0	0	2	0	0	2	0	0	2
Total	0	10	11¾	0	8	9	0	9	11½	0	8	0	0	9	2½	0	9	2
Amount *per annum*	28	10	11	22	15	0	25	17	10	20	16	0	23	18	10	23	16	8
Earnings per Week.	£.	s.	d.	£.	s.	d.	£.	s.	d.	£.	s.	d.	£.	s.	d.	£.	s.	d.
The Man earns (harvest excepted)	0	7	0	0	7	0	0	7	0	0	7	0	0	7	0	0	7	0
The Woman - - - - -	0	1	0	Parish pay	1	6	0	1	0	0	0	4	0	0	6	0	0	4
The Children - - - -	0	2	0	0	0	0	0	2	0	0	0	0	0	2	0	0	2	0
Total	0	10	0	0	8	6	0	10	0	0	7	4	0	9	6	0	9	4
Amount *per annum*	26	0	0	22	2	0	26	0	0	19	1	4	24	14	0	24	5	4
Extra earnings in harvest	3	4	0	1	10	0	3	8	0	2	0	0	5	4	0	1	10	0
Total Earnings	29	4	0	23	12	0	29	8	0	21	1	4	29	18	0	25	15	4
	£.	s.	d.	£.	s.	d.	£.	s.	d.	£.	s.	d.	£.	s.	d.	£.	s.	d.
To the above Amount of Expences *per annum* -	28	10	11	22	15	0	25	17	10	20	16	0	23	18	10	23	16	8
Add Rent, Fuel, Clothing, &c.	6	19	6	3	3	0	6	14	0	6	14	0	4	16	0	7	10	0
Total Expences *per annum* -	35	10	5	25	18	0	32	11	10	27	10	0	28	14	10	31	6	8
Total Earnings *per annum* -	29	4	0	23	12	0	29	8	0	21	1	4	29	18	0	25	15	4
Deficiency of Earnings	6	6	5	2	6	0	3	3	10	6	8	8	1	3	2 Surplus	5	11	4

CRAWLEY PARISH, IN HAMPSHIRE.

ACCOUNT OF THE FAMILIES.

No. 1. A man, his wife, and fix children, the eldeft a boy thirteen years of age, the youngeft an infant.

No. 2. A man and five children, (his wife being dead) the eldeft a girl thirteen years old, the youngeft fix years.

No. 3. A man his wife, and five children, the eldeft a boy eleven years of age, the youngeft $2\frac{1}{2}$ years.

No. 4. A man, his wife, and four children, the eldeft five years of age, the youngeft an infant.

No. 5. A man, his wife, and five children, the eldeft a boy ten years of age, the youngeft an infant.

No. 6. A man, his wife, and four children, the eldeft a boy fourteen years of age, the youngeft an infant.

	£.	s.	d.
Price of the half-peck loaf of wheaten bread - - - -	0	1	0
Price of the gallon of flour - -	0	0	10½
Price of a week's labour - -	0	7	0

I have made the calculations through the whole at the above rates, though in reality the half peck loaf is at this time 12½d. and the gallon of flour 11d.

Where a man has no reaping in harveft, he is allowed 12s. a week for fix weeks: he commonly reaps and mows by the acre.

ANNUAL EXPENCES.

		£.	s.	d.	£.	s.	d.
No. 1.	Rent - -	2	0	0			
	Fuel - - -	0	9	6			
	Shoes - - -	1	10	0			
	Clothes, &c. -	3	0	0			
					6	19	6
No. 2.	Rent - - -	0	0	0			
	Fuel - - -	0	8	0			
	Shoes - - -	0	15	0			
	Clothes, &c. -	2	0	0			
					3	3	0
No. 3.	Rent - - -	2	0	0			
	Fuel - - -	0	14	0			
	Clothes, &c. -	4	0	0			
					6	14	0
No. 4.	Rent - - -	2	2	0			
	Fuel - - -	1	2	0			
	Clothes, &c. -	3	10	0			
					6	14	0
No. 5.	Rent* - - -	0	0	0			
	Fuel - - -	0	14	0			
	Clothes, &c. -	4	2	0			
					4	16	0
No. 6.	Rent - - -	2	0	0			
	Fuel - - -	1	10	0			
	Clothes, &c. -	4	0	0			
					7	10	0

Rent of a cottage is 2l.—Fuel at the loweft eftimation muft be reckoned at 1l.; to make a family comfortable, it ought to be double of this. Clothing may be nearly the fame as in the printed eftimate for Barkham, except the article of fhoes, which is too low, efpecially if there is a boy who goes to plough, as he wears more than one pair per annum: a pair of man's nailed fhoes is here 8s.

I have chofen thofe who are efteemed the beft managers, as all buy their flour by the bufhel; and Nos. 1, 3, and 4, either fat a hog, or buy one whole by the fcore.

The reafon that I have put the firing at fo different rates is, becaufe in fome families the girls are employed in bringing fticks from coppices.

* This is the firft year that No. 5 has not paid rent, 2l.

LONG PARISH, IN HAMPSHIRE.

[BY THE REV. LASCELLES IREMONGER, APRIL 1789.]

EXPENCES AND EARNINGS OF SIX FAMILIES OF LABOURERS, BY THE WEEK, AND BY THE YEAR.

	No. 1. 7 Persons.			No. 2. 7 Persons.			No. 3. 6 Persons.			No. 4. 5 Persons.			No. 5. 5 Persons.			No. 6. 4 Persons.		
Expences per Week.	£.	s.	d.	£.	s.	d.	£.	s.	d.	£.	s.	d.	£.	s.	d.	£.	s.	d.
Bread or Flour - - - -	0	6	6	0	7	0	0	5	0	0	4	3	0	4	0	0	4	2
Yeast and Salt - - - -	0	0	3	0	0	3	0	0	3	0	0	2	0	0	2	0	0	1
Bacon or other Meat - -	0	1	0	0	1	0	0	1	0	0	0	8	0	1	0	0	0	4
Tea, Sugar, and Butter -	0	0	7	0	0	8	0	0	6	0	0	9	0	0	8	0	0	7
Cheese - - - - - - -	0	0	5	0	0	10	0	0	5	0	0	0	0	0	0	0	0	5
Beer - - - - - - - -	0	0	6	0	0	9	0	0	0	0	0	2	0	0	6	0	0	0
Soap, Starch, and Blue -	0	0	6	0	0	6	0	0	2	0	0	3	0	0	8	0	0	$3\frac{1}{4}$
Candles - - - - - - -	0	0	2	0	0	3	0	0	2	0	0	2	0	0	2	0	0	2
Thread, Thrum, Worsted -	0	0	3	0	0	3	0	0	3	0	0	3	0	0	3	0	0	2
Total	0	10	2	0	11	6	0	7	9	0	6	8	0	7	5	0	6	$2\frac{1}{4}$
Amount *per annum*	26	8	8	29	18	0	20	3	0	17	6	8	19	5	8	16	1	9
Earnings per Week.	£.	s.	d.	£.	s.	d.	£.	s.	d.	£.	s.	d.	£.	s.	d.	£.	s.	d.
The Man earns at a medium	0	8	0	0	8	0	0	8	0	0	8	0	0	7	0	0	7	6
The Woman - - - - -	0	0	0	0	1	0	0	1	0	0	0	6	0	1	6	0	0	6
The Children - - - -	0	1	6	0	4	6	0	0	0	0	0	0	0	0	6	0	0	0
Total	0	9	6	0	13	6	0	9	0	0	8	6	0	9	0	0	8	0
Amount *per annum*	24	14	0	35	2	0	23	8	0	22	2	0	23	8	0	20	16	0
	£.	s.	d.	£.	s.	d.	£.	s.	d.	£.	s.	d.	£.	s.	d.	£.	s.	d.
To the above Amount of Expences *per annum* -	26	8	8	29	18	0	20	3	0	17	6	8	19	5	8	16	1	9
Add Rent, Fuel, Clothes, Lying-in, &c. - -	7	0	0	7	0	0	7	0	0	7	0	0	7	0	0	7	0	0
Total Expences *per annum* -	33	8	8	36	18	0	27	3	0	24	6	8	26	5	8	23	1	9
Total Earnings *per annum* -	24	14	0	35	2	0	23	8	0	22	2	0	23	8	0	20	16	0
Deficiencies of Earnings	8	14	8	1	16	0	3	15	0	2	4	8	2	17	8	2	5	9

LONG PARISH, IN HAMPSHIRE.

ACCOUNT OF THE FAMILIES.

No. 1. A man, his wife, and five children, the eldeſt nine years of age, the youngeſt an infant.

No. 2. A man, his wife, and five children, the eldeſt fourteen years of age, the next a boy aged thirteen, the reſt unable to earn any thing.

No. 3. A man, his wife, and four children, the eldeſt under nine years of age, the youngeſt an infant.

No. 4. A man, his wife, and three ſmall children, the eldeſt not quite ſix years of age, and the youngeſt only one year.

No. 5. A man, his wife, and three children, the eldeſt near ten years old.

No. 6. A man, his wife, and two ſmall chidren, unable to earn any thing.

ANNUAL EXPENCES.

	£.	s.	d.
Cottage rent and fuel, both very high and ſcarce, ſo that they greatly exceed the eſtimate in the Barkham paper, and one pound may be added at the leaſt to the expences in the Berkſhire account.			
Rent, fuel, clothing, &c. -	7	0	0
Price of the half-peck loaf of wheaten bread - - -	0	1	0½

No. 5. Waſhes for two young men.

LONG PARISH, IN HAMPSHIRE.

MONK-SHERBORNE AND BASING PARISHES, IN HAMPSHIRE, 1789.

EXPENCES AND EARNINGS OF SIX FAMILIES OF LABOURERS, BY THE WEEK, AND BY THE YEAR.

	No. 1. 7 Persons.			No. 2. 7 Persons.			No. 3. 6 Persons.			No. 4. 5 Persons.			No. 5. 5 Persons.			No. 6. 4 Persons.		
Expences per Week.	£.	s.	d.	£.	s.	d.	£.	s.	d.	£.	s.	d.	£.	s.	d.	£.	s.	d.
Flour, Yeast, and Salt - -	0	7	0	0	7	0	0	6	0	0	5	0	0	5	0	0	4	0
Bacon, &c. - - - - -	0	1	2	0	1	2	0	1	2	0	1	0	0	1	0	0	1	0
Cheese - - - - - -	0	0	0	0	0	0	0	0	0	0	0	6	0	0	6	0	0	8
Sugar and Butter - - -	0	0	$4\frac{1}{2}$	0	0	$4\frac{1}{2}$	0	0	$4\frac{1}{2}$	0	0	6	0	0	6	0	0	6
Beer in hay-time and harvest	0	1	0	0	1	0	0	1	0	0	0	10	0	0	10	0	0	10
Soap, Starch, and Blue - -	0	0	3	0	0	3	0	0	3	0	0	3	0	0	3	0	0	3
Candles - - - - - -	0	0	$3\frac{1}{2}$	0	0	$3\frac{1}{2}$	0	0	$3\frac{1}{2}$	0	0	3	0	0	3	0	0	3
Thread, Worsted, &c. - -	0	0	3	0	0	3	0	0	3	0	0	2	0	0	2	0	0	2
Total	0	10	4	0	10	4	0	9	4	0	8	6	0	8	6	0	7	8
Amount *per annum*	26	17	4	26	17	4	24	5	4	22	2	0	22	2	0	19	18	8
Earnings per Week.	£.	s.	d.	£.	s.	d.	£.	s.	d.	£.	s.	d.	£.	s.	d.	£.	s.	d.
The Man - - - - -	0	8	6	Parish pay	4	0	0	8	6	0	8	6	0	8	6	0	8	6
The Woman - - - - -	0	1	6	0	1	6	0	1	0	0	0	9	0	0	9	0	1	6
The Children - - - -	0	0	0	0	3	6	0	0	0	0	0	0	0	0	0	0	0	0
Total	0	10	0	0	9	0	0	9	6	0	9	3	0	9	3	0	10	0
Amount *per annum*	26	0	0	23	8	0	24	14	0	24	1	0	24	1	0	26	0	0
	£.	s.	d.	£.	s.	d.	£.	s.	d.	£.	s.	d.	£.	s.	d.	£.	s.	d.
To the above Amount of Expences *per annum* -	26	17	4	26	17	4	24	5	4	22	2	0	22	2	0	19	18	8
Fuel, Clothes, &c. [Rent to No. 4, 5, 6] - - - -	4	10	0	4	10	0	4	10	0	6	0	0	6	0	0	6	0	0
Total Expences *per annum* -	31	7	4	31	7	4	28	15	4	28	2	0	28	2	0	25	18	8
Total Earnings *per annum* -	26	0	0	23	8	0	24	14	0	24	1	0	24	1	0	26	0	0
Deficiencies of Earnings	5	7	4	7	19	4	4	1	4	4	1	0	4	1	0			
Exceedings																0	1	4

MONK-SHERBOURN AND BASING PARISHES, IN HAMPSHIRE, 1789.

ACCOUNT OF THE FAMILIES.

No. 1. A man, his wife, and five children, the eldeſt nine years of age, the youngeſt an infant.

No. 2. A woman, whoſe huſband is dead, and ſix children, the eldeſt a boy fourteen years of age, the next a girl twelve years, the remainder too young to work.

No. 3. A man, his wife, and four ſmall children, the eldeſt ſeven years of age, the youngeſt an infant.

No. 4. A man, his wife, and three ſmall children, the eldeſt five years of age, the youngeſt an infant.

No. 5. A man, his wife, and three children, the eldeſt five years of age, the youngeſt an infant.

No. 6. A man, his wife, and two children, the eldeſt ſix years of age, the youngeſt four years.

ANNUAL EXPENCES.

	£.	s.	d.
Price of the half-peck loaf*	0	1	$1\frac{1}{2}$
Price of a gallon of flour	0	1	0
A week's labour in winter	0	7	0
Hay time, hoeing, and harveſt, ſuppoſed to make it average at - - - -	0	8	6

The annual expences are ſimilar to thoſe in the Berkſhire account, except that in this neighbourhood, the pariſh pays the rents for families of the deſcription of No. 1, 2, 3.

This calculation was made from two pariſhes, Monk-Sherbourn and Baſing, both in Hampſhire, on account of the families being of the ſame number.

* Bread or flour is 2d. per half-peck dearer than in 1787.

LANCASHIRE, FEB. 1789.

[COMMUNICATED THROUGH THOMAS STANLEY, ESQ; M. P.]

EXPENCES AND EARNINGS OF THREE FAMILIES OF LABOURERS, BY THE WEEK, AND BY THE YEAR.

	No. 1. 7 Persons.			No. 2. 7 Persons.			No. 3. 6 Persons.					
Expences per Week.	£.	s.	d.	£.	s.	d.	£.	s.	d.			
Bread from Oatmeal - -	0	3	0	0	3	0	0	3	0			
Potatoes - - - - - - -	0	0	6	0	0	9	0	0	6			
Salt - - - - - - - -	0	0	1½	0	0	3	0	0	3			
Bacon or other Meat - -	0	0	4	0	0	4	0	0	6			
Tea, Sugar, Treacle, Butter	0	1	2	0	0	11½	0	0	11			
Beer and Milk - - - -	0	0	5½	0	0	5	0	0	2			
Soap, Starch, and Blue -	0	0	2½	0	0	4	0	0	4			
Candles - - - - - - -	0	0	3½	0	0	3½	0	0	3½			
Thread, Thrum, Worsted -	0	0	2	0	0	2	0	0	2			
Total	0	6	3	0	6	6	0	6	1½			
Amount *per annum*	16	5	0	16	18	0	15	18	6			
Earnings per Week.	£.	s.	d.	£.	s.	d.	£.	s.	d.			
The Man earns at a medium	0	7	0	0	6	6	0	7	6			
The Woman - - - - -	0	1	0	0	1	0	0	1	6			
The Children - - - -	0	0	6	0	2	0	0	0	6			
Total	0	8	6	0	9	6	0	9	6			
Amount *per annum*	22	2	0	24	14	0	24	14	0			
	£.	s.	d.	£.	s.	d.	£.	s.	d.			
To the above Amount of Expences *per annum* -	16	5	0	16	18	0	15	18	6			
Add Rent, Fuel, Clothes, Lying-in, &c. - -	9	0	0	10	7	0	9	2	2			
Total Expences *per annum* -	25	5	0	27	5	0	25	0	8			
Total Earnings *per annum* -	22	2	0	24	14	0	24	14	0			
Deficiencies of Earnings	3	3	0	2	11	0	0	6	8			

LANCASHIRE.

ACCOUNT OF THE FAMILIES.

TOWNSHIP OF GREAT ECCLESTON, AND PARISH OF ST. MICHAEL'S.

No. 1. A man, his wife, and five children, the eldeſt a boy twelve years of age, the next a girl ten years, the next eight, and the youngeſt an infant of two years old.

TOWNSHIP OF BARTON, PARISH OF PRESTON.

No. 2. A man, his wife, and five children, the eldeſt a girl eleven years of age, the next a girl nine years, the youngeſt an infant of two years.

TOWNSHIP OF KIRKLAND, PARISH OF GARSTANG.

No. 3. A man, his wife, and four children, the eldeſt a girl eleven years of age, the next a girl nine years, the youngeſt two.

ANNUAL EXPENCES OF No. 1.

	£.	s.	d.
Rent of a cottage and garden -	2	2	0
Fuel, 24 falls of turf - - - - -	1	5	0
Man's clothing - - - - - -	1	8	0
Woman's ditto - - - - - -	0	17	0
The five children's clothing - -	1	16	0
Lying-in, ſickneſs, &c. loſs of time in bad weather, &c. - - - -	1	12	0
	£. 9	0	0

ANNUAL EXPENCES OF No. 2.

	£.	s.	d.
Rent of a cottage and garden - -	2	0	0
Fuel, altogether coals - - - -	3	0	0
Man's clothing - - - - - -	1	6	6
Woman's ditto - - - - - -	0	15	0
The five children's clothing - -	1	13	6
Lying-in, ſickneſs, &c. loſs of time in bad weather, &c. - - - -	1	12	0
	£. 10	7	0

ANNUAL EXPENCES OF No. 3.

	£.	s.	d.
Rent of a cottage and garden - -	1	8	0
Fuel, 30 falls of turf - - - -	1	6	0
Man's clothing - - - - - -	1	8	0
Woman's ditto - - - - - -	1	2	8
The four children's clothing - -	2	5	6
Lying-in, ſickneſs, &c. loſs of time in bad weather, &c. - - - -	1	12	0
	£. 9	2	2

PARISH OF WINWICK,

IN THE TOWNSHIP OF LOWTON, LANCASHIRE.

[COMMUNICATED BY JOHN BLACKBURNE, ESQ; M. P.]

EXPENCES AND EARNINGS OF ONE FAMILY OF LABOURERS, CONSISTING OF A MAN, HIS WIFE, AND FIVE CHILDREN, THE ELDEST EIGHT YEARS OF AGE, THE YOUNGEST AN INFANT, BY THE WEEK, AND BY THE YEAR.

	No. 1. 7 Persons.					
Expences per Week.	£. s. d.					
Meal and Flour - - - -	0 5 0					
Potatoes - - - - - - -	0 1 0					
Yeast and Salt - - - -	0 0 4					
Bacon or other Meat - -	0 1 4					
Milk and Butter - - - -	0 1 10					
Soap, Starch, and Candles -	0 0 5					
Thread and Woollen Yarn -	0 0 3					
Total	0 10 2					
Amount *per annum*	26 8 8					
Earnings per Week.	£. s. d.					
The Man earns - - - -	0 9 0					
The Woman - - - - -	0 1 6					
The Children - - - -	0 0 0					
Total	0 10 6					
Amount *per annum*	27 6 0					
	£. s. d.					
To the above Amount of Expences *per annum* -	26 8 8					
Add Rent 3l. Fuel 1l. Clothing 6l. Lying-in, Sickness, Loss of Time, &c. 2l. -	12 0 0					
Total Expences *per annum* -	38 8 8					
Total Earnings *per annum* -	27 6 0					
Deficiency of Earnings	11 2 8					

MARSHAM, NORFOLK, JANUARY 1790.

BY MR. JOHN KIDDLE.

The pariſh of Marſham, in the Eaſtern part of the county of Norfolk, is (with many other pariſhes in the ſame diſtrict) greatly burthened with the poor-rates, which have ſome years amounted to 10s. in the pound, rack rent; that is, a farm rented at 100l. per annum has paid (ſince my reſidence in the pariſh) 50l. in the year to the poor-rates, excluſive of the church-rate and ſurveyors; but on an average for the ſeven years paſt, they have been at 9s. in the pound, rack rent, and are not likely to be reduced lower.

The common price of labour in the diſtrict is a ſhilling a day to thoſe who have families; if there be no children, and they aſk employment of the pariſh, it is uſual to diminiſh of that price, according to circumſtances, from eightpence a day, which is commonly paid to a ſingle man who comes to the pariſh for work; which is countenanced by the magiſtrate.

I have a labourer who drives a team for me, that is, has the care of five horſes, from ſix o'clock in the morning until nine in the evening; whoſe ſituation is envied by half the labourers in the pariſh, becauſe his wages are 7s. a week through the year; this man has a wife and ſix ſmall children now living, and has buried three, ſupports himſelf and family with that wages, and pays his rent of 2l. 5s. a year, and has done ſo theſe ſix years paſt, without aſking relief of the pariſh, to my certain knowledge, he having been with me that time.

The common price of labour when a farmer chooſes his labourers from the ſtrongeſt and beſt workmen in the pariſh, is to give them 6s. a week the winter half year, and 7s. the ſummer.

The uſual pariſh allowance to a man advanced in years, is 2s. a week, and to find them clothes, firing, and ſometimes the uſe of the poor-houſe.

The allowance for widows is, to thoſe without any children, a ſhilling per week, houſe-rent and firing, unleſs they are paſt doing any labour; and then it is uſual to give them 2s.

If they have one child, 1s. 6d. if two children, 2s. &c.

BRINGTON, IN THE COUNTY OF NORTHAMPTON.

EXPENCES AND EARNINGS OF THREE FAMILIES OF LABOURERS, BY THE WEEK, AND BY THE YEAR.

	No. 1. 9 Persons.			No. 2. 6 Persons.			No. 3. 12 Persons.					
Expences per Week.	£.	s.	d.	£.	s.	d.	£.	s.	d.			
Bread and Flour - - -	0	8	0	0	3	6	0	13	0			
Bacon and Meat on a Sunday	0	2	6	0	1	1	0	0	9			
Tea, Sugar, Soap, Starch, Blue, Candles, Thread, and Worsted - - -	0	4	0	0	1	5	0	3	8			
Cheese, Butter, Milk, Oatmeal	0	1	0	0	0	5	0	1	6			
Malt and Beer - - - -	0	0	10	0	0	4	0	0	5			
Total	0	16	4	0	6	9	0	19	4			
Amount *per annum*	42	9	4	17	11	0	50	5	4			
Earnings per Week.	£.	s.	d.	£.	s.	d.	£.	s.	d.			
The Man at a medium - -	0	6	6	0	6	6	0	6	0			
Eldest Son - - - - -	0	2	0	0	0	0	0	6	0			
Other Children - - - -	0	2	0	0	0	0	0	2	0			
Woman - - - - - - -	0	0	0	0	1	8	0	0	0			
Lodger and Parish Allowance	0	5	0	0	0	0	0	2	6			
Total	0	15	6	0	8	2	0	16	6			
Amount *per annum*	40	6	0	21	4	8	42	18	0			
	£.	s.	d.	£.	s.	d.	£.	s.	d.			
To the above Amount of Expences *per annum* -	42	9	4	17	11	0	50	5	4			
Add Rent, Clothing, &c. &c.	5	16	0	5	16	0	5	16	0			
Total Expences *per annum* -	48	5	4	23	7	0	56	1	4			
Total Earnings *per annum* -	40	6	0	21	4	8	42	18	0			
Deficiency of Earnings	7	19	4	2	2	4	13	3	4			

BRINGTON, IN THE COUNTY OF NORTHAMPTON.

ACCOUNT OF THE FAMILIES.

No. 1. T. Taylor, his wife, and fix children, the eldeft fourteen years of age a boy, the next a girl twelve years, the youngeft about two years; with a man, a lodger, who is placed there by the parifh at 5s. per week, board, lodging, wafhing, and mending.

No. 2. Thomas Mailer, a wife, and four children; the eldeft feven years of age, the youngeft about eighteen months.

No. 3. George Capel, a wife, and ten children; the eldeft a youth twenty years old; the next a girl thirteen years; the next a girl twelve years; the next a girl ten years; the next a girl eight; the next a boy feven; the youngeft two years.

ANNUAL EXPENCES.

	£.	s.	d.
Rent of cottages from 1l. to 5s. per annum - - -	1	0	0
Fuel, about 26s. per annum	1	6	0
Coals are here fold at fourpence per cwt. lefs than prime coft; the gift of Earl Spencer.			
The clothing is generally bought fecond-hand; and a great many gowns, petticoats, and fhifts, are annually diftributed by the Countefs Spencer to the poor families:—Call what is bought - - - - - -	2	0	0
Allow for lying-in and cafualties - - - - - - - -	1	10	0
	£.5	16	0

The parifh pays the rent of No. 1; and generally makes up the deficiency of No. 3.

An allowance of a twelve-penny loaf and 8lbs. of beef, for four weeks at Chriftmas, is given by Earl Spencer to Nos. 1 and 3.

CASTOR, NEAR PETERBOROUGH, NORTHAMPTONSHIRE,

FEBRUARY 6, 1794.

[COMMUNICATED BY THE REV. CH. HODGSON, RECTOR OF MARHOLM, AND CURATE OF CASTOR.]

EXPENCES AND EARNINGS OF SIX FAMILIES OF LABOURERS, BY THE WEEK, AND BY THE YEAR.

	No. 1. 6 Persons.			No. 2. 5 Persons.			No. 3. 4 Persons.			No. 4. 6 Persons.			No. 5. 6 Persons.			No. 6. 7 Persons.		
Expences per Week.	£.	s.	d.	£.	s.	d.	£.	s.	d.	£.	s.	d.	£.	s.	d.	£.	s.	d.
Bread and Flour - - - -	0	5	0	0	4	1	0	4	0	0	5	6	0	4	3	0	6	6
Salt - - - - - - - -	0	0	1½	0	0	0¾	0	0	1½	0	0	1	0	0	1	0	0	2
Meat - - - - - - - -	0	1	6	0	1	6	0	1	0	0	1	6	0	1	6	0	1	3
Tea, Sugar, and Butter -	0	0	6	0	1	7	0	1	0	0	0	8	0	1	1	0	1	2
Cheese (sometimes) - -	0	0	5½	0	0	0	0	0	0	0	0	0	0	0	5	0	0	0
Beer (seldom any) - - -	0	0	0	0	0	0	0	0	0	0	0	0	0	0	0	0	0	0
Soap ¼lb. Starch, &c. - -	0	0	2½	0	0	2½	0	0	2	0	0	4½	0	0	2½	0	0	3
Candles ½lb. Thread, &c.	0	0	6	0	0	5	0	0	4	0	0	5½	0	0	6	0	0	8
Total	0	8	3½	0	7	10¼	0	6	7½	0	8	7	0	8	0½	0	10	0
Amount *per annum*	21	11	2	20	8	5	17	4	6	22	6	4	20	18	2	26	0	0

Earnings per Week.	£.	s.	d.	£.	s.	d.	£.	s.	d.	£.	s.	d.	£.	s.	d.	£.	s.	d.
The Man earns at a medium	0	7	6	0	6	6	0	8	0	0	6	6	0	7	6	0	9	0
The Woman - - - - -	0	0	4	0	0	0	0	1	0	0	0	3½	0	0	10	0	0	8
The Children - - - -	0	0	0	0	0	3	0	0	0	0	1	3	0	0	4	0	0	3
Total	0	7	10	0	6	9	0	9	0	0	8	0½	0	8	8	0	9	11
Amount *per annum*	20	7	4	17	11	0	23	8	0	20	18	2	22	10	8	25	15	8

	£.	s.	d.	£.	s.	d.	£.	s.	d.	£.	s.	d.	£.	s.	d.	£.	s.	d.
To the above Amount of Expences *per annum* -	21	11	2	20	8	5	17	4	6	22	6	4	20	18	2	26	0	0
Add Rent, Fuel, Clothes, &c.	7	10	0	7	10	0	7	10	0	7	10	0	7	10	0	7	10	0
Total Expences *per annum* -	29	1	2	27	18	5	24	14	6	29	16	4	28	8	2	33	10	0
Total Earnings* *per annum* -	20	7	4	17	11	0	23	8	0	20	18	2	22	10	8	25	15	8
Deficiencies of Earnings	8	13	10	10	7	5	1	6	6	8	18	2	5	17	6	7	14	4

To the Earnings may be added what is got by gleaning.

CASTOR, NEAR PETERBOROUGH, NORTHAMPTONSHIRE.

ACCOUNT OF THE FAMILIES.

No. 1. A man, his wife, and four children, the eldeſt eleven years of age, the youngeſt an infant.

No. 2. A man, his wife, and three children, the eldeſt thirteen years of age, the youngeſt an infant.

No. 3. A man, his wife, and two children, the eldeſt ſix years of age, the youngeſt an infant.

No. 4. Henry Snow, his wife, and four children, the eldeſt ten years of age, the youngeſt an infant.

No. 5. A man, his wife, and four children, the eldeſt twelve years of age, the youngeſt an infant.

No. 6. A man, his wife, and five children, the eldeſt fourteen years of age, the youngeſt an infant.

ANNUAL EXPENCES.

	£.	s.	d.
Rent of a cottage only from 1l. 10s. to 2l. 2s. - - - - - -	1	15	0
Fuel and coals - - - - - -	1	10	0
Clothing, the man's and family -	2	15	0
Lying-in, loſs of time, &c. - -	1	10	0
	£.7	10	0

Price of a week's labour in winter	0	6	0
Ditto in ſummer - - - - - -	0	8	0
Ditto in hay time - - - - - -	0	9	0
Ditto in harveſt time - - - - -	0	10	6

Coals are, in this part of the kingdom, a very dear article: poor people cannot buy any now under a ſhilling a buſhel, beſides the expence of getting them home; and the price of wood bears a conſiderable proportion to that of coals. But when a poor man is at wood-work, he is then allowed a faggot per day, for his own uſe, beſides his wages.

In No. 2, the wife can add nothing to her huſband's earnings by her own induſtry, being ſo much diſabled as not to do any profitable kind of work whatever.

PARISH OF HOLWELL, SOMERSETSHIRE.

[COMMUNICATED BY MR. RADCLIFFE, 1789.]

EXPENCES AND EARNINGS OF TWO FAMILIES OF LABOURERS, BY THE WEEK, AND BY THE YEAR.

	No. 1. 7 Persons.			No. 2. 8 Persons.						
Expences per Week.	£.	s.	d.	£.	s.	d.				
Bread or Flour - - - -	0	7	0	0	4	8				
Potatoes and Vegetables -	0	0	6	0	0	5				
Cheese and Salt - - - -	0	1	1¾	0	0	4				
Bacon or other Meat - -	0	1	6	0	0	7				
Tea, Sugar, and Butter - -	0	0	10	0	0	*2				
Soap, Starch, and Candles -	0	0	8	0	0	5				
Thread and Woollen Yarn -	0	0	3½	0	0	1				
Total	0	11	11¼	0	6	8				
Amount *per annum*	31	0	9	17	6	8				
Earnings per Week.	£.	s.	d.	£.	s.	d.				
The Man earns at a medium	0	6	6	0	5	6				
The Woman and Children -	0	7	0	0	2	6				
Total	0	13	6	0	8	0				
Amount *per annum*	35	2	0	20	16	0				
	£.	s.	d.	£.	s.	d.				
To the above Amount of Expences *per annum* -	31	0	9	17	6	8				
Add Clothes - - - - - -	5	9	9	4	16	8				
Total Expences *per annum* -	36	10	6	22	3	4				
Total Earnings *per annum* -	35	2	0	20	16	0				
Deficiency of Earnings	1	8	6	1	7	4				

* In No. 2, no Sugar or Butter.

PARISH OF HOLWELL, SOMERSETSHIRE.

ACCOUNT OF THE FAMILIES.

No. 1. A man, his wife, and ſix children, the eldeſt fourteen years of age, the youngeſt two.

The clothing of this family was as follows:

	£.	s.	d.
Man: coat and breeches - -	0	11	0
2 pair ſhoes, and repairing them	0	16	0
Shirts, 8s. ſtockings 3s. - - -	0	11	0
Woman: gown and petticoats -	0	8	6
Shifts 7s. ſhoes 3s. 9d. - - -	0	10	9
Stockings 1s. 6d. apron, caps, and handkerchiefs 6s. - - - -	0	7	6
Children's clothes - - - -	2	5	0
	£. 5	9	9

N. B. The man's wages are only 5s. per week in the winter, and 6s. in the ſummer: but he is often abroad with his maſter's waggon, and has then ſome little additional advantages. The woman alſo informs me, that ſhe makes ſome money by geeſe, and now and then receives a ſhilling from a kind relation. The eldeſt ſon earns 2s. 6d. per week, and expends in clothes about 20s. a year.

No. 2. A man, his wife, and ſix children, the eldeſt thirteen years of age, the youngeſt an infant.

The clothing of this family was as follows:

	£.	s.	d.
Man: coat and breeches - - -	0	8	0
2 pair ſhoes, and repairing them	0	16	0
Shirts 12s. ſtockings 3s. 6d. -	0	15	6
Spade, ſhovel, &c. for trenching	0	4	0
Woman: gown and petticoats -	0	6	0
Shifts 9s. ſhoes, 3s. 8d. ſtockings 1s. 6d. - - - - - - - -	0	14	2
Apron, cap, and handkerchiefs -	0	5	0
Lying-in - - - - - - - -	0	8	0
Children's clothes - - - -	1	0	0
	£. 4	16	8

The man has a ſmall garden, which is of ſome advantage. The children are rather of the diminutive kind, and never wear ſhoes or ſtockings.

Houſe-rent and fuel coſt neither of theſe families any thing. The former is paid by the pariſh; the latter is procured by gathering cow-dung, and breaking their neighbours' hedges. No beer, and very ſeldom any cyder.

The men, whoſe families I have deſcribed, are of the common run of labourers, but are many days in the year without employment.

P. S. I have examined the ſtate of another poor family, which conſiſts of a man, his wife, and three children, the eldeſt nine years of age, and the youngeſt one. Their annual expences are, in proviſions 16l. 5s. in clothes, &c. 4l. 6s. total 20l. 11s. The man earns 6s. a week, and the woman 1s. 6d. which produce in the year 19l. 10s.

	£.	s.	d.
Total expences *per annum* -	20	11	0
Total earnings *per annum* -	19	10	0
Deficiency of earnings -	1	1	0

N. B. The half-peck loaf of wheaten bread, is valued in the foregoing accounts at 1s. 2d. and a ſtone of flour 2s. 4d.

SIDLESHAM PARISH, SURRY

[COMMUNICATED BY JOHN FARHILL, ESQ; 1793.]

EXPENCES AND EARNINGS OF SIX FAMILIES OF LABOURERS, BY THE WEEK, AND BY THE YEAR.

	No. 1. 6 Persons.	No. 2. 6 Persons.	No. 3. 6 Persons.	No. 4. 6 Persons.	No. 5. 5 Persons.	No. 6. 6 Persons.
Expences per Week.	£. s. d.	£. s. d.	£. s. d.	£ s. d.	£. s. d.	£. s. d.
Bread and Flour - - -	0 4 0	0 4 2	0 4 3	0 3 11	0 3 9	0 4 9
Yeast and Salt - - - -	0 0 0½	0 0 0½	0 0 0½	0 0 0½	0 0 1	0 0 0½
Bacon and other Meat - -	0 2 0	0 1 9	0 1 10	0 2 3	0 2 1	0 3 0
Tea and Sugar - - - -	0 0 7	0 1 2	0 0 7	0 0 7	0 0 7½	0 0 8
Butter - - - - - - - -	0 0 9	0 0 6	0 0 9	0 0 9	0 0 8½	0 0 9
Cheese - - - - - - -	0 1 0	0 0 6	0 1 3	0 1 0	0 1 2	0 0 11
Soap, Starch, and Blue -	0 0 2	0 0 1	0 0 1½	0 0 1½	0 0 1	0 0 1½
Candles - - - - - - -	0 0 2½	0 0 2½	0 0 1½	0 0 2½	0 0 2	0 0 1½
Thread, Worsted, &c. - -	0 0 1	0 0 0½	0 0 0½	0 0 0½	0 0 0½	0 0 1
Total	0 8 10	0 8 5½	0 9 0	0 8 11	0 8 8½	0 10 5½
Amount *per annum*	22 19 4	21 19 10	23 8 0	23 3 8	22 12 10	27 3 10
Earnings per Week.	£. s. d.	£. s. d.	£. s. d.	£. s. d.	£. s. d.	£. s. d.
Total	0 10 0	0 12 0	0 11 0	0 11 6	0 11 0	0 12 0
Amount *per annum*	26 0 0	31 4 0	28 12 0	29 18 0	28 12 0	31 4 0
	£. s. d.	£. s. d.	£. s. d.	£. s. d.	£. s. d.	£. s. d.
Expences *per annum* - -	22 19 4	21 19 10	23 8 0	23 3 8	22 12 10	27 3 10
Rent and Fuel - - - -	3 13 6	2 0 0	1 15 0	7 6 0	4 1 0	6 3 6
Total Expences *per annum* -	26 12 10	23 19 10	25 3 0	30 9 8	26 13 10	33 7 4
Total Earnings *per annum* -	26 0 0	31 4 0	28 12 0	29 18 0	28 12 0	31 4 0
	0 12 10 Deficient	7 4 2 Surplus	3 9 0 Surplus	0 11 8 Deficient	1 18 2 Surplus	2 3 4 Deficient

SIDLESHAM PARISH, SURRY.

ACCOUNT OF THE FAMILIES.

No. 1. John Hart, his wife, and four children, the eldeſt a girl ten years old, another four, a boy two, and the youngeſt an infant. Earn about 10s. per week.

No. 2. William Lock, his wife, and four children, the eldeſt a boy five years old, another four, a girl two, and the youngeſt an infant. Earn about 11s. per week, 1s. ditto of the pariſh.

No. 3. John Homer, his wife, and four children, the eldeſt a girl twelve years old, a boy nine, another ſix, and a girl four. Earn about 10s. per week, and 1s. of the pariſh.

No. 4. Henry Mabbs, his wife, and four children; the eldeſt a boy eleven years old, another nine, a third ſeven, and the youngeſt one. Earn about 10s. per week, 1s. allowed by the pariſh, 6d. lodgers.

No. 5. William Dawtry, his wife, and three children, the eldeſt a boy eight years old, another ſix, and the youngeſt an infant. Earn about 11s. per week.

No. 6. Jeremiah Meal, his wife, and four children. Earns about 11s. 6d. per week, wife 6d.

ANNUAL EXPENCES.

No. 1.	Rent - - -	1	2	6				
	Coals 1l. 10s. } Wood 1l. 1s. }	2	11	0				
						3	13	6

Brews 6 buſhels of malt, 4lb. hops.

No. 2. Rent - - - - - - -		2	0	0

Brews 5 buſhels of malt, 2½lb. hops.

No. 3.	Rent - - -	0	0	0				
	Wood - -	0	14	0				
	Coals - - -	1	1	0				
						1	15	0

Beer about 5s. per annum, the reſt of the year drinks water.

No. 4.	Rent - - -	3	3	0				
	Fuel - - -	4	3	0				
						7	6	0

Brews about 9 buſhels of malt, 6lb. hops.

No. 5.	Rent - - -	1	0	0				
	Fuel - - -	3	1	0				
						4	1	0

Brews about 9 buſhels of malt, 8lb. hops.

No. 6.	Rent - - -	3	13	6				
	Fuel - - -	2	10	0				
						6	3	6

Shoes 2l. 10s. yearly.

Nos. 1, 2, 3, 4, take in lodgers which leſſens their rents, and for whom the wives waſh and mend, which is not included in the weekly earnings, and which contributes to account for making up the deficiencies.

No. 5 is a ſheep-ſhearer, which increaſes the total of his earnings beyond the average of 11s. per week.

N. B. Many labourers, whoſe work is with pick-axe and ſhovel, ſuſtain very often an expence of not leſs than from 6d. to 9d. per week for the repair of tools, excluſive of their coſt.

TUNTINGTON, SUSSEX, AND SIDLESHAM, SURRY.

[COMMUNICATED BY JOHN FARHILL, ESQ; 1793.]

EXPENCES AND EARNINGS OF SIX FAMILIES OF LABOURERS, BY THE WEEK, AND BY THE YEAR.

	No. 1. 3 Persons.			No. 2. 6 Persons.			No. 3. 5 Persons.			No. 4. 7 Persons.			No. 5. 6 Persons.			No. 6. 5 Persons.		
Expences per Week.	£.	s.	d.	£.	s.	d.	£.	s.	d.	£.	s.	d.	£.	s.	d.	£.	s.	d.
Bread and Flour - - - -	0	2	4	0	4	0	0	4	6	0	5	6	0	3	6	0	3	6
Yeast and Salt - - - -	0	0	1	0	0	1	0	0	0½	0	0	0½	0	0	0½	0	0	0½
Bacon and other Meat - -	0	2	0	0	3	1½	0	1	10	0	2	7	0	2	0	0	2	6
Tea and Sugar - - - -	0	0	8½	0	0	7	0	0	5	0	1	5	0	0	4	0	0	9
Butter - - - - - -	0	0	4½	0	0	7	0	0	7	0	0	8½	0	1	0	0	0	8½
Cheese - - - - - -	0	0	2¼	0	0	7½	0	0	7	0	1	0	0	1	1	0	1	1
Soap, Starch, and Blue - -	0	0	2	0	0	2½	0	0	2	0	0	2½	0	0	3	0	0	2
Rushes dipt in grease, instead of Candles - -	0	0	0	0	0	2	0	0	1½	0	0	3	0	0	3	0	0	2
Thread, Worsted, &c. - -	0	0	1	0	0	1	0	0	1	0	0	2	0	0	1	0	0	1
Total	0	5	11¼	0	9	5½	0	8	4	0	11	10½	0	8	6½	0	9	0
Amount *per annum*	15	8	9	24	11	10	21	13	4	30	17	6	22	4	2	23	8	0
Earnings per Week. (Including every Means)	£.	s.	d.	£.	s.	d.	£.	s.	d.	£.	s.	d.	£.	s.	d.	£.	s.	d.
Total	0	10	0	0	12	6	0	11	0	0	15	6	0	10	0	0	10	0
Amount *per annum*	26	0	0	32	10	0	28	12	0	40	6	0	26	0	0	26	0	0
	£.	s.	d.	£.	s.	d.	£.	s.	d.	£.	s.	d.	£.	s.	d.	£.	s.	d.
Expences *per annum* - -	15	8	9	24	11	10	21	13	4	30	17	6	22	4	2	23	8	0
Rent and Fuel - - - -	3	12	0	5	0	0	3	5	0	5	6	0	5	15	6	1	16	0
Total Expences *per annum* -	19	0	9	29	11	10	24	18	4	36	3	6	27	19	8	25	4	0
Total Earnings *per annum* -	26	0	0	32	10	0	28	12	0	40	6	0	26	0	0	26	0	0
	6	19	3	2	18	2	3	13	8	4	2	6	1	19	8	0	16	0
	Surplus			Surplus			Surplus			Surplus			Deficient			Surplus		

TUNTINGTON, SUSSEX, AND SIDLESHAM, SURRY.

ACCOUNT OF THE FAMILIES.

No. 1. John Marſhall of Tuntington, near Chicheſter, his wife, and one child. Earns about 10s. per week.

No. 2. James Fielder, of ditto, his wife, and four children, the eldeſt eight years old, another ſix, a third three, and the youngeſt an infant. Man earns about 12s. per week.

No. 3. Henry Penfold, of ditto, his wife, and ſix children, the three eldeſt in the common work-houſe, one of three years old, another two, and the youngeſt one, at home. Man earns about 11s. per week.

No. 4. Nicholas Crowter, North-Munden, his wife, and five children, the eldeſt ſeventeen years old earns 4s. 6d. per week, a girl fifteen earns 1s. 6d. father 9s. 6d. a girl twelve, another nine, and the youngeſt a boy two.

No. 5. John Barns, of Sidleſham, his wife, and four children, the eldeſt a girl twelve years old, another nine, a third ſix, and the youngeſt four. Man earns 10s. per week.

No. 6. William King, of ditto, his wife, and three children, the eldeſt a girl twelve years old, a boy ten, and a girl two. Man earns 10s. per week, nearly.

ANNUAL EXPENCES.

		£	s.	d.	£	s.	d.
No. 1.	Rent - - -	3	0	0			
	Fuel - - -	0	12	0			
					3	12	0

Brews 5 buſhels of malt, 3lb. of hops.

		£	s.	d.	£	s.	d.
No. 2.	Rent - - -	3	0	0			
	Fuel - - -	2	0	0			
					5	0	0

Brews 4 buſhels of malt, 2lb. of hops.

		£	s.	d.	£	s.	d.
No. 3.	Rent - - -	2	10	0			
	Fuel - - -	0	15	0			
					3	5	0

Brews 3 buſhels of malt, 1½lb. of hops.

N. B. The difference in amount of fuel No. 1, 2, and 3, is, No. 1 has a right of cutting furze. No. 2, a hard-working man, and generally works at all kinds of labour by taſk, ſo that late hours prevents procuring fuel by his own hands.

		£	s.	d.	£	s.	d.
No. 4.	Rent - - -	2	0	0			
	Wood - - -	1	15	0			
	Coals - - -	1	11	0			
					5	6	0

Brews 10 buſhels of malt, 11lb. of hops.

		£	s.	d.	£	s.	d.
No. 5.	Rent - - -	3	3	0			
	Fuel - - -	2	12	6			
					5	15	6

Brews 6 buſhels of malt, 5lb. of hops.

		£	s.	d.	£	s.	d.
No. 6.	Rent - - -	0	0	0			
	Wood - - -	0	6	0			
	Coals - - -	1	10	0			
					1	16	0

Brews 8 buſhels of malt, 4½lbs. of hops.

N. B. Not one of the labourers were able to aſcertain what ſums they expended very exactly for drink, clothes, ſickneſs, lying-in, or burials: yet No. 1, 2, and 3, think the expence of ditto, &c. not far from exactneſs as ſet down in the printed eſtimate for Barkham.

PARISH OF MARTON, WESTMORELAND.

JANUARY 1790.

[COMMUNICATED BY THE REV. GILPIN GORST, RECTOR OF MARTON.]

EXPENCES AND EARNINGS OF SIX FAMILIES OF LABOURERS, BY THE WEEK, AND BY THE YEAR.

	No. 1. 7 Persons.			No. 2. 7 Persons.			No. 3. 6 Persons.			No. 4. 5 Persons.			No. 5. 5 Persons.			No. 6. 4 Persons.		
Expences per Week.	£.	s.	d.	£.	s.	d.	£.	s.	d.	£.	s.	d.	£.	s.	d.	£.	s.	d.
Bread and Flour - - - -	0	4	6	0	4	6	0	4	3	0	4	0	0	3	10	0	3	6
Salt - - - - - - - -	0	0	1	0	0	1	0	0	1	0	0	1	0	0	1	0	0	1
Tea, Sugar, and Butter -	0	1	2	0	1	3	0	1	0	0	1	4	0	0	10	0	0	8
Cheese - - - - - - -	0	0	0	0	0	8	0	0	5	0	0	9	0	0	6	0	0	9
Milk - - - - - - - -	0	1	2	0	1	2	0	1	0	0	0	9	0	0	8	0	0	7
Soap, Candles, and Thread -	0	0	3	0	0	3	0	0	3	0	0	3	0	0	3	0	0	3
Potatoes - - - - - - -	0	1	3	0	1	3	0	1	0	0	0	7	0	0	6	0	0	7
Meat - - - - - - - -	0	0	0	0	0	0	0	0	0	0	0	0	0	0	0	0	0	0
Total	0	8	5	0	9	2	0	8	0	0	7	9	0	6	8	9	6	5
Amount *per annum*	21	17	8	23	16	8	20	16	0	20	3	0	17	6	8	16	13	8
Earnings per Week.	£.	s.	d.	£.	s.	d.	£.	s.	d.	£.	s.	d.	£.	s.	d.	£.	s.	d.
The Man earns - - - -	0	8	0	0	8	0	0	8	0	0	8	0	0	8	0	0	8	0
The Woman - - - - -	0	0	6	0	0	6	0	0	6	0	0	6	0	0	6	0	0	6
The Children - - - -	0	0	0	0	0	0	0	0	0	0	0	0	0	0	0	0	0	0
Total	0	8	6	0	8	6	0	8	6	0	8	6	0	8	6	0	8	0
Amount *per annum*	22	2	0	22	2	0	22	2	0	22	2	0	22	2	0	22	2	0
	£.	s.	d.	£.	s.	d.	£.	s.	d.	£.	s.	d.	£.	s.	d.	£.	s.	d.
To the above Amount of Expences *per annum* -	21	17	8	23	16	8	20	16	0	20	3	0	17	6	8	16	13	8
Add Rent, Fuel, Clothes, Lying-in, &c. - -	8	4	5	8	4	5	8	4	5	8	4	5	8	4	5	8	4	5
Total Expences *per annum* -	30	2	1	32	1	1	29	0	5	28	7	5	25	11	1	24	18	1
Total Earnings *per annum* -	22	2	0	22	2	0	22	2	0	22	2	0	22	2	0	22	2	0
Deficiencies of Earnings	8	0	1	9	19	1	6	18	5	6	5	5	3	9	1	2	16	1

PARISH OF MARTON, WESTMORELAND.

ACCOUNT OF THE FAMILIES.

No. 1. A man, his wife, and five children, the eldeſt ten years old, the youngeſt an infant.

No. 2. A man, his wife, and five children, the eldeſt nine years old, the youngeſt an infant.

No. 3. A man, his wife, and four children, the eldeſt ſeven years old, the youngeſt an infant.

No. 4. A man, his wife, and three children, the eldeſt ſix years old, the youngeſt an infant.

No. 5. A man, his wife, and three children, the eldeſt five years old, the youngeſt an infant.

No. 6. A man, his wife, and two young children, the eldeſt three years old, the youngeſt an infant.

ANNUAL EXPENCES.

	£.	s.	d.
Rent 1l. fuel 7s. - - - - - - - - -	1	7	0
Man's clothes - - - - - - - - -	1	10	0
Two ſhirts 6s. pair of ſhoes 6s. 6d. -	0	12	6
Two pair of wooden ſhoes - - - -	0	8	7
Hat and handkerchief - - - - -	0	2	6
Three pair of ſtockings - - - - -	0	3	0
Woman's clothes: gown and petticoat	0	8	0
Two ſhifts 6s. two aprons 2s. 4d. - -	0	8	4
Pair of ſhoes 4s. 6d. ditto wooden 3s.	0	7	6
Two pair of ſtockings 2s. caps 3s. - -	0	5	0
Handkerchiefs - - - - - - - -	0	2	0
Children's clothes and ſhoes - - -	1	15	0
Lying-in, &c. - - - - - - - -	0	15	0
	£.8	4	5

Bread eaten by this claſs of people, is made of rye and barley. Their chief diet is milk and bread, oatmeal porridge, commonly called haſty-pudding, and potatoes. There is no kind of manufactory carried on in this neighbourhood; for which reaſon women and children earn little, except in hay and corn harveſt. Old milk cheeſe is eaten pretty generally, and coſts about 2½d. per lb. Inſtead of ſoap, human urine is made uſe of. Bacon is not uſually eaten by this claſs of people.

The average price of barley, rye, and oats, in January 1790, per buſhel Wincheſter meaſure, was as under:

Barley 3s.—Rye 4s. 3d.—Oats 2s.

Fuel, in the townſhip of Marton, conſiſts entirely of turf, taken from a common adjoining the town, and, as near as I can calculate, coſts a labouring family 7s. annually.

The ſum of 1l. 10s. allowed for clothing a poor labouring man, is meant for coat, waiſtcoat, and breeches, and the making thereof. If this ſum exceeds what is allowed in the more ſouthern counties, ſuch diſparity will perhaps be beſt accounted for, by conſidering, that in warm dry counties fewer clothes will be required, than in thoſe that are cold and wet.

PARISHES OF THORNER AND CHAPEL-ALLERTON, YORKSHIRE.

[COMMUNICATED BY MR. WILLIAM KAYE, NOV. 1791.]

EXPENCES AND EARNINGS OF SIX FAMILIES OF LABOURERS, BY THE WEEK, AND BY THE YEAR.

	No. 1. 7 Persons.			No. 2. 4 Persons.			No. 3. 9 Persons.			No. 4. 6 Persons.			No. 5. 7 Persons.			No. 6. 4 Persons.		
Expences per Week.	£.	s.	d.	£.	s.	d.	£.	s.	d.	£.	s.	d.	£.	s.	d.	£.	s.	d.
Bread and Flour - - - -	0	5	3	0	4	0	0	6	0	0	4	9	0	5	6	0	3	6
Yeast and Salt - - - -	0	0	3½	0	0	3	0	0	4	0	0	3	0	0	3	0	0	2
Bacon and other Meat - -	0	1	9	0	1	2	0	1	6	0	1	0	0	1	6	0	1	2
Tea and Sugar - - - -	0	1	0	0	0	6	0	1	0	0	1	0	0	1	0	0	1	0
Cheese (seldom any) - -	0	0	0	0	0	0	0	0	0	0	0	0	0	0	0	0	0	4½
Beer (seldom any) - - -	0	0	0	0	0	2	0	0	0	0	0	0	0	0	4	0	0	4
Soap, Starch, and Blue - -	0	0	4	0	0	2	0	0	4	0	0	4	0	0	4	0	0	2
Candles - - - - - -	0	0	3	0	0	3	0	0	3	0	0	3	0	0	3	0	0	3
Thread, Worsted, &c. - -	0	0	3	0	0	2	0	0	3	0	0	3	0	0	3	0	0	2
Milk - - - - - - -	0	0	0	0	1	0	0	1	3	0	0	6	0	1	0	0	0	7
Total	0	9	1½	0	7	8	0	10	11	0	8	4	0	10	5	0	7	8½
Amount *per annum*	23	14	6	19	18	8	28	7	8	21	13	4	27	1	8	20	0	10
Earnings per Week.	£.	s.	d.	£.	s.	d.	£.	s.	d.	£.	s.	d.	£.	s.	d.	£.	s.	d.
The Man earns at a medium	0	8	0	0	7	6	0	8	6	0	8	0	0	9	0	0	8	0
Woman - - - - - - -	0	0	0	0	0	6	0	0	6	0	0	0	0	0	6	0	0	6
The Children - - - -	0	1	0	0	0	4	0	1	6	0	0	6	0	1	6	0	0	0
Total	0	9	0	0	8	4	0	10	6	0	8	6	0	11	0	0	8	6
Amount *per annum*	23	8	0	21	13	4	27	6	0	22	2	0	28	12	0	22	2	0
	£.	s.	d.	£.	s.	d.	£.	s.	d.	£.	s.	d.	£.	s.	d.	£.	s.	d.
To the above Amount of Expences *per annum* -	23	14	6	19	18	8	28	7	8	21	13	4	27	1	8	20	0	10
Add Rent, Fuel, Clothes, and Lying-in - - -	6	12	0	6	12	0	6	12	0	6	12	0	6	12	0	6	12	0
Total Expences *per annum* -	30	6	6	26	10	8	34	19	8	28	5	4	33	13	8	26	12	10
Total Earnings *per annum* -	23	8	0	21	13	4	27	6	0	22	2	0	28	12	0	22	2	0
Deficiencies of Earnings	6	18	6	4	17	4	7	13	8	6	3	4	5	1	8	4	10	10

THORNER AND CHAPEL-ALLERTON, YORKSHIRE.

ACCOUNT OF THE FAMILIES.

No. 1. A man, his wife, and five children, the eldeſt fifteen years old, the youngeſt an infant.

No. 2. A man, his wife, and two children, the eldeſt nine years old, lame, and the youngeſt ſix.

No. 3. A man, his wife, and ſeven children, the eldeſt fourteen years old, the two youngeſt twins, ſix months.

No. 4. A man, his wife, and four children, the eldeſt eight years old, the youngeſt four.

No. 5. A man, his wife, and ſeven children, five of the youngeſt conſtantly at home, the eldeſt fourteen years old, the youngeſt four.

No. 6. A man, his wife, and two children, the eldeſt three years old, the youngeſt an infant.

[Nos. 1, 2, 3, 4, live in the townſhip of Thorner, about five or ſix miles from Leeds in Yorkſhire. Nos. 5 and 6 live at Chapel-Allerton, three miles from Leeds.]

ANNUAL EXPENCES.

	£.	s.	d.
Rent of a cottage and garden from 1l. to 2l. per annum:—ſay -	1	10	0
Fuel: coals are generally uſed, which coſt 9d. a horſe-load, about 3 buſhels; the expence of each family per annum -	1	0	0

Although coals are plentiful, yet it is an obſervation, that the habit of making large fires makes the expence of fuel greater than in places where it is much ſcarcer.

	£.	s.	d.
Clothing for each family - - -	2	10	0
Lying-in, ſickneſs, &c. - - -	1	12	0
	£.6	12	0

	£.	s.	d.
Price of the half-peck loaf - -	0	1	0
—— of 14lb. of flour - - -	0	2	0
—— of a week's labour in winter	0	7	0
—— of ditto the year through -	0	8	0

The tea uſed by each family is from 1 oz. to 1½oz. at 2d. or 3d. per oz.

Soft ſugar ½lb. at 7d. or 8d. per lb.

Salt butter ½lb. at 7d. to 9d. per lb.

In No. 1, the reaſon why there is nothing ſet down for milk is, they keep a ſmall Scotch cow upon the waſte, which ſupplies them with milk, and ſomething to ſpare.

PARISHES OF LLANDEGLA AND LLANARMON, DENBIGHSHIRE.

[COMMUNICATED BY MR. JOHN EDWARDS, 1788.]

EXPENCES AND EARNINGS OF THREE FAMILIES OF LABOURERS, BY THE WEEK, AND BY THE YEAR.

	No. 1. 8 Persons.			No. 2. 7 Persons.			No. 3. 6 Persons.		
Expences per Week.	£.	s.	d.	£.	s.	d.	£.	s.	d.
Meal of Barley or Oats - -	0	5	0	0	4	2	0	3	8
Butter - - - - - -	0	1	9	0	1	4	0	1	3
Milk - - - - - - -	0	0	7	0	0	6	0	0	5
Potatoes - - - - - -	0	0	6	0	0	5	0	0	5
Salt, Soap, and Tallow - -	0	0	4½	0	0	4	0	0	4
Bread - - - - - - -	0	0	1½	0	0	1	0	0	1
Total	0	8	4	0	6	10	0	6	2
Amount *per annum*	21	13	4	17	15	4	16	0	8
Earnings per Week.	£.	s.	d.	£.	s.	d.	£.	s.	d.
The Man earns at a medium	0	6	0	0	0	0	0	6	0
The Woman - - - - -	0	1	0	Parish pay	4	0	0	0	6
The Children - - - -	0	0	9	0	0	0	0	0	0
Total	0	7	9	0	4	0	0	6	6
Amount *per annum*	20	3	0	10	8	0	16	18	0
	£.	s.	d.	£.	s.	d.	£.	s.	d.
To the above Amount of Expences *per annum* -	21	13	4	17	15	4	16	0	8
Add Rent, Fuel, Clothing, Lying-in, &c. - -	6	1	0	5	10	0	5	0	0
Total Expences *per annum* -	27	14	4	23	5	4	21	0	8
Total Earnings *per annum* -	20	3	0	10	8	0	16	18	0
Deficiency of Earnings	7	11	4	12	17	4	4	2	8

PARISHES OF LLANDEGLA AND LLANARMON, DENBIGHSHIRE.

ACCOUNT OF THE FAMILIES.

No. 1. A man, his wife, and ſix children, the eldeſt a boy thirteen years of age, the youngeſt three; five of the children too young to earn any thing.

No. 2. A woman, whoſe huſband is dead, and five children, the eldeſt ten years of age, the youngeſt two.

No. 3. A man, his wife, and four children, the eldeſt under eight years of age, the youngeſt an infant.

The poor women of this country are generally employed in ſpinning flax and wool, which turns out to but very little advantage. The children in this county are not employed ſo early as in the neighbouring counties: becauſe in Merionethſhire, &c. they learn to knit as ſoon as they can talk. Begging is alſo an old-eſtabliſhed trade in this county, as well as the neighbouring counties: the dole they receive is barley; in ſhearing time they have wool, but hardly enough to make ſtockings.

ANNUAL EXPENCES.

				£.	s.	d.
Rent of a cottage and garden, from 1l. to 1l. 10s.—ſay				1	5	0
Fuel, very dear in this county: conſiſts chiefly of coals, three cart loads will ſerve a family for a year: eſtimated from 7s. to 10s. a load:—ſay				1	1	0
Clothing: moſt poor families buy wool and manufacture it themſelves, rated at	1	10	0	2	5	0
Shoes, hats, &c.	0	15	0			
Lying-in, &c.				1	10	0
				£. 6	1	0

Average price of a meaſure of barley, (viz. forty quarts) of which poor people make bread, 5s.

The above quantity will ſerve a family, conſiſting of ſeven or eight perſons, for a week.

Tea is but ſeldom drunk in poor families in Wales, except in the towns where milk is ſcarce.

To eke out ſoap they uſe chamber-lye.

Butter is bought all the year round from 7d. to 8d. per lb. There is not at any time of the year above 1d. per lb. difference between freſh and ſalt butter in Denbighſhire.

PARISHES OF LLANFAWR AND LLANGEIL, MERIONETHSHIRE, NORTH-WALES.

[COMMUNICATED BY S. LLOYD, CURATE OF LLANDGLA IN YALE, 1788.]

EXPENCES AND EARNINGS OF TWO FAMILIES OF LABOURERS, BY THE WEEK, AND BY THE YEAR.

	No. 1. 6 Persons.			No. 2. 8 Persons.					
Expences per Week.	£.	s.	d.	£.	s.	d.			
Meal of Barley or Oats - -	0	4	6	0	5	0			
Butter - - - - - - -	0	1	8	0	1	6			
Sugar - - - - - - -	0	0	1	0	0	0			
Salt - - - - - - -	0	0	1	0	0	1½			
Milk - - - - - - -	0	0	6	0	0	6			
Potatoes - - - - - -	0	0	5	0	0	6			
Soap, &c. - - - - - -	0	0	1	0	0	2			
Tallow - - - - - -	0	0	2½	0	0	2			
Total	0	7	6½	0	7	11½			
Amount *per annum*	19	12	2	20	13	10			
Earnings per Week.	£.	s.	d.	£.	s.	d.			
The Man earns at a medium	0	6	6	0	6	0			
The Woman - - - - -	0	0	9	0	1	0			
The Children - - - -	0	0	3	0	1	0			
Total	0	7	6	0	8	0			
Amount *per annum*	19	10	0	20	16	0			
	£.	s.	d.	£.	s.	d.			
To the above Amount of Expences *per annum* -	19	12	2	20	13	10			
Add Clothes, Rent, Fuel, and other extras - -	4	10	0	5	0	0			
Total Expences *per annum* -	24	2	2	25	13	10			
Total Earnings *per annum* -	19	10	0	20	16	0			
Deficiencies of Earnings	4	12	0	4	17	10			

PARISHES OF LLANFAWR AND LLANGEIL, MERIONETHSHIRE.

ACCOUNT OF THE FAMILIES.

No. 1. A man, his wife, and four children, the eldeſt ten years old.

No. 2. A man, his wife, and ſix children, the eldeſt nine years old.

It is preſumed that the two families above ſpecified are ſufficient to give a general idea of the labouring poor. Thoſe that cannot, or will not work, are ſupported by pariſh relief, and by begging, which is an old-eſtabliſhed trade, to which men, women, and children, devote themſelves without the leaſt degree of ſhame. One reaſon to which we may attribute ſo much begging in this and the neighbouring counties, is the want of profitable manufactories. The knitting of coarſe woollen ſtockings chiefly employs boys, girls, and grown perſons of both ſexes, in the inland part of Merionethſhire.

That it is an unprofitable manufacture is evident, as they knit, walking, talking, begging, without hardly ever looking at their work; and though they exhibit an inſtance of unexampled induſtry, yet they are obliged to beg to make up the deficiencies of their earnings.

ANNUAL EXPENCES.

	£.	s.	d.
Rent of a cottage and garden from 18s. to 1l. 5s.—ſay - - -	1	1	0
Fuel, dear in this country, conſiſting chiefly of turf and peat, the aſhes eſtimated at a ſmall value - - - - - - - -	1	5	0
Clothing is often manufactured by poor families for their own uſe, with the wool which they beg in ſhearing time; ſome few articles, ſuch as ſhoes, they buy, which we ſhall eſtimate at - -	1	6	0
Lying-in, &c. as in the Barkham account - - - - - - - -	1	15	0
	£. 4	17	0

Average price of a buſhel (Wincheſter) of oatmeal, of which the poor make bread, 5s.

The above quantity will ſerve a family, conſiſting of ſix or ſeven perſons, for a week.

In general tea is not drunk in poor families in Wales, except in the towns where milk is ſcarce.

To eke out ſoap, they uſe chamber-lye.

Butter is bought at an average for 6½d. all the year round. There is not at any time of the year above 1d. per lb. difference between freſh and ſalt butter in Merionethſhire.

Pariſh rates in this county are from 3s. 6d. to 4s. Widows and their families receive ſome pariſh relief, but are chiefly ſupported by begging from door to door. The dole which they receive is oatmeal.

GENERAL STATE OF THE EXPENCES AND EARNINGS OF THE PEASANTRY IN THE NORTH PART OF ABERDEENSHIRE.

TRANSMITTED BY DR. FINDLAY, OF FRASERBURGH.

[COMMUNICATED BY THE REVEREND JAMES RAMSAY, JAN. 1789.]

THE Peaſantry in Aberdeenſhire may be ranked in three claſſes, viz.

1ſt. Cottars, or merely Day-Labourers.

2dly. Tradeſmen, being Sub-Tenants.

3dly. The very pooreſt, being old Men or Widows, whoſe Children (if they had any) are gone to ſervice, have families of their own, gone to trades, or have left the country.

CLASS FIRST—Rent a houſe, a cottage, a cabbage garden, and two or three acres of land from the farmer.

	£.	*s.*	*d.*
He ploughs their land, brings home their peats (fuel;) for this, they pay him in caſh at a medium 10s. per acre of the ground	1	10	0
The man gives his work in harveſt, receiving two meals a day, and one firlot of meal, (32lbs.) for harveſt ſupper home to his family; his harveſt wages being valued at - - - - - - -	1	0	0
He gives three days work at caſting the farmer's peats, and forming his ſheep or cattle folds - - - - - at 8d.	0	2	0
Annual clothing to ſelf, wife, and children - - - - -	1	0	0
He buys two bolls of meal (256lbs.) more than the produce of his land, at 12s. - - - - - - - -	1	4	0
He uſes ſalt 5s.; fiſh 4s.; ſoap, ſtarch, blue, hardly any—ſay 1s. -	0	10	0
In lyings-in, burials, or other incidents - - - - -	1	0	0
Lamp-oil 4s.; ruſhes dipt in it for candles 0; tea, ſugar, butchers meat, none; treacle or melaſſes when ſick, 1s. - - - - -	0	5	0
Total expences £.	6	11	0

Suppoſe

	£.	s.	d.
Suppofe him to have five children under eight years, which, as the mothers nurfe at leaft twelve months, is the hardeft cafe poffible, deducting the work above given to his mafter, and the time employed in his own ground, he may hire himfelf in the year 120 days at 8d.	4	0	0
He rears a calf yearly, which at the year old is worth from 20s. to 25s.	1	1	0
The eldeft child attends the youngeft, while the mother earns at fpinning 6d. per week - - - - - - - - - -	1	6	0
Two or three hens will produce in eggs and chicken - - -	0	4	0
In the long winter evenings, the hufband cobbles fhoes, mends the family clothes, and attends the children while the wife fpins—Some hufbands fpin or knit ftockings, make horfe or oxen harnefs of ftript and dried rufhes, &c. for fale.			
Total earnings £.	6	11	0

The produce of their garden and lands, and cow, give them what more meal they want above the two bolls already mentioned, with milk, potatoes, turnips, cabbage, greens, and ale at Chriftmas;—butchers meat none.

If by ficknefs, lofs of cow or calf, or other accidents, they are reduced to poverty and real want, the Kirk Seffion and private charity fupport them during that time only:—or if their lofs and wants be too much for the ordinary feffion charities, the minifter intimates a collection to be made for them only next Sunday at church.

The fame perfon, after his eldeft child, whether boy or girl, is eight years old, begins to hold up his head; the boy keeps cattle or fheep, the girl fpins linen yarn, and earns 6d. per week, fome more. As the other children advance he becomes ftill more independant. When all boys, many of them learn to fpin or knit ftockings at a very early age.

Class second.—Tradefmen, who have like houfes, gardens, and grounds, for the like rent and fervices:—The only difference is, his employing his own time at his trade, which is generally more profitable, and enables him to live better.

In cafe of ficknefs or misfortune, he is relieved and fupported as the other.

Class third—Have a hut, near a peat-mofs, from a farmer, for which they pay him from 12d. to 20d. a year, and what is called a rick (fmoak) hen to the landlord, for the privilege of taking fuel of peats from the mofs.

While

While able, they beg through the pariſh and neighbourhood, and often live more comfortably than the firſt claſs. When through age or infirmity they cannot go out to beg, they are poorly off, if they have not laid up any thing in their begging days, (but this many of them do) being only ſupported by private charity or the Kirk Seſſion, whoſe higheſt charity allowance is 1s. per week.

This Kirk Seſſion Fund, which anſwers all the purpoſes of poor-rates, (aſſiſted by private charity and occaſional Sunday collections for particular perſons) from the beſt information, does not, one country pariſh with another, exceed 15l. ſterling a year. Some very few ſuch pariſhes have a fund of 50l. or 100l. ſterling benefactions of individuals, the intereſt of which goes in addition;—yet true it is that moſt pariſhes have more or leſs ſavings at intereſt from 50l. to 200l. ſterling to anſwer bad years or great emergencies; and but for which, in 1783, ſome poor muſt have periſhed for want.

This is the trueſt ſtate of our Country Peaſantry. I meddle not with Towns, where tea and gin are introduced among the meaneſt;—their wages are higher, and conſtant employment more certain;—but gin debauches the morals of both ſexes, and they are in general much leſs comfortable than the Country Peaſants.

You have that moſt burthenſome, and miſapplied, and miſmanaged charity, *poor rates*, to encourage idleneſs and luxury, and, in addition to gin, to debauch morals and induſtry. The poor here, knowing the extent of what they have to expect from the kirk ſeſſion, the great uncertainty of private charities, and that there is no legal obligation on the pariſh or publick for their ſupport, [and inſtigated by a certain pride not to beg charity, or be on the poor liſt, which is looked on as degrading to their children] exert every nerve, and often indeed live poorly, to ſupport themſelves, and they ſucceed. We have extremely few wretched poor, nor ever heard of any part of a family ſtarving for want.

We are indeed peſtered with Highland Beggars throughout the ſummer, who ſow their own grounds at home, then lock their doors, and come, man, wife, and children, to *ſorn* till harveſt on the Low Country; and had we police (the name of which only is known here) to prevent theſe and other ſtrollers, every pariſh could ſupport their own poor comfortably in their own houſes, at a leſs expence than theſe ſtrangers coſt the country, (which is often plundered by them) and we ſhould have no beggars.

A. F.

OBSERVATIONS

OBSERVATIONS BY J. R.

The *Kirk Seſſion Fund* ariſes from the ordinary Sunday collections, which are conſtantly made at church, each perſon according to his inclination contributing a farthing, a halfpenny, or penny.

It is worthy of being remarked, that the comfort of the firſt claſs ariſes chiefly from their having little ſpots of ground attached to their gardens, which helps out the maintenance of their family.

EAST-LOTHIAN.

ACCOUNTS OF TWO FAMILIES, BY H. SANGSTER, SEPT. 1789.

[COMMUNICATED BY MR. DEMPSTER, M. P.]

SIR,

AT your deſire I have ſent you the incloſed calculations, which have been made with as much care as poſſible from the different reports I have got. As we ſeldom meet with a family more numerous than a man, his wife, and four children under age, I have fixed upon it as the moſt expenſive.

The income of both labourer and ploughman is above his expences, and ſhould certainly be ſufficient for procuring the mere neceſſaries of life. And you will ſee it is ſo, from the copies which are ſent you along with this, of the articles of ſome ſocieties in this county, the ſubſcribers to which are moſtly ploughmen and day-labourers. There are more of theſe ſocieties in this county; and in a ſhort time, it is almoſt certain, every labourer and ploughman will ſubſcribe, as much benefit has been already derived from them, and their ſtocks are increaſing faſt.

Ten-pence per day, which is the higheſt rate of wages in this county, is ſtated without any deduction for loſs by bad weather, becauſe the labourer has the chance of increaſed wages for hay and harveſt-work, and threſhing in winter.

I have not ſtated, in the article of income, that the farmer furniſhes ground for ſowing a half peck of lintſeed, and ground alſo for laying on their aſhes for potatoes or barley, both of which might have been ſet down at twelve ſhillings.

The wife is ſuppoſed to work in harveſt when ſhe has a child that needs a keeper; for this reaſon, ſhe gets a young girl to wait on her child, and her allowance for food, which is the ſame as a man's, is nearly ſufficient for them both.

Nothing is ftated for lying-in, or burials;—the former can only be calculated at an average of two fhillings yearly: the latter tends to leffen the expences of the family.

YEARLY EXPENCES OF A LABOURER, HIS WIFE, AND FOUR CHILDREN UNDER AGE.

	£.	s.	d.
Eight bolls of meal, at 10d. per peck - - - - - -	5	6	8
Two bolls of barley, at 16s. per boll; Two bolls of peafe, at 12s. ditto } for bread - - -	2	16	0
Salt 9s. 9d.—foap 8s. 8d.—candles 2s. 4d. - - - -	1	0	9
One boll of barley, for the pot - - - - - - -	0	17	0
Coals 11s. 8d.—butcher's meat 10s. - - - - -	1	1	8
Clothing - - - - - - - - - - - - -	2	0	0
	£. 13	2	1

HIS YEARLY INCOME.

	£.	s.	d.	£.	s.	d.
The man earns 10d. per day - - -	£. 13	0	0			
His wife works 20 days in harveft, as rent for the houfe; her earnings therefore can only be -	2	9	0	15	9	0
Income above his expences				£. 2	6	11

THE YEARLY INCOME OF A FARMER'S PLOUGH-SERVANT, WITH A WIFE, AND FOUR CHILDREN UNDER AGE.

	£.	s.	d.
Money - - - - - - - - - - - - -	£. 3	8	0
Six bolls and a half of oat-meal - - - - - - -	4	6	8
One boll, three firlots of barley, at 16s. - - - - - -	1	8	0
Three firlots of peafe, at 12s. - - - - - - - - -	0	9	0
A cow - - - - - - - - - - - - -	4	0	0
His wife earns - - - - - - - - - - -	2	9	0
	17	4	8
His expences the fame as a labourer's	13	2	1
Income above his expences	£. 4	2	7

N. B. A boll is about fix bufhels, five firlots make a boll.

ACCOUNT OF SIX FAMILIES IN THE COUNTY OF SUTHERLAND.

FROM MR. JOHN BOOKLESS TO JOHN FRASER, ESQ; CAMBUSMORE.

[COMMUNICATED BY HUGH SCOTT, ESQ.]

DEAR SIR, *Dunrabin Caſtle, 21ſt Auguſt,* 1789.

INCLOSED I ſend you an exact account of the earnings of ſix different Day-Labourers, which I have extracted from the books that I keep, for three years back; theſe ſent are the medium earnings. The additional aid of wife or children I took from the men's own reports, which I have reaſon to believe to be pretty exact:—Alſo, as to their expences, I think them equally juſt. Theſe ſix families may be a ſufficient rule for all the labourers that I have a concern with, to the number of eighty; and by what I can learn from others who employ labourers in Sutherland, I find a great ſimilarity in their earnings, method of living, &c. I have not calculated the weekly earnings, owing to want of time; but that may be eaſily done from the year's earnings. I have allowed nothing for houſe or land rent: You know that the generality of labourers take up their reſidence bordering on ſome muir, and moſs—there they find materials for building a houſe, and plenty of moſs for fuel, beſides paſtures for their beaſts. Thoſe that have not theſe advantages, you will ſee how they live. No. 2, 3, 4, beſides their real income, have an additional aid from the ſea, when low water; ſuch as lobſter, crab, muſcle, cockle, limpet, wilk, ſand-eel, &c. make a very conſiderable ſupport to their families. Salt water is a ſubſtitute in place of ſalt; and you know that it is laid down as an invariable rule, never to exceed their annual income; never to contract debts, excepting on account of indiſpoſition or uncommon calamity; in ſuch a caſe they take credit for a boll or two of bear or meal, which they regularly pay out of their next year's earnings. What enables them to build a houſe—purchaſe a cow—and ſome ſheep; alſo the needful houſhold furniture; is explained in No. 6.

(Signed) JOHN BOOKLESS.

EXPENCES

EXPENCES AND EARNINGS OF SIX FAMILIES, BY THE YEAR, IN THE COUNTY OF SUTHERLAND, 1789.

No. I. A man, his wife, and three children, the eldeſt ſix years of age, the youngeſt a ſucking infant.

EARNINGS.

	£.	s.	d.
The man earns each year, for three years back, at an average	5	10	0
The wife earns by ſpinning lint when able, and what ſpare-time ſhe may have after the neceſſary attention to her children and other houſhold affairs - -	0	15	0
A calf is reared yearly, and ſold when two years old, brings at an average - - - -	1	5	0
	£ 7	10	0

EXPENCES.

	£.	s.	d.
Six bolls of bear and oat-meal at 14s. per boll - -	4	4	0
Ground-rent to a tenant for liberty to plant four pecks of potatoes	0	4	0
A raw hide bought for ſhoes, to which he gives a kind of dreſſing, coſts 12s. which ſerves him and his family two years for ſhoes - - -	0	6	0
Making the ſhoes - - -	0	2	6
Wool bought 10s. beſides what is ſhorn from a few ſheep that he has paſturing on the hills and commons, affords clothing for the whole family - - -	0	10	0
The wife ſpins the wool, and dyes the cloth for the different purpoſes. Dye ſtuffs - -	0	2	6
Pays for the weaving and dreſſing	0	5	0
To the taylor for making - -	0	5	0
Soap and blue, needles and pins -	0	2	0
Handkerchiefs 1s. 6d. apron 1s. 6d. linen for a kips 1s. 6d. a bonnet which laſts two years 1s. -	0	5	0
At Chriſtmas holidays, and chriſtenings, &c. cheeſe 2s. whiſky 2s. ale 3s.—Poultry they rear themſelves, which with potatoes compoſe the entertainment on theſe occaſions - - - -	0	7	0
Potatoes bought for family uſe and feed - - - - -	0	7	0
	£ 7	0	0

No. II. A man, his wife, and four children, the eldeſt twelve, the next ten years of age, the reſt infants.

EARNINGS.

	£.	s.	d.
The man earns yearly - -	6	0	0
The wife by waſhing earn - -	1	5	0
The two eldeſt children being employed in planting and lifting potatoes, handhoing turnips and potatoes, earns about - - -	1	10	0
	£. 8	15	0

EXPENCES

	£.	s.	d.
Eight bolls of bear and oat-meal at 14s. - - - -	5	12	0
Ground-rent for potatoes - -	0	6	0
Shoes for man and family - -	0	10	6
For cloth of different kinds - -	1	0	0
Taylor for making and mending clothes - - - -	0	6	6
Soap, blue, needles, and pins -	0	10	0
A bonnet, handkerchief, apron, and linen for a cap - - -	0	5	0
Chriftening entertainment - -	0	5	0
	£. 8	15	0

No. III. A man, his wife, and one boy, the boy fourteen years of age.

EARNINGS.

The man earns yearly -	5	15	0
The wife by fpinning, and fundry little works in the fields, fuch as planting potatoes, &c. -	2	5	0
The fon at fchool earns nothing			
	£. 8	0	0

EXPENCES.

Five bolls of oat-meal at 14s. -	3	10	0
Ground rent for potatoes -	0	3	0
Shoes for himfelf, wife, and fon -	0	6	0
Clothes of different kinds - -	1	0	0
Taylor for making and mending -	0	5	0
Soap, blue, needles and pins -	0	2	0
A bonnet, handkerchiefs, apron, &c.	0	5	0
School fees for his fon - -	0	5	0
Potatoes bought - - -	0	16	0
Money faved - - -	1	8	0
	£. 8	0	0

No. IV. A man, his wife, and two children, the eldeft four years old, the youngeft two years.

EARNINGS.

The man earns yearly - -	6	15	0
The wife, by her attention to her children, a cow, and a few fheep, earns nothing - -	0	0	0
Sells a cow every fecond year at 3l.	1	10	0
	£. 8	5	0

EXPENCES.

Six bolls of bear and oat-meal, at 14s.	4	4	0
For fhoes - - - -	0	4	0
Wool produced from the fheep which he fhears twice a year, affords clothing for himfelf and family, the wife fpins and dyes it for the different purpofes. Dye ftuffs bought - - -	0	2	6
Pays for weaving and dreffing -	0	5	0
Taylor for making and mending	0	5	0
Soap, needles and pins - -	0	2	0
Bonnet, handkerchief, apron, &c.	0	5	0
Chriftening entertainment and holidays - - - -	0	10	6
Potatoes bought for feed, and ufe of family - - - -	0	18	0
Money faved - - - -	1	9	0
	£. 8	5	0

No. V. A man, his wife, and five children, the eldeft fix years of age, the two youngeft fucking infants and are twins.

EARNINGS.

The man earns yearly - -	5	2	0
The wife nothing - - -	0	0	0
	5	2	0

EXPENCES.

	£.	s.	d.
Six bolls of bear and oat-meal, at 12s. is - - - -	3	12	0
Ground-rent for potatoes - -	0	6	0
Shoes for himſelf and wife -	0	3	4
Clothing of different kinds -	0	15	0
To the taylor for making and mending - - - -	0	5	0
Soap, blue, needles and pins, &c.	0	2	0
Entertainment at lying-in - -	0	5	0
Bonnet, handkerchief, apron, &c.	0	5	0
Potatoes for feed and family uſe -	0	16	0
In debt - - - - - -	1	7	4
	£. 6	9	4

No. VI. A man unmarried.

	£.	s.	d.
Earns yearly - - - -	6	18	5
EXPENCES.			
Two bolls one firlot of oat-meal	1	11	6
Potatoes bought - - -	0	10	0
Shoes, two pair - - -	0	3	4
Clothes of different kinds - -	1	0	0
Pays for waſhing 1s. ſoap for ſhaving, razor, &c. 6d. - -	0	1	6
Buys a little milk where it can be got - - - - -	0	2	0
At particular times to make merry with his friends, ſpends - -	0	5	0
Saves annually, which enables him to take up houſe - - -	3	5	1
	£. 6	18	5

For EU product safety concerns, contact us at Calle de José Abascal, 56–1°,
28003 Madrid, Spain or eugpsr@cambridge.org.

www.ingramcontent.com/pod-product-compliance
Ingram Content Group UK Ltd.
Pitfield, Milton Keynes, MK11 3LW, UK
UKHW050455190625
459647UK00035B/2849

* 9 7 8 1 1 0 8 0 2 4 7 4 7 *